THE M. & E. HANDBOOK SERIES

OPERATIONAL RESEARCH

W. M. HARPER,
A.C.M.A., A.M.B.I.M.

MACDONALD AND EVANS

MACDONALD & EVANS LTD.
Estover, Plymouth PL6 7PZ

First published May 1975
Reprinted (with amendments) April 1976
Reprinted in this format 1977
Reprinted 1979

©
MACDONALD & EVANS LIMITED
1975

ISBN: 0 7121 1514 5

Printed in Great Britain by Richard Clay (The Chaucer Press) Ltd
Bungay, Suffolk

PREFACE

More and more the operations of business concerns are being subjected to mathematical analysis. Inevitably, therefore, the student of business is required to look ever more closely at the concepts and techniques that have emerged from prior studies of this sort, and examining bodies expect ever-increasing knowledge and comprehension in this field. For the mathematically-minded young full-time student with an extensive academic background this new demand by business presents little in the way of problems, but for his more practical contemporary whose time and effort have been more directed towards doing a job than researching it, it is a totally different matter. With only a relatively elementary mathematical education (and one often concluded many years previously at that) and a lack of familiarity with "throwing around" mathematical concepts, expressions and formulae, these new methods of analysing the business he understands only too well in an empirical way appear incomprehensible and impractical and, worst of all, lacking any clearly defined and easily-found logical path that will take him to a point where he can obtain a confident grasp of their purpose and relevance.

It is for this latter student that this book has been written. It assumes only elementary mathematical knowledge (and much of that is revised). Such additional knowledge that is required to appreciate how the techniques "work" is given in the first section of the book—which, incidentally, avoids any mathematics which is felt to be irrelevant to this objective. One branch of mathematics, probability theory, is so fundamental to operational research that a whole section of the book—the second—is devoted to it, and again it is assumed that the student has no more initial comprehension of this topic than the layman. Only then, after the mathematical and probability theory introductions, are the operational research techniques themselves discussed, and such discussion is wholly in terms of the ordinary business world and employs no mathematics not previously covered.

What's in a name? The introduction of relatively advanced mathematics into business analysis is, on an historical time-scale, so new that the terminology is still unstandardised. As will be clear from Chapter I in my own view it is possible that this book would be more appropriately titled "Quantitative Techniques," since it is this aspect of the broader topic of operational research that is discussed. Nevertheless quantitative techniques are so widely believed to represent the whole of operational research that a person looking for a first text on the subject of quantitative techniques would be more likely to expect to find what he was looking for under the title "Operational Research" than any other. For this reason I have given the book this title. Whilst possibly academically inaccurate, it does at least describe the book in terms the potential reader would probably use himself and in this sense is an accurate indication of the book's contents.

"Ballads, songs and snatches." It should, perhaps, be made clear that operational research is essentially practical even though mathematical theory is used in its application. This means the subject grew as a series of more or less disconnected techniques. In consequence one chapter does not necessarily lead logically to the next—rather each chapter stands relatively independent of whatever preceded it. Of course, a later chapter may use some of the mathematical theory developed in an earlier chapter and many use the probability theory discussed in the middle section. Nevertheless extensive back-reference tends to be the exception rather than the rule. As a result it is not necessary to understand fully one chapter before reading further in the book. Some chapters are relatively more difficult than others and if the student finds one that is rather hard to grasp at first reading he should nevertheless proceed to the next chapter in good heart for in all probability the earlier insurmountable hurdles will not again appear in the book.

Progress Tests. Most of the chapters conclude with a Progress Test which usually involves practical work. This work is very often designed not only to test the student's comprehension but also to illustrate additional points relevant with the topic covered by the chapter, particularly in connection to the approach to problem solutions. Ideally the student should attempt all these tests but if he feels he has grasped the main points in the chapter and time is short then although he may not attempt the tests he should at least study the questions and answers to ensure this additional material is not overlooked.

Bibliography
For further study, the student is referred to the following books:
For general reading which parallels this book:

L. W. T. Stafford, *Business Mathematics* (M. & E. Handbook series)

M. S. Makower and E. Williamson, *Teach yourself operational research* (English Universities Press)

Albert Battersby, *Mathematics in Management* (Pelican)

N. W. Marsland, *Quantitative techniques for business* (Polytech Publishers)

Kemeny, Schleifer, Snell, Thompson, *Finite mathematics with business applications* (Prentice Hall)

For a greater emphasis on probability and statistics in quantitative techniques:

> Bierman, Bonini, Fouraker, and Jaedicke, *Quantitative analysis for business decisions* (Richard D. Irwin)
>
> R. Schlaifer, *Probability and statistics for business decisions* (McGraw-Hill)

For a more detailed treatment of stock control:
> Albert Battersby, *A guide to stock control* (Pitman)

For a more detailed treatment of network analysis:
> K. G. Lockyer, *An introduction to critical path analysis* (Pitman)

For a set of case studies illustrating the use of quantitative techniques:
> Phillip G. Carlson, *Quantitative techniques for management* (Harper & Row)

Acknowledgments

I gratefully acknowledge permission to quote from the past examination papers of the following bodies:

> Institute of Cost and Management Accountants (ICMA)
> Institute of Chartered Accountants in England and Wales—Certificate in Management Information examination (CMI)

February 1975   W.M.H.

CONTENTS

PART THREE: PROBABILITY

LIST OF ILLUSTRATIONS

PART ONE
INTRODUCTION

CHAPTER I

THE ROLE OF OPERATIONAL RESEARCH IN THE BUSINESS WORLD

INTRODUCTION

Operational research has been used in business for many years now but it is still a relatively new subject and the student can be forgiven for wondering just what it is all about, where it fits into the conventional business structure, and how it links up with the other accepted commercial subjects.

Unfortunately there are no authoritative answers to these sort of questions. Like other practical subjects operational research was introduced into business on an *ad hoc* basis. It was, in effect, used where useful and fitted as best it could without formal expression into the existing organisational framework. However, to enable the student to integrate this subject logically with the many other subjects he must study, we will in this chapter put forward a tentative scheme that suggests the subject matter of operational research and also the relationships between operational research and the other aspects of business. This scheme is diagrammatically illustrated in Fig. 1.

1. Data for decisions. Managers must manage. Moreover they must manage effectively and efficiently. Managing involves making decisions and to do this sound information is needed. There is no limit to the sources managers can tap for such information—indeed, a manager's performance depends very much on his skill at locating and exploiting sources of information. They must, therefore, be continually on the look-out for fresh and worthwhile information sources.

2. Emergence of operational research. For very many years there have been a number of sources that have been providing managers with the information necessary for their work. These sources lie within the subject matter of economics,

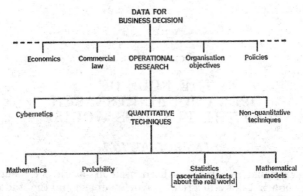

FIG. 1.—*The place of operational research in the business situation.*

accountancy, commercial law, industrial relations, production techniques, human relations, etc. In addition, when making decisions a manager has to take into account the organisation's objectives and policies.

Since the last war, however, managers have become increasingly aware that their performance can be improved by a more careful study of the way they run their *operations*. Previously operations were regarded in what may be referred to as "engineering" terms—you put your foot on the brake, for example, and the machine was effectively and efficiently stopped. But then managers began to question whether or not putting one's foot on the brake was the best way to stop the machine, or whether, in fact, the machine should be stopped—or even if the organisation should be in the machine stopping business at all. In other words they questioned not the engineering but the *operational* aspect. To answer such questions it was, of course, necessary to have information relating to the consequences of the existing and alternative methods of operating. And to obtain this information management needed to research into the operational side of the business. So *operational research* came into being.

3. Techniques of operational research. Operational research uses *any technique that helps in the analysis of operations.*

Arbitrarily these techniques can be classified as follows:

(a) *Quantitative techniques.* The most obviously useful operational research techniques are those involving the careful *measurement* of operational requirements and returns, for valid measurement enables objective comparisons to be made between alternatives. This aspect of operational research is further discussed in the next paragraph.

(b) *Non-quantitative techniques.* Unfortunately many operating factors cannot be quantified. It is not possible, for example, to measure how one kind of organisation structure compares with another. Nevertheless research is possible and operational research workers will often use analogies (non-mathematical models) with non-business situations to enable them to find more effective operational methods. For example, organisational structure can be modelled in terms of the nervous system, and traffic flow can be modelled in terms of liquid flow in channels.

(c) *Cybernetics.* Cybernetics is the theory of control and effective control is, of course, essential for effective operations. This wide and complex subject, then, must be included in operational research.

A distinctive feature of operational research (which tends to have been lost sight of in recent years) is its inter-disciplinary nature. Because operations involve a broad variety of sciences such as economics, accounting, engineering, mathematics, statistics, psychology, etc.—and even law and medicine—an effective operational research team needs to be composed of people with these various disciplines. There is, therefore, no science of operational research—only operational research problems and solutions.

4. Quantitative techniques. As we said in the previous paragraph, if we can measure operational factors it makes the task of comparing one alternative with another very much more objective. Quantitative techniques, then, embrace all the operational techniques that lend themselves to such quantitative measurement, and to this end employs the following subjects and techniques:

(a) *Mathematics.* Measuring involves numbers and relationships between numbers. This, of course, is the domain of mathematics and so mathematical techniques are frequently used in quantitative techniques.

(b) *Probability*. Nothing is certain in this uncertain world and consequently any analysis of potential operations must cater for this uncertainty. Probability theory, therefore, is also frequently used in quantitative techniques.

(c) *Mathematical models*. As will be seen later in the book a mathematical model simply depicts the actual working of the real world in mathematical terms. If we can measure the factors involved in operations then we can build mathematical models of such operations. Mathematical models, therefore, play a fundamental role in quantitative techniques.

(d) *Statistics*. In order to build effective mathematical models of the operational world as it really is, it is necessary to have numerical data about that world. Unfortunately it is prohibitively expensive to obtain such data in absolute terms—all that is practical is its inference from appropriately selected samples. Moreover, the real world is not deterministic (at least, not for practical purposes) and factual data can only be expressed in terms of probabilities (*e.g.* daily demand for a product, delivery times of materials from suppliers). Obtaining information both from samples and in terms of probability patterns is, of course, the function of statistics.

5. Models. We have already referred to the importance of models, but these are so basic to operational research work as to warrant a special emphasis. Indeed, operational research can virtually be defined as model building and analysis. In a typical research study the researchers broadly try to:

(a) Ascertain the facts surrounding the operation (a step that often leans heavily on the collection and interpretation of statistical data).

(b) Quantify the various factors.

(c) Construct a valid model of the operation.

(d) Analyse the model to see if a better way of operating can be found.

6. Plan of this book. This book has been laid out in Parts, the first being this Introduction. In the second and third Parts the mathematics and probability theory necessary to handle the quantitative techniques later discussed are respectively outlined. In the fourth Part the most commonly used quantitative techniques are examined. The book, then, is fully self-contained—only an elementary knowledge of statistics (of which there is in fact very little) being expected of the student.

DEFINITIONS

There are a few words which are so often used in operational research that they warrant some initial discussion. In this section we look at these words.

7. Variables. A *variable* is obviously something that varies. When using quantitative techniques we are concerned with putting values on variables so as to obtain measures such as cost, frequency, distance, speed, etc. Some variables are not, unfortunately, quantifiable (*e.g.* morale) but in this book we will only consider those that are.

Variables can be classified in different ways of which the most important are discrete/continuous and dependent/independent. These can be defined as follows:

(*a*) Discrete/Continuous variable.

(*i*) *Discrete variable.* This is a variable that in real life *cannot* take fractional unit values. For example, we cannot have half a person in a room. Numbers of people in rooms, then, is a discrete variable. Essentially we have a discrete variable whenever we are counting. Note, though, we can sometimes count in fractional units, *e.g.* ½ps, but since we cannot have a fraction of a ½p in real life the variable is a discrete one.

(*ii*) *Continuous variable.* This is a variable that can take fractional values (*e.g.* 5·068921). Virtually all units of measurement of physical characteristics (distance, weight, time, temperature) give us continuous variables.

(*b*) Dependent/independent variable.

(*i*) *Dependent variable.* This is a variable whose values depend on another (independent) variable. In a study of, say, advertising and subsequent sales, the sales are clearly the dependent variable since the sales values will depend upon the advertising.

(*ii*) *Independent variable.* This is a variable whose values are independent of those taken by the dependent variable.

8. Optimisation and optimality. The primary purpose of operational research is obviously to see if it is possible to identify the best way of operating. Such a best way is referred to as the *optimum* way. Consequently in operational research we talk about *optimisation* which means identifying the optimum way of operating, and of *optimality* studies which, of course, are studies aimed at such an identification.

9. Sub-optimisation. Although the issue does not arise in this book, the student should be warned of the possible danger inherent in optimality studies. Frequently in such studies we tend to find the optimum way of operating in respect of a relatively narrow aspect of the whole business situation (*e.g.* find the most economical re-order quantity without reference to the effect of such a quantity on our suppliers). We refer to such a "narrow" optimisation as a *sub-optimisation* (*i.e.* an optimisation of a sub-section of the whole) and a little thought will show that a sub-optimisation could possibly result in injury to the organisation outside these narrow confines. In other words, sub-optimisation in each and every section of the organisation does not *necessarily* lead to optimum operation of the business as a whole, and it should never be assumed that it does.

PROGRESS TEST 1

(Figures in brackets at the end of the questions relate to the paragraph number in the chapter where the answer may be found.)

1. Distinguish between the following variables: discrete; continuous; dependent; independent   **(7)**
2. What is meant by:
   (*a*) Optimisation   **(8)**
   (*b*) Sub-optimisation   **(9)**

PART TWO

THE MATHEMATICS OF
OPERATIONAL RESEARCH

CHAPTER II

READING AND MANIPULATING ALGEBRAIC EXPRESSIONS

Operational research of necessity frequently employs algebraic expressions and it is essential, therefore, that students can read and manipulate such algebraic expressions. These expressions are really only statements in a kind of shorthand, and though they sometimes take on a most fearsome appearance *a patient and methodical decoding of the symbols* often reveals them to be very tame paper tigers. For example $\sum_{i=1}^{\infty} i$ simply means add up all the numbers from 1 to infinity. (Note, incidentally, that while reading the expression may involve only a little trouble, working out the answer may be quite a different thing.)

Not only, however, must the student be able to read algebraic expressions—he must also be able to manipulate them. This is often necessary since the initial expression may not be in the most useful or most simple form. While reading expressions is just a matter of learning the symbols, manipulation does involve a little practice and skill. Nevertheless, by the end of this chapter the student should be able to read the majority of expressions used in operational research and be able to manipulate the simpler and most common kinds of expressions.

COMMON SYMBOLS

First we will explain the more common and simple symbols.

1. Equalities and inequalities. A number of symbols indicate how one value relates to another. These symbols are as follows:

SYMBOL	*Meaning*	*Example*
$=$	Equal to	$3 \times 4 = 12$
$\neq$	Not equal to	$3 \times 4 \neq 15$
$\doteqdot$	Approximately equal to	$\frac{501}{1000} \doteqdot \frac{1}{2}$
$<$	Less than	Sum of any two whole numbers under 5 < 9
$\leqslant$	Less than or equal to	Sum of any two whole numbers under 5 $\leqslant 8$
$>$	Greater than	Sum of any two whole numbers over 5 > 11
$\geqslant$	Greater than or equal to	Sum of any two whole numbers over 5 $\geqslant 12$

Note, incidentally, how we can use the inequality symbols to define a range. If, for example, we wished to refer to x within the range 5 to 35 we could write $5 \leqslant x \leqslant 35$—*i.e.* 5 is less than or equal to x (so x cannot be less than 5) and x is less than or equal to 35 (and so x cannot be greater than 35).

2. Word symbols. Some symbols simply represent words or phrases:

SYMBOL	*Words*
$\therefore$	"Therefore"
$\because$	"Because"
δ	"A little bit more of," *e.g.* δx means "a little bit more of x." (Note it does not represent a figure—it stands solely for the phrase given just as "$\therefore x$" stands for "Therefore x" and not "$\therefore \times x$".)
$\int$	"Integrate." This word is discussed in Chapter VI.

3. ... A row of dots (. . .) means one of two things:

(a) The number it follows goes on and on and on—*e.g.* $\frac{8}{3} = 2 \cdot 66. \ldots$ (If a decimal recurs a dot is sometimes placed over the recurring part—*e.g.* $\frac{8}{3} = 2 \cdot 66\dot{6}$ and $\frac{1}{11} = 0 \cdot 90\dot{9}0\dot{9}$.)

(b) The pattern established by the first few parts of the expression repeats itself until the last term is reached, *e.g.* $1 + 2 + 3 + 4 \ldots + 9$ means $1 + 2 + 3 + 4 + 5 + 6 + 7 + 8 + 9$. A row of dots used in this way, of course, does require the reader to use a little common sense, but not only does the symbol save space (imagine $1 + 2 + 3 + 4 \ldots + 1000$ written out in full) but it also draws the reader's attention to the pattern which, in more complex expressions, helps the reader to gain insight into the situation being analysed.

4. ! The symbol ! is the factorial symbol. When this symbol follows a number (*e.g.* 5!—which speaking aloud we call "5 factorial" or "factorial 5") it indicates that you must list all the numbers in the form of a count-down from the number given to 1—and then multiply all the numbers together. For example, $5! = 5 \times 4 \times 3 \times 2 \times 1 = 120$ and

$$7! \div 4! = (7 \times 6 \times 5 \times 4 \times 3 \times 2 \times 1) \div (4 \times 3 \times 2 \times 1) = 210$$

Note, incidentally, one very important (though seemingly illogical) fact—namely that $0! = 1$.

5. Constants. Some symbols stand for numbers (which are always the same) and nothing more. The commonest are:

∞	Infinity
π	$3 \cdot 14159\ldots$ Found by dividing the circumference of a circle by its diameter
e	$2 \cdot 71828$ Called "exponential *e*." Found by calculating $1 + \frac{1}{1!} + \frac{1}{2!} + \frac{1}{3!} \cdots + \frac{1}{\infty!}$

6. Limits. Assume a factory-worker earns £3 a day plus 1p a unit he produces. If we let $x =$ number of units produced then clearly his pay for any given day would be (in £s) $3 + 0 \cdot 01x$.

Fairly obviously, the smaller x becomes, the less his daily pay, and the nearer x is to zero, the nearer his pay is to his basic £3. Indeed, at the extreme limit when x *is* zero his pay is exactly £3. Algebraically we can show this rather trivial result as follows:

$$\underset{x \to 0}{L} \ (3 + 0{\cdot}01x) = 3,$$

the symbol L being read as "the limit when x becomes 0."
$\underset{x \to 0}{}$

Let's take a slightly less simple example. What if we total

the series $1 + \dfrac{1}{2} + \dfrac{1}{2^2} + \dfrac{1}{2^3} + \dfrac{1}{2^4} \ldots$ etc. Of course the answer

depends upon the length of the series, but we can say with certainty that if we go on to infinity the total will be 2, *i.e.*:

$$\underset{x \to \infty}{L} \left(1 + \frac{1}{2} + \frac{1}{2^2} + \frac{1}{2^3} + \ldots + \frac{1}{2^x} \right) = 2.$$

(If you don't believe this, try it and you'll find each additional fraction halves the gap between the total to that point and 2—so by the time you reach infinity the total will just reach 2.)

7. $\dbinom{n}{x}$. In operational research we often need to know how many combinations can be made out of a number of different items (say n) taking a given number at a time (say x). The shorthand for the number of combinations possible is $\dbinom{n}{x}$. We will discuss this further in Chapter V. (Note, incidentally, the symbol is *not* $\left(\dfrac{n}{x} \right)$, which would mean $n \div x$.)

GENERALISING

Apart from being useful as a form of shorthand, algebraic symbols also enable us to generalise—and the ability to do this makes our techniques much more useful and powerful. We must, then, briefly explain what is meant by generalising.

8. The meaning of "generalising." *Generalising* is stating a relationship between figures that holds true for all cases. When we said in **6** that the worker's daily pay was £$(3 + 0.01x)$ we were generalising since this held true for any and every value x could have taken. (Well, almost—though a pure mathematician would add "when $x \geqslant 0$," *i.e.* point out the generalisation was only true as long as the worker was not producing a negative number of units!) Again, since we can always find the weight of an object in ounces by multiplying its weight in pounds by 16, we can generalise and say "weight in ounces $= 16a$, where $a = $ weight in pounds."

In short, then, generalising involves finding a pattern that applies generally, and expressing the pattern in algebraic symbols.

9. Generalisations and dots. We have already seen that a row of dots in an expression indicates a pattern, and usually the reader is left to work out the pattern for himself. If, however, the pattern is a little complex and not, perhaps, immediately apparent, the writer sometimes generalises the pattern in the middle of the dots. For example, suppose the expression ran as follows:

$$1 + 2 + 3 + 5 + 8 + 13 + 21 \ldots \ldots \ldots \ldots + 377.$$

Here the pattern is not easily seen so the writer may show the expression as follows:

$$1 + 2 + 3 + 5 + 8 + 13 + 21 \ldots + x + y + (x + y)$$
$$\ldots + 377.$$

Now the reader can see each term is found by adding the two previous terms.

INDICES

Sometimes we wish to multiply a number by itself (*e.g.* 6×6) —and perhaps even repeat the multiplication more than once. Rather than write the same number over and over again we indicate the number of times we wish to multiply it by itself with a small *index*—*e.g.* 6×6 is shown as 6^2 and $6 \times 6 \times 6$ as 6^3. Indices are sometimes referred to as *powers* or *exponentials*.

NOTE: The converse of multiplying a number by itself is finding what figure, when multiplied by itself, will give the initial number. For example, what figure when multiplied by itself will give 64? The answer is, of course, 8. The computed figure is called the *root* of the initial number. If the root is multiplied by itself twice to give the initial number we have the square root ($\sqrt{}$); three times, the cube root ($\sqrt[3]{}$); four times, the fourth root ($\sqrt[4]{}$). So we can say: $\sqrt{64} = 8$; $\sqrt[3]{64} = 4$; $\sqrt[6]{64} = 2$.

10. The index scale—zero and negative indices. Each time we add one more multiplication on to an index number expression we increase the index by 1. It follows, then, each time we make a *division* we must decrease the index by 1—*e.g.* $6^4 \div 6 = 6^3$. Let us push the logic of this as far as we can—that is, keep dividing and keep reducing the index by 1 each time:

If we start with:	*and divide by 6:*	*we get:*	*decreasing the index by 1:*
$6^3 = 6 \times 6 \times 6$	$\div 6$	$= 6 \times 6$	6^2
$6^2 = 6 \times 6$	$\div 6$	$= 6$	6^1
$6^1 = 6$	$\div 6$	$= 1$	6^0
$6^0 = 1$	$\div 6$	$= 1/6$	6^{-1}
$6^{-1} = 1/6$	$\div 6$	$= 1/6^2$	6^{-2}
$6^{-2} = 1/6^2$	$\div 6$	$= 1/6^3$	6^{-3}

Studying this pattern we find:

(*a*) $6^1 = 6$, *i.e.* an ordinary 6 really should be written 6^1. For convenience, however, we omit the index 1.

(*b*) $6^0 = 1$.

(*c*) 6 to any *negative* index is simply 1 over what we'd have had if the minus sign hadn't been there in the first place. So generalising we can say that where *a* represents any figure we care to choose:

$$a^1 = a$$
$$a^0 = 1$$
$$a^{-x} = \frac{1}{a^x}, \text{ where } x \text{ is any index.}$$

11. Fractional indices. Next note that if we square a figure we double the index—*e.g.* $6^1 \times 6^1 = 6^2$; $6^2 \times 6^2 = 6^4$; $6^3 \times 6^3 = 6^6$ etc. Clearly, then, if we *halve* the index we must obtain the square root of the initial figure—*e.g.*:

If we start with:	*and halve the index:*	*we get the square root of the initial figure, i.e.:*
16^8	16^4	$\sqrt{16^4 \times 16^4}$
16^4	16^2	$\sqrt{16^2 \times 16^2}$
16^2	16^1	$\sqrt{16^1 \times 16^1}$
16^1	$16^{\frac{1}{2}}$	$\sqrt{16} = 4$
$16^{\frac{1}{2}}$	$16^{\frac{1}{4}}$	$\sqrt{4} = 2$

Clearly, then, if we see a figure carrying an index of $\frac{1}{2}$ we know we need the square root of that figure.

We can, however, go further, for in the last line of our table we note that $16^{\frac{1}{4}} = 2$. Now since $2 = \sqrt[4]{16}$, then the index $\frac{1}{4}$ indicates here the 4th root of our initial figure. And, indeed, what is true here is true generally, so we can say that the denominator (lower part) of a fractional index indicates the root to be found—*i.e.* $a^{\frac{1}{x}} = \sqrt[x]{a}$.

We now just have one last small step—if halving an index, for example, gives us the square root of our initial figure, then we can write the square root of a^3 (*i.e.* $\sqrt{a^3}$) as $a^{\frac{3}{2}}$. And $\sqrt{a^5}$ as $a^{\frac{5}{2}}$ (or, if we wish, $a^{2\frac{1}{2}}$). Generalising again, then we can say:

$$a^{\frac{x}{y}} = \sqrt[y]{a^x}$$

12. Negative fractional indices. Finally we can put together the two previous conclusions to obtain an overall generalisation for a negative fractional index, *i.e.*:

$$a^{\frac{-x}{y}} = \frac{1}{\sqrt[y]{a^x}}$$

Students should now be able to read any index expression that they will normally meet.

SUFFIXES

Indices are, of course, written in small print at the top right of the figure of the symbol concerned. However, we frequently come across small print at the *bottom* right (*e.g.* x_2). Such numbers are called suffixes, and we must now turn our attention to these.

13. Purpose of a suffix. Suffixes serve one purpose and one purpose only—to *identify* which of a group of possible figures is the one referred to. They do *not* enter into any of the calculations themselves in any way.

14. How suffixes work. Imagine we wish to measure the height of six people. If we wished to generalise we could perhaps say "Let a = height of 1st person, b = height of 2nd person, c = height of 3rd person ... etc." But this would be very lengthy and tedious (and, indeed, in any situation with more than 26 items, involve us in finding new symbols other than alphabetical letters). It would be much easier, in fact, to say "Let h = height of a person and h_1 = height of 1st person, h_2 = height of 2nd person, h_3 = height of 3rd person ... etc." In other words the suffix would indicate which person's height was under discussion.

This, then, is how suffixes work. If we had 100 people we would have suffixes running from 1 to 100, and if, for example, we wished to add the height of the last three people we would write "$h_{98} + h_{99} + h_{100}$."

15. Symbol suffixes. As most students know, $\bar{x}$ is the symbol we use for the arithmetic mean. Assume now that you have three different groups (*e.g.* Americans, British and Chinese) which you identify by the symbols a, b and c respectively. If you wished to refer to the mean of the first group you could write $\bar{x}_a$, *i.e.* this would be read as "the mean of group a." Similarly we could write $\bar{x}_b$ and $\bar{x}_c$ for the means of the other two groups. (Students of statistics will now appreciate—if they didn't before—why the standard error of the mean is symbolised as $\sigma_{\bar{x}}$, for reading this literally we have "the σ which relates to a distribution of $\bar{x}$'s," *i.e.* the standard deviation of the sampling distribution of the mean.)

16. Time suffixes. There is another context in which symbol suffixes are useful and this relates to a time series. The principle employed here is, in fact, identical to that used in military terminology when the day of an attack is symbolised as D-day, the two days after the attack as $D + 1$ and $D + 2$ respectively, and the day before as $D - 1$. In mathematics we usually symbolise a particular moment in time as t, and $t + 1$ and $t + 2$ represent one and two periods later and $t - 1$ one period earlier. If, for example, we're discussing sales, which we symbolise as S, then S_t will be sales in the chosen period while $S_{t + 1}$ and $S_{t - 1}$ will identify the sales in the following and preceding periods respectively.

17. Matrix suffixes. A matrix, as we will see in Chapter VIII, is simply a layout of figures in rows and columns. Clearly it is possible to identify a particular figure by specifying which row and column it happens to be in. For example, assume there are figures in each of the following squares:

If we wished to refer to the figure in the square with a tick in it, then, since it lies in the 2nd row and 3rd column we identify it as the 2·3 figure. If, to generalise, we have called all the figures in the squares x's, then this particular x could be symbolised as $x_{2.3}$ (though with matrices with less than ten rows and columns we often miss out the dot in the suffix and just write x_{23}). Similarly, the figure in the square with the cross in will be symbolised as x_{38}. Indeed, all the figures in the matrix would be identified as follows:

x_{11}	x_{12}	x_{13}	x_{14}	x_{15}	x_{16}	x_{17}	x_{18}
x_{21}	x_{22}	x_{23}	x_{24}	x_{25}	x_{26}	x_{27}	x_{28}
x_{31}	x_{32}	x_{33}	x_{34}	x_{35}	x_{36}	x_{37}	x_{38}

THE $\sum$ NOTATION

A symbol continually met in operational research is $\sum$. In this section we explain how to read this ubiquitous symbol.

18. $\sum$. Assume we need to add together all the heights of a group of people (*e.g.* we wish to find the average height). We could, as we've seen, write "$h_1 + h_2 + h_3 + h_4 \ldots$" However, adding together a series of figures occurs so commonly in mathematics that a special symbol exists to indicate this operation. The symbol is $\sum$ (pronounced "sigma") and means "Add together." If, then, we write "$\sum h$" this can be interpreted as "Add together all the h's."

19. Where to start and stop. Useful as this symbol is as it stands, though, it is limited to situations where we add all the figures in a series together. However, we often wish to add only a part of the series—*e.g.* the heights of the first six people, or, using our suffix convention, h_1, h_2, h_3, h_4, h_5 and h_6. How can we adapt the $\sum$ symbol to indicate where we start and where we end?

This is really no problem. If we generalise the *suffix* number and call it, say, i, and then write the first value i takes below the $\sum$ symbol and the last value above, we have the required information. For example, writing $\sum_{i=1}^{6} h_i$ means "Add together all the h's starting at $i = 1$, that is h_1, and stopping at $i = 6$, that is h_6." (Note the figures are inclusive, *i.e.* both h_1 and h_6 are included in the group to be added.)

20. The multi-role of i. It should perhaps be pointed out that the i in the $\sum$ notation is not restricted to suffixes. If desired i can be a value in the algebraic expression. For example, if we wish to add together all the numbers from 3 to 10 we could write $\sum_{i=3}^{10} i$ since this would read "Add together all the i's starting at $i = 3$ and stopping at $i = 10$."

Since our i can play two roles there can clearly be occasions when it plays both at once. For example, assume you had four groups of people, the number in each group being symbolised as g_1, g_2, g_3 and g_4 respectively. To each of the people in the first group you intend to give £1, those in the second group £2, in the third £3 and in the fourth £4. How much will you need? Here the expression $\sum_{i=1}^{4} i g_i$ gives the answer. This perhaps can be more clearly seen if we assume the groups contain, say, 6, 10, 8 and 3 people respectively (*i.e.* $g_1 = 6$; $g_2 = 10$; $g_3 = 8$; $g_4 = 3$), for $\sum_{i=1}^{4} ig_i$ means "Add together all the ig's from $i = 1$ to $i = 4$" which gives us: $1g_1 + 2g_2 + 3g_3 + 4g_4$

$$= (1 \times 6) + (2 \times 10) + (3 \times 8) + (4 \times 3) = £62.$$

Note, incidentally, we are not limited to payments which increase by £1 for each group. As long as there is a regular pattern a little ingenuity will enable us to form a $\sum$ expression. For example, if we want to pay £6, £7, £8 and £9 to the people in the respective groups we can depict this by the expression $\sum_{i=1}^{4}(5 + i)g_i$. Again, if our payments are to be £40, £35, £30 and £25 we could write $\sum_{i=1}^{4}5(9 - i)g_i$. (Test it and see.)

21. Double summation. Let's go one step further. Assume we wish to add together all the x's in the *left-hand half* of the matrix on p. 19. We could do this by taking each column in turn and totalling the x's—and then adding together the totals for the first four columns only. Symbolically we could show this as follows:

$$\sum_{i=1}^{3}x_{i1} + \sum_{i=1}^{3}x_{i2} + \sum_{i=1}^{3}x_{i3} + \sum_{i=1}^{3}x_{i4}$$

(since letting i progress from 1 to 3 in each case gives us $(x_{11} + x_{21} + x_{31}) + (x_{12} + x_{22} + x_{32}) + (x_{13} + x_{23} + x_{33}) + (x_{14} + x_{24} + x_{34})$.

But we can take yet a further short-cut since all four of the above $\sum$ expressions are the same except for the second figure in the suffix—and that progresses regularly from 1 to 4. We can, therefore, write instead $\sum_{j=1}^{4} \sum_{i=1}^{3} x_{ij}$. This expression is termed a *double summation* and is read as follows: "Set j at 1 and keeping it at this value, progress i from 1 to 3 in the expression x_{ij}. Next set j at 2 and progress i from 1 to 3, then set j at 3 and again progress i from 1 to 3, and then set j at 4 and again progress i from 1 to 3. Finally add up all the results."

To ensure the student has the knack of handling double summations we give a further example.

EXAMPLE:

Find
$$\sum_{j=1}^{3} \sum_{i=0}^{4} ji^{j}$$

$$\sum_{j=1}^{3} \sum_{i=0}^{4} ji^{j} = (1 \times 0^1 + 1 \times 1^1 + 1 \times 2^1 + 1 \times 3^1 + 1 \times 4^1) +$$
$$(2 \times 0^2 + 2 \times 1^2 + 2 \times 2^2 + 2 \times 3^2 + 2 \times 4^2) +$$
$$(3 \times 0^3 + 3 \times 1^3 + 3 \times 2^3 + 3 \times 3^3 + 3 \times 4^3)$$
$$= 10 + 60 + 300$$
$$= \underline{\underline{370}}$$

MANIPULATING ALGEBRAIC EXPRESSIONS

Being able to read mathematical expressions is one thing but being able to manipulate them is another and rather more difficult matter. Usually the rules of manipulation are covered during school education, but the importance of this ability in operational research warrants a brief summary of these rules.

22. Definitions. To discuss the manipulation of algebraic expressions we need to know the following definitions:

Expression. A linked group of algebraic symbols—*e.g.* $3x + 4y + z$.

Term. One "bit" of an expression—*e.g.* the terms in the expression just given are $+ 3x$, $+ 4y$ and $+ z$.

Equation. An algebraic statement asserting that two expressions are equal—*e.g.* $3x + 4y + z = 6a + b$.

Inequality. An algebraic statement asserting that two expressions are *not* equal—*e.g.* $3x + 4y + z \neq 6a + b$. Often an inequality is expressed by asserting one expression is greater or less than the other—*e.g.* $3x + 4y + z > 6a + b$ or $3x + 4y + z < 6a + b$.

23. Collecting like terms. If two or more algebraic terms which are to be added or subtracted have *exactly the same symbols* (including indices), the ordinary numbers that form part of the terms can be added and subtracted in the normal way.

EXAMPLE:
$$4x + 3y + 7x - 2y + 5xy - xy + 2x^2 - 3x^2$$
$$= 11x + y + 4xy - x^2$$

24. The multiplication convention. The multiplication sign used in arithmetic ($\times$) is often omitted in algebra (since it tends, particularly in script, to be confused with the letter x), symbols to be multiplied simply being placed alongside each other—*e.g.* ax means $a \times x$ and $5x$ means $5 \times x$. Note that this rule extends to bracketed expressions so that $(a + b)(c + d)$ means $(a + b) \times (c + d)$.

25. Multiplying and dividing symbols with indices. If two or more terms which are to be multiplied or divided have exactly the same symbols other than the indices then they can be combined by adding or subtracting the indices. Thus $x^3x^2 = x^{3 + 2} = x^5$, and $x^3 \div x^2 = x^{3 - 2} = x^1$. (This is immediately obvious if one writes out the terms in full—*i.e.* $x^3x^2 = (x \times x \times x) \times (x \times x) = x \times x \times x \times x \times x = x^5$ and

$$x^3 \div x^2 = \frac{x \times x \times x}{x \times x} = x.)$$

Generalising, then, we can say:

$$x^ax^b = x^{a + b}$$
$$x^a/x^b = x^{a - b}$$

26. Order of operations. In the mathematics of operational research there are essentially five operations—addition, subtraction, multiplication, division and raising to a power (index). By convention, in any expression involving a mixture of these operations, we must always take the operations in the following order:

(*a*) Raise any numbers, symbols or expressions to their powers.

(*b*) Carry out all multiplication and division operations.

NOTE: Generally speaking it does not matter which order one multiplies or divides—*e.g.* if you have $6 \times 8 \div 2$ you finish with the same answer whether you first multiply the 6 and 8 and then divide by 2, or first divide the 8 by 2 and then multiply by 6.

(*c*) Carry out all addition and subtraction operations. (Again note the order here is not important—$5 + 6 - 2 = 9$ whether one first adds the 5 and the 6 and then subtracts the 2, or first subtracts the 2 from 6 and then adds the 5.)

To illustrate this order of operations we will simplify the expression:
$$26 + 5 \times 4^2 \div 8 - 1 + 3^2 \times 100 \div 5^2 + 9 - 7 \times 64^{\frac{1}{2}}.$$

(a) Raising to powers we get:
$$26 + 5 \times 16 \div 8 - 1 + 9 \times 100 \div 25 + 9 - 7 \times 8$$

(b) Multiplying and dividing we get:
$$26 + 10 - 1 + 36 + 9 - 56$$

(c) Adding and subtracting we get: 24.

27. Use of brackets. In addition to the rules so far given on the order of operations there is the additional rule that figures inside a pair of brackets must be worked out before operations involving figures *outside* the brackets can be undertaken. If there happens to be brackets within brackets then the inner brackets must be dealt with first.

EXAMPLES:
$$3 \times (6 + 1) = 3 \times 7 = 21$$
$$(12 - 8)(5 + 2) = 4 \times 7 = 28$$
$$4(5^2 - 2^2) = 4(25 - 4) = 4 \times 21 = 84$$
$$4(5 - 2)^2 = 4 \times 3^2 = 4 \times 9 = 36$$
$$6[3 + (4 \times 4 - 6)] = 6[3 + 10] = 6 \times 13 = 78$$
$$6 + [1 + (\tfrac{3}{4})^2 - (\tfrac{1}{4})^2]^2[4(6 - 5)^5]^3$$
$$= 6 + [1 + \tfrac{9}{16} - \tfrac{1}{16}]^2 [4 \times 1^5]^3$$
$$= 6 + [1\tfrac{1}{2}]^2[4]^3 = 6 + \tfrac{9}{4} \times 64$$
$$= 6 + 144$$
$$= 150$$

28. The minus rules. When manipulating expressions special care is needed wherever there is a minus. The rules for handling minuses are as follows:

(a) Two minuses always make a plus—*e.g.* $5 - (-1)$ $= 5 + 1 = 6$; $-4 \times -3 = +12$; $\dfrac{-8}{-2} = +4$;

(b) A plus and a minus always make a minus—*e.g.* $5 + (-1) = 5 - 1 = 4$; $-4 \times 3 = -12$; $\dfrac{8}{-2} = -4$.

29. Removal of brackets. We have said that where expressions involve brackets, the terms within the brackets must be worked out first. Unfortunately, if we have algebraic expressions this is rarely possible, and so, in order to enable further simplification or manipulation to proceed, it is necessary to have a set of rules that enable us to remove the brackets as a first step rather than as a last step. These rules are as follows:

(a) If the expression in brackets is to be multiplied by a single term, then *multiply every term inside the brackets by this term*—e.g. $5(x + 2y) = 5x + 10y$;
$3x^2(4p - 5q) = 12x^2p - 15x^2q$.

(b) If the bracket is preceded by a plus then every sign inside the bracket will remain the same. If, however, the bracket is preceded by a *minus* then every sign inside the bracket will *reverse*—e.g. $10 + (x - 2y) = 10 + x - 2y$;
$10 - (x - 2y) = 10 - x + 2y$;
$3z - 4x(3 - 5y) = 3z - 12x + 20xy$.

(c) If pairs of brackets are themselves multiplied together then start by re-writing the whole expression so that *each* term in the first pair of brackets is shown immediately in front of the whole of the second pair of brackets (which means the second brackets will be re-written as many times as there are terms in the first brackets)—and then apply rules (a) and (b).

EXAMPLE:
$$(x - 4y + 2z)(3p - 5r)$$
$$= x(3p - 5r) - 4y(3p - 5r) + 2z(3p - 5r)$$
$$= 3xp - 5xr - 12yp + 20yr + 6zp - 10zr.$$

(d) If there are whole groups of brackets and symbols multiplied together, then arbitrarily put square brackets round pairs of the ordinary brackets and then work out the pairs—so progressively reducing the number of brackets until all brackets have been removed.

EXAMPLE:
$$5(2x + y)(3x - 2y)(4x + 3y)(x + y)$$
$$= [5(2x + y)](3x - 2y)[(4x + 3y)(x + y)]$$
$$= [10x + 5y](3x - 2y)[4x(x + y) + 3y(x + y)]$$
$$= [(10x + 5y)(3x - 2y)][4x^2 + 4xy + 3xy + 3y^2]$$
$$= [10x(3x - 2y) + 5y(3x - 2y)][4x^2 + 7xy + 3y^2]$$
$$= [30x^2 - 20xy + 15xy - 10y^2][4x^2 + 7xy + 3y^2]$$
$$= [30x^2 - 5xy - 10y^2][4x^2 + 7xy + 3y^2]$$
$$= 30x^2[4x^2 + 7xy + 3y^2] - 5xy[4x^2 + 7xy + 3y^2]$$
$$- 10y^2[4x^2 + 7xy + 3y^2]$$
$$= 120x^4 + 210x^3y + 90x^2y^2 - 20x^3y - 35x^2y^2 - 15xy^3$$
$$- 40x^2y^2 - 70xy^3 - 30y^4$$
$$= 120x^4 + 190x^3y + 15x^2y^2 - 85xy^3 - 30y^4$$

30. Taking a value out of the brackets. A complex expression can often be simplified by what is termed "taking a value out of the brackets"—the value involved being a number or symbol that can be divided *exactly* into each and every term. The operation is performed by dividing the selected value into every term, putting a bracket round the answer and then writing the selected value *outside* the brackets.

EXAMPLES:

$3 + 9x = 3(1 + 3x)$

$6xy + 7xz - x^2 = x(6y + 7z - x)$

$12x^4y^2 + 24x^3y^3 - 40x^2y^4 + 32xy^2 = 4xy^2(3x^3 + 6x^2y$
$$- 10xy^2 + 8)$$

Note that when the operation is complete removing the brackets must give us back our original expression. If it doesn't we have made an error somewhere. Note, too, we can take a value out of the brackets for just part of the expression if we wish.

EXAMPLE:

$$6x^2 + 4xz - 3xy - 2yz$$

Take $2x$ out of the first two terms and $-y$ out of the latter two:

$$2x(3x + 2z) - y(3x + 2z)$$

And now we can take out $(3x + 2z)$:

$$(3x + 2z)(2x - y).$$

31. Manipulating equalities. When faced with an unsatisfactory-looking equation it is quite permissible to treat it in any way one wishes and still keep the equality as long as one always remembers that *whatever is done to one side must be done to the other*. For example, take the equation:

$$5x^2 - 6x - 12 = 2x^2 - 15x + 21$$

We can simplify this by taking the following steps:

(*a*) Remove the x^2's from the right-hand side by deducting $2x^2$ from each side to give:

$$3x^2 - 6x - 12 = -15x + 21$$

(*b*) Remove the x's from the right-hand side by adding $15x$ to each side to give:

$$3x^2 + 9x - 12 = 21$$

(c) Remove the 12 from the left-hand side by adding 12 to each side to give:

$$3x^2 + 9x = 33.$$

(d) Make all the figures smaller by dividing each side by 3 to give:

$$x^2 + 3x = 11$$

And this, as can be seen, is a much simpler equation than the original one. (We can, indeed, go one step further in our simplification by taking x "out of the brackets" and writing $x(x + 3) = 11$.)

32. Manipulating inequalities. Just as we can manipulate equations, so we can manipulate inequalities as long as we keep to the same all-important rule, *i.e.* do the same to each side. There is, however, one additional important rule and that is when manipulating a "greater than" or "lesser than" inequality *multiplying or dividing by a negative value reverses the inequality symbol*. Thus $6 > -2$, but if we multiply both sides by -3 we get -18 and 6 respectively, and obviously $-18 < 6$, not >6.

Again, if we have $6a^2 - ax < 4a^2 - 3ya$ and we divide both sides by $-a$ we have $-6a + x > -4a + 3y$ (or, more neatly, $x - 6a > 3y - 4a$). And, of course, we can go further here by adding $4a$ to both sides to get $x - 2a > 3y$.

PROGRESS TEST 2

NOTE: Values of negative and fractional powers of e. In operational research we often need to know the value of e when it carries a negative and/or fractional index. Since e is a constant it is possible to construct tables from which the necessary values can be directly read off. Such a table is given in Appendix I and the student should familiarise himself with this table before proceeding to the Progress Test.

None of the first four expressions below have any practical value other than for practice in reading mathematical symbols.

1. If $y = 64x^{-1\frac{1}{3}} + (64x)^{-1\frac{1}{3}} + 3^{0.5x}$, find the value of y when $x = 8$.

2. If $h = \sum_{j=1}^{5} jN_j$, find the value of h when $N_1 = 7$, $N_2 = 3$, $N_3 = 5$, $N_4 = 2$ and $N_5 = 1$.

3. If $L = \sum_{r=1}^{5} a_r r^{r-3}$, find the value of L when $a_r = 6 - r$.

4. If $y = \sum_{i=1}^{3} \sum_{j=2}^{4} ij$, find the value of y.

5. The formula for the Poisson distribution is as follows:
$P(x) = e^{-a} \dfrac{a^x}{x!}$. If $a = 1{\cdot}2$ find the value of $P(x)$
when: (i) $x = 0$ (ii) $x = 1$ (iii) $x = 2$ (iv) $x = 3$ (v) $x = 4$.

6. An adaptation of the formula for the Binomial distribution is
as follows: $P(x \leqslant 2) = \sum_{x=0}^{2} \binom{n}{x} p^x (1 - p)^{n-x}$.
If $n = 5$ and $p = \frac{1}{2}$, find the value of $P(x \leqslant 2)$.

CHAPTER III

CURVE CONSTRUCTION

One of the most effective devices for gaining insight into the way a dependent variable is affected by an independent variable (*see* p. 7) is to show the relationship in the form of a curve on a graph. Curve construction, then, is a vital weapon in the armoury of those who employ operational research.

1. Definition of a curve. When we refer to a *curve* on a graph we mean any line of the graph depicting the relationship between two variables. In this context, therefore, even a straight line will be called a curve.

2. Procedure for constructing a curve. The procedure for constructing a curve is as follows:

(*a*) Set down the mathematical relationship between the two variables in the form:

Dependent variable = Some expression containing the independent variable.

(*b*) Give the independent variable a succession of selected values within the range it is desired to investigate and compute the resulting values of the dependent variable.

(*c*) Prepare a graph with the dependent variable on the vertical axis and the independent variable on the horizontal axis.

(*d*) Plot the values of the independent variable against the resulting values of the dependent variable.

(*e*) Join the plotted points in the form of a curve.

3. A simple example. Assume we wish to gain some insight into the relationship between x and y in the range $x = -4$ to $x = +3$ where $y = x^3 + x^2 - 4x + 1$. Adopting the above procedure gives us the following:

(*a*) $y = x^3 + x^2 - 4x + 1$

(*b*) Taking selected values of x in the range -3 to $+4$ we obtain:

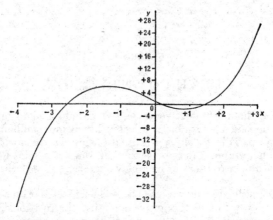

(a) Curve of $y = x^3 + x^2 - 4x + 1$.

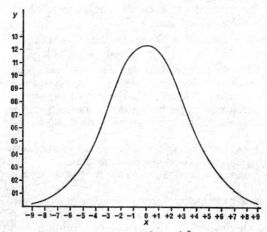

(b) Curve of $y = \dfrac{1}{\sqrt{10} \times \sqrt{2\pi}}\, e^{-\frac{1}{2}\left(\frac{x - o}{\sqrt{10}}\right)^2}$ (normal curve).

FIG. 2.—*Curve construction.*

Selected values of

x	x^3	$+x^2$	$-4x$	$+1$	y
-4	-64	$+16$	$+16$	$+1$	-31
-3	-27	$+9$	$+12$	$+1$	-5
-2	-8	$+4$	$+8$	$+1$	$+5$
$-1\frac{1}{2}$	$-3\cdot375$	$+2\cdot250$	$+6$	$+1$	$+5\cdot875$
-1	-1	$+1$	$+4$	$+1$	$+5$
$-\frac{1}{2}$	$-0\cdot125$	$+0\cdot250$	$+2$	$+1$	$+3\cdot125$
0	0	0	0	$+1$	$+1$
$+\frac{1}{2}$	$+0\cdot125$	$+0\cdot250$	-2	$+1$	$-0\cdot625$
$+1$	$+1$	$+1$	-4	$+1$	-1
$+1\frac{1}{2}$	$+3\cdot375$	$+2\cdot250$	-6	$+1$	$+0\cdot625$
$+2$	$+8$	$+4$	-8	$+1$	$+5$
$+3$	$+27$	$+9$	-12	$+1$	$+25$

(*c*), (*d*) and (*e*) (*see* Fig. 2(*a*)).

4. Constructing the normal curve. Finally we show that curve construction is in itself a simple technique (if rather lengthy at times) by illustrating the construction of the, *on the face of it*, complex normal curve. To ease the burden of the arithmetic we will construct a normal curve having a mean ($\bar{x}$) of zero and a standard deviation (σ) of $\sqrt{10}$ between the limits $x = \pm 9$.

(*a*) The normal curve formula is:

$$y = \frac{1}{\sigma\sqrt{2\pi}}\, e^{-\frac{1}{2}\left(\frac{x-\bar{x}}{\sigma}\right)^2}$$

Substituting our values for $\bar{x}$ and σ we have:

$$y = \frac{1}{\sqrt{10} \times \sqrt{2\pi}} \cdot e^{-\frac{1}{2}\left(\frac{x-0}{\sqrt{10}}\right)^2} = \frac{1}{\sqrt{20\pi}} \cdot e^{-\frac{1}{2} \times \frac{x^2}{10}}$$

$$= \frac{1}{\sqrt{20 \times 3\cdot14159}}\, e^{-\frac{x^2}{20}} = \frac{1}{8}\, e^{-\frac{x^2}{20}}$$

(*b*) Taking selected values of x in the range ± 9 gives us:

1	2	3	4	5
SELECTED VALUES OF x	x^2	$\frac{x^2}{20}$	$e^{\frac{-x^2}{20}}$	$\frac{1}{8}e^{\frac{-x^2}{20}}$
−9	81	4.05	0.017	0.002
−7	49	2.45	0.086	0.011
−5	25	1.25	0.287	0.036
−3	9	0.45	0.638	0.080
−1	1	0.05	0.952	0.119
0	0	0	1.000	0.125
+1	1			0.119
+3	9			0.080
+5	25			0.036
+7	49			0.011
+9	81			0.002

NOTE: Column 4 is found from our table of exponential values (Appendix I), interpolating where necessary, being the value of e to the negative power of the figure in column 3. Column 5 is column 4 × $\frac{1}{8}$. Since the curve is symmetrical (as can be seen from the symmetry of x^2 in column 2), there is no need to complete the lower parts of columns 3 and 4.

(c), (d) and (e) (see Fig. 2(b)).

PROGRESS TEST 3

1. Construct curves for the following expressions:

	Expression	Limits of x	Comments
(a) (i)	$y = 2x$	0, 9	On same graph.
(ii)	$y = 2x + 4$	0, 9	(Maximum
(iii)	$y = \frac{1}{2}x + 4$	0, 9	value of y is 22)
(b) (i)	$y = x^2$	−8, +8	On same graph
(ii)	$y = 2^x$	−2, +6	
(c)	$y = e^x$	0, 4	See Appendix I
(d)	$y = e^{-x}$	0, 4	See Appendix I
(e)	$y = \binom{n}{x}p^x(1 - p)^{n-x}$	0, 5	When $n = 5$, $p = 0.8$ and x is discrete.

(f) $y = e^{-a}\dfrac{a^x}{x!}$ 0, 4   When $a = 1 \cdot 2$ (see Progress Test 2, question 5).

(g) $y = KR^{R^x}$ $-4, +6$ When $K = 1000$ and $R = \frac{1}{2}$

(h) $y = \dfrac{1}{\sigma\sqrt{2\pi}} \cdot e^{-\frac{1}{2}\left(\frac{x - \bar{x}}{\sigma}\right)^2}$

                                  $-3, +3$ When $\sigma = 1$ and $\bar{x} = 0$

CHAPTER IV

PROGRESSIONS

A mathematical pattern commonly found in work involving operational research is one in which there are a series of figures such that each figure differs from its neighbours in a regular fashion. Such a series is called a *progression* and the individual figures, *terms*, and a knowledge of the features of progressions and terms frequently proves useful in the analysis of mathematical business situations. The two most important progressions are the arithmetic and the geometric and these we will now study.

ARITHMETIC PROGRESSIONS

An *arithmetic progression* is a series in which each term is the previous term *plus* a constant (though note we can have a negative constant). For example, the series 5, 7, 9, 11, . . . is an arithmetic progression since each term is the previous term plus the constant 2—as is the series 24, 21, 18, 15. . . . where the constant is -3. These progressions are not limited to whole numbers—the series $1\frac{1}{2}, 2\frac{1}{4}, 3, 3\frac{3}{4}, 4\frac{1}{2}$ . . . is an arithmetic progression with a constant of $\frac{3}{4}$. Note that progressions can start anywhere and end anywhere.

1. The value of the nth term of an arithmetic progression. The value of the nth term (*e.g.* 2nd, 3rd, 4th, 5th . . .) of an arithmetic progression is given by the following formula:

Value of the nth term = 1st term $+ (n-1) \times$ constant.

EXAMPLE:
Value of 7th item of the progression 5, 7, 9, 11 and 13 . . .
$$= 5 + (7-1) \times 2 = 17$$

2. The sum of an arithmetic progression. The "sum of an arithmetic progression" is the total obtained if all the terms are added together. Such a sum can be calculated from the following formula:

Sum of an arithmetic
progression = (first term + last term) × No. of terms ÷ 2

EXAMPLE:

$$\text{Sum of the series 5, 7, 9, 11 and 13}$$
$$= (5 + 13) \times 5 \div 2$$
$$= \frac{18 \times 5}{2} = 45$$

Although the formula can be taken as given, its validity can be confirmed by inspecting any arithmetic progression, for if one takes the terms in pairs, one from each extreme end of the series and deleting each term as it is taken, then it can be quickly seen the sums of each pair are all equal (*e.g.* 18 in the case just examined). So the total of the whole series must be this figure (which is given at once by the sum of the first and last terms) halved times the number of terms.

A word of warning here—be careful to count the number of terms in the series correctly. For example, in the series 10, 11, 12, 13 . . . 22 there are *thirteen*, not twelve, terms.

GEOMETRIC PROGRESSIONS

A *geometric progression* is a series in which each term is the previous term *multiplied* by a constant. For example, the series 10, 20, 40, 80, 160 . . . is a geometric progression since each term is the previous term multiplied by 2. Again, the progressions are not limited to whole numbers—the series 64, 32, 16, 8, 4, 2, 1, $\frac{1}{2}$, $\frac{1}{4}$, $\frac{1}{8}$, $\frac{1}{16}$ . . . forming a geometric progression where the constant is $\frac{1}{2}$.

3. The value of the nth term of a geometric progression. The value of the nth term of a geometric progression is given by the formula:

Value of the nth term = 1st term × constant $^{n-1}$

EXAMPLES:
Value of 5th term of the series 10, 20, 40 . . . = $10 \times 2^{5-1} = 160$
Value of 5th term of the series 64, 32, 16 . . . = $64 \times (\frac{1}{2})^{5-1} = 4$

4. The sum of a geometric progression. The sum of a geometric progression is given by the formula:

Sum of a geometric progression =

$$\frac{\text{First term} \times (1 - \text{Constant}^{\text{No. of terms}})}{1 - \text{Constant}}$$

EXAMPLES:

Sum of the series 10, 20, 40, 80, 160

$$= \frac{10(1 - 2^5)}{1 - 2} = \frac{10 \times -31}{-1} = 310$$

Sum of the series 64, 32, 16, 8, 4, 2, 1, $\frac{1}{2}$

$$= \frac{64[1 - (\frac{1}{2})^8]}{1 - \frac{1}{2}} = \frac{64[1 - \frac{1}{256}]}{\frac{1}{2}} = 127\frac{1}{2}$$

5. Sum of a geometric progression to infinity. If the constant in a geometric progression is less than 1, then it is possible to find the sum of such a progression even when it extends to infinity. This is because as we raise a number less than 1 to higher and higher powers we obtain a progressively *smaller* figure (*e.g.* $(\frac{1}{2})^2 = \frac{1}{4}$; $(\frac{1}{2})^3 = \frac{1}{8}$; $(\frac{1}{2})^4 = \frac{1}{16}$). A fraction to the power of infinity, therefore, reduces to zero, or as we can say using our limit symbol (*see* p. 14):

$\underset{x \to \infty}{L} a^x = 0$, where $a < 1$ (though greater, of course, than 0).

Applying this to our formula, then, we find:

Sum of geometric progression to infinity where constant is

less than 1 $$= \frac{\text{1st term} \times (1 - \text{Constant}^\infty)}{1 - \text{Constant}}$$

$$= \frac{\text{1st term} \times (1 - 0)}{1 - \text{Constant}} = \frac{\text{1st term}}{1 - \text{Constant}}$$

EXAMPLE:

Sum of series 64, 32, 16, . . . to infinity

$$= \frac{64}{1 - \frac{1}{2}} = \frac{64}{\frac{1}{2}} = 128$$

(Not much more, in fact, than the same but much shorter series summed in the previous paragraph. But, of course, once our terms fall below 1 we are adding progressively tinier fractions to our total.)

PROGRESS TEST 4

1. Find the sums of the following series:
   (a) 20, 24, 28, 32, ... 100
   (b) 5, 7, 10, 12, 15, 17, ... 47

2. Three foremen issue requisitions using their own pad of requisitions. At the end of the month the following sequences had been used:

	Foreman		
	A	B	C
First requisition	132	288	344
Last requisition	145	296	377

   (a) What would be the hash total of all the used requisitions?
   (b) If the hash total were as follows, what do you think the explanation would be?
   (i) 16,461; (ii) 17,121; (iii) 14,196.

   NOTE: A "hash total" is a total of a series of figures which in itself has no real meaning but which can be used for cross-checking purposes. In this instance the hash total is simply the total obtained by adding together all the serial numbers of the used requisitions.

3. The rate of growth of transport costs in an organisation is such that each year the costs are 40% more than the previous year. If these costs are £2000 this year what will they be in 16 years' time?

4. In exponential smoothing the following formula is used:

$$A_t = ax_t + (1 - a)A_{t-1}.$$

   (It follows, then, that

$$A_{t-1} = ax_{t-1} + (1 - a)A_{t-2}$$

   and

$$A_{t-2} = ax_{t-2} + (1 - a)A_{t-3} \text{ etc.})$$

a and $(1 - a)$ are known as "weights." Prove that if the formula is expanded so that only x's appear—i.e. so we have

$$ax_t + (1 - a)(ax_{t-1} + (1 - a)[ax_{t-2} + (1 - a)\{ax_{t-3} \ldots,$$

then the sum of the weights of an infinitely long series is 1.

   NOTE: This question is harder than usual but the answer provides a useful proof that the sum of the weights of an exponentially smoothed average *are* equal to 1—(*see* Chapter XXI).

CHAPTER V

PERMUTATIONS AND COMBINATIONS

Imagine there are 5 people (labelled A to E) in a courtyard. You intend to call them into a room, three at a time to have their photographs taken in groups. In the room there are three chairs in a row on which the selected people can sit for the photograph. How many different group photographs can you take?

If you try to answer this question you will quickly become aware of an ambiguity in its phrasing for it is not clear what the word "different" means. Clearly a photograph of A, B and C is different from one of A, B and D. But is a photograph of A, B and C with A sitting in the left-hand chair "different" from one of the same three people but with A now sitting in the middle chair?

The answer here depends on what we want the word "different" to mean. If by "different" we mean different in every respect *including the order in which the people sit*, then we are concerned with the number of *permutations* we can have. Conversely, if we only mean different groups and regard all photographs of the same three people as being the "same," *i.e.* we *disregard the order in which they sit*, then we are concerned with the number of *combinations* we can have.

Keeping this distinction between permutations and combinations clearly in mind, we can see how to find the answer to our initial question (as to how many different group photographs we can take) in both contexts.

PERMUTATIONS

First let us look at permutations—*i.e.* in terms of our illustration, find out how many different photographs we can take where the order of sitting is significant.

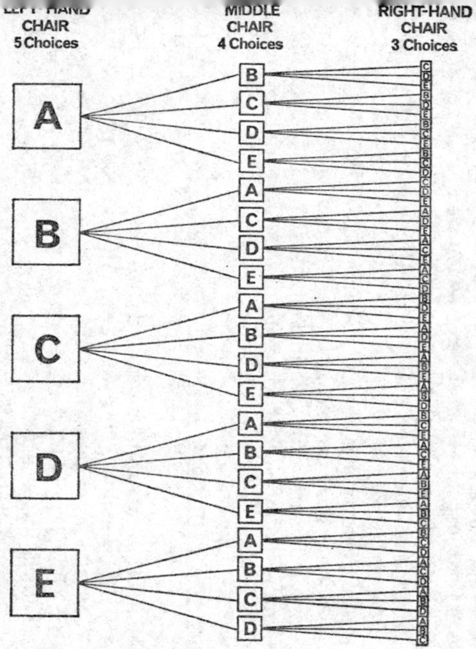

ABC Group	ABE Group	ACE Group	BCD Group	BDE Group
A B C	A B E	A C E	B C D	B D E
A C B	A E B	A E C	B D C	B E D
B A C	B A E	C A E	C B D	D B E
C A B	B E A	C E A	C D B	D E B
C B A	E A B	E C A	D B C	E B D
	E B A		D C B	E D B

ABD Group	ACD Group	ADE Group	BCE Group	CDE Group
A B D	A C D	A D E	B C E	C D E
A D B	A D C	A E D	B E C	C E D
B A D	C A D	D A E	C B E	D C E
B D A	C D A	D E A	C E B	D E C
D A B	D A C	E A D	E B C	E C D
D B A	D C A	E D A	E C B	E D C

(b) Combinations. As can be seen, our 60 "photographs" relate to a total of only 10 different groups. The number of combinations, then, can be found by dividing the total number of permutations by the number of permutations that can be made within each separate group.

LEFT-HAND CHAIR 5 Choices — MIDDLE CHAIR 4 Choices — RIGHT-HAND CHAIR 3 Choices

Total permutations = 5 × 4 × 3 = 60

(a) Permutations.

Fig. 3.—Taking 5 items, 3 at a time.

1. Number of permutations of n objects taking x at a time.
The easiest way to tackle our photographic problem here is to
imagine all three chairs empty and then consider how many
different people could sit on the left-hand side chair. The
answer is, of course, 5. Sitting one of these in the left-hand
chair, then, means we have only 4 people left whom we can put
in the middle chair. So the total number of different pairs we
make is only 5×4 (*see* Fig. 3). However, we still have to fill
the last chair—and now we have only 3 people left to choose
from. So each of our pairs can be joined by any one of 3 remaining people—and this gives us a total of $5 \times 4 \times 3 = 60$
different photographs.

The procedure in this situation, then, is fairly obvious. All
one needs to do to find the total number of permutations is
write down the total number of people in the courtyard, and
then start a count-down which stops when you have as many
numbers as there are chairs, and then multiply all the numbers
together. If, then, for example, there were 20 people in the
courtyard and 5 chairs, the number of permutations would be
$20 \times 19 \times 18 \times 17 \times 16 = 1,860,480$.

2. $^{n}P_{x}$. Let us now try and generalise this procedure.

It takes only a moment's thought to see that some sort of
factorial expression is involved—indeed, if we say there are n
people in the courtyard then the expression we want is going to
be something like $n!$. But the trouble is, the "count-down"
doesn't run to 1—it cuts off before that. How can we cut off the
tail of a factorial?

Actually the answer is absurdly simple—we just divide by a
lower factorial. For example, if we want to cut off $20!$ at 16 (as
in the previous paragraph) we just divide it by $15!$. This becomes immediately clear if we write out the factorials in full,
i.e.

$$\frac{20!}{15!} = \frac{20 \times 19 \times 18 \times 17 \times 16 \times 15 \times 14 \times 13 \times 12 \times 11 \times 10 \times 9 \times 8 \times 7 \times 6 \times 5 \times 4 \times 3 \times 2 \times 1}{15 \times 14 \times 13 \times 12 \times 11 \times 10 \times 9 \times 8 \times 7 \times 6 \times 5 \times 4 \times 3 \times 2 \times 1}$$

Cancelling the two right-hand ends we have $20 \times 19 \times 18
\times 17 \times 16$—which is what we want. All we need now, then,
is to know the lower factorial. But this is no problem, either,
since if we have, say, 5 chairs in the room we want to cut off the
main factorial after 5 terms—*i.e.* $20 - 5 = 15$, or *the total
number of people minus the total number of chairs.*

Now at last we can write down our general expression and say that the number of permutations we can make from n items taking x at a time (symbolised as ^nP_x) and without replacement (see next paragraph) can be found from the following formula:

$$^nP_x = \frac{n!}{(n-x)!}$$

3. With and without replacement. So far we've made the common-sense assumption that having taken one of the people (say A) out of the courtyard and sat him on one of the chairs, he is no longer in the courtyard available for further selection. We have, therefore, been what is technically termed as *selecting without replacement*.

Imagine, however, we are prepared to take our photograph by three separate exposures. Now we can take our first exposure with A sitting in the left-hand chair and then *send him out into the courtyard again so he is available for further selection* before we select someone for the second exposure. In this situation we are *selecting with replacement—i.e.* after we select each item we replace it in the group before making our next selection of an item. Note that selecting with replacement means we can have a photograph with A sitting in all three chairs.

Selecting with replacement is not common but where it applies $^nP_x = n^x$. This can be seen if we consider our 5 people and 3 chairs, since we can sit any one of the 5 in the left-hand chair, any one of the 5 in the middle chair and any one of the 5 in the right-hand chair—*i.e.* a total of $5 \times 5 \times 5$ permutations $= 5^3$ or n^x.

EXAMPLES:

How many three-letter car registration numbers can be made from the 26 letters of the alphabet:

    (a) selecting without replacement? $26 \times 25 \times 24 = 15,600$
    (b) selecting with replacement? 26^3 $= 17,576$

COMBINATIONS

Now we turn to seeing how many distinct groups we can photograph where the order of sitting is ignored.

4. Permutations within groups. We will start to solve this problem by imagining we begin our photographic session by calling into the room just one group of 3 and then taking as many different photographs of the one group as possible. How many photographs can we take? Clearly, if our group is A, B and C we can arrange them on the chairs in the following ways: ABC, ACB, BAC, BCA, CAB and CBA. Indeed, all we have done, of course, is listed all the permutations we have if we have 3 items and take them 3 at a time—*i.e.* $n = 3$ and $x = 3$, so

$$^nP_x = \frac{n!}{(n-x)!} = \frac{3!}{(3-3)!} = \frac{3!}{0!} = 3! = 6$$

(Recall that $0! = 1$ (*see* page 13).)

So after 6 photographs we have exhausted all the permutations possible with our first group. We then turn to our second group (which can, of course, still include two people from our original group) and again we find we can take just 6 different photographs. Indeed every group will involve exactly 6 photographs (*see* Fig. 3).

5. $\binom{n}{x}$. Now imagine our stack of photographs at the end of the day. For every group we will have 6 photographs. But in total we will have all the different numbers of photographs it is possible to take—*i.e.* we will have all the permutations of 5 people taken 3 at a time (if every possible group was taken in every possible sitting arrangement then every possible photograph will have been taken). And this means, then, the total number of permutations will be six times the number of groups —or, more importantly, the number of groups will be the number of permutations ÷ 6. Which means in this case we will have $60 \div 6 = 10$ groups.

Let us try and generalise from this. Since every group of x people will be able to form $x!$ permutations (there's no need to cut off the factorial "tail" here since everybody in the group is included in the arrangement) and since collectively there will be ^nP_x permutations, then:

The number of combinations (groups) that can be formed from n items taking x items at a time without replacement (symbolised as $\binom{n}{x}$) is given by the formula:

$$\binom{n}{x} = {}^nP_x \div x!$$

$$= \frac{n!}{(n-x)!} \div x!$$

$$= \frac{n!}{(n-x)!x!}$$

This is an important formula and should be carefully memorised.

EXAMPLE:

How many combinations of 3 letters (*i.e.* disregarding the order) can we form from an alphabet of 26 letters?

$$\binom{26}{3} = \frac{26!}{(26-3)!3!}$$

$$= \frac{26!}{23!3!}$$

$$= \frac{26 \times 25 \times 24 \times 23!}{23! \times 3 \times 2 \times 1}$$

And since the 23!'s cancel we have

$$\frac{26 \times 25 \times 24}{3 \times 2 \times 1} = \underline{\underline{2600}}$$

PROGRESS TEST 5

1. Find $\sum_{i=0}^{n} \binom{n}{i}$ when:

(a) $n = 4$; (b) $n = 6$.

2. Seven capital projects are under discussion. How many different programmes ("arrangements") must be considered in each of the following circumstances:

(a) Projects are to be started at one-year intervals;

(*b*) Four projects can be started now and the other three at one-year intervals.

3. A special recurring job requires 4 men. If there are 19 men in the department, how many different teams can be arranged, and in how many will a given individual appear?

CHAPTER VI

CALCULUS

On occasions calculus can be of considerable use to the operational research worker. The subject divides essentially into differential calculus and integral calculus, and, as the student is no doubt aware, can extend to considerable depth. In this chapter we shall examine the relevant aspects only in very elementary terms.

DIFFERENTIAL CALCULUS

Differential calculus is often of use when it is necessary to identify the value a particular factor must take in order to obtain an optimum result, such as maximising a profit or minimising a cost.

1. Measuring slope. Before turning to the calculus involved it is necessary to appreciate how the mathematician measures slopes on a graph. Actually the method is essentially the same as that used in day-to-day practical life for we will often refer to the slope of a hill as, say, 1 in 10 which simply means there is a rise of 1 vertical foot per 10 horizontal feet. The only difference is that mathematicians would write 1 in 10 as $\frac{1}{10}$. A slope on a graph, then, is measured by *change in value of* y *(vertical change)* ÷ *change in value of* x *(horizontal change)* (*see* Fig. 4). Note, incidentally, that if *y decreases* as *x* increases the slope is negative. Thus the sign before the slope figure indicates the *direction* of the slope.

2. The slope of a curve. Look at the curve of the expression $y = 5 + 2x$ in Fig. 5. It is clear that y rises by 2 units for every 1 unit of x and so the slope is $\frac{2}{1} = 2$.

For a straight line, then, measuring the slope is no problem. Look now, however, at the curve $y = 10x - x^2 - 5$ in the same Fig. Obviously the slope of this curve is changing all the

45

time. If we want to measure this slope, then, we must specify at just which point the measurement must be made—such as where $x = 3$. It so happens that the tangent to the curve at that point gives the slope, but the problem is how to calculate the slope of this tangent.

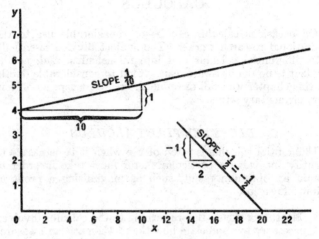

FIG. 4.—*Measuring slopes.*

3. Differentiation. We state without proof (though the proof is not difficult—just rather irrelevant) that by *differentiating* an expression we obtain a second expression that enables us to measure the slope directly. To differentiate an expression written in the form "y = some expression containing an x" (where y can be "Total cost" or "Profit" or "No. of orders" etc. and x can be "No. of workers" or "age of machine" or "% of items inspected" etc.), take each x term in turn in the expression and subject it to the following manipulation:

(a) Multiply the whole term by the *index number* of x.
(b) Reduce the x index number by 1.

Thus, for example, x^2 becomes $2 \times x^{2-1} = 2x$, and $10x^4$ becomes $4 \times 10x^{4-1} = 40x^3$.

Generalising we can say ax^b becomes bax^{b-1}.

Note the following additional minor points:

(i) The whole operation is referred to as "differentiating y with respect to x" symbolised as "$\dfrac{dy}{dx}$" and spoken as "dy by dx"—x being the variable whose index numbers are involved in the process.

(ii) Every term in the expression to be differentiated must include an x with an index number. For example, take the expression $x^2 - 4x + 21$. The "x^2" obviously gives no trouble but "$4x$" must be written as "$4x^1$." As for "21," at first glance it seems impossible to squeeze an x into the term— until we remember that $x^0 = 1$ and since $21 = 21 \times 1$ we can write "21" as "$21x^0$").

EXAMPLES:

(a) Differentiate $y = 5x^3 - 6x^2 + 10x - 8$.

Now we can write this as:
$$y = 5x^3 - 6x^2 + 10x^1 - 8x^0$$
$$\therefore \frac{dy}{dx} \text{ (i.e. slope)} = 3 \times 5x^{3-1} - 2 \times 6x^{2-1} + 1 \times 10x^{1-1}$$
$$- 0 \times 8x^{0-1}$$
$$= 15x^2 - 12x^1 + 10x^0 - 0$$
$$= 15x^2 - 12x + 10$$

(b) Differentiate
$$y = x^3 + 6x^{1\frac{1}{2}} - 4x^{\frac{3}{4}} + x^{-1} + 7x^{-2} - 2x^{-4} + 4x^{-6\frac{1}{2}}$$
$$\frac{dy}{dx} = 3x^{3-1} + 9x^{1\frac{1}{2}-1} - 3x^{\frac{3}{4}-1} + (-1 \times x^{-1-1})$$
$$+ (-2 \times 7x^{-2-1}) - (-4 \times 2x^{-4-1})$$
$$+ (-6\frac{1}{2} \times 4x^{-6\frac{1}{2}-1})$$
$$= 3x^2 + 9x^{\frac{1}{2}} - 3x^{-\frac{1}{4}} - x^{-2} - 14x^{-3} + 8x^{-5} - 26x^{-7\frac{1}{2}}$$

4. Differential expressions and the slope. Having obtained a differentiated expression the slope of the original curve at any point can be found by *substituting the value of x at that point in the differentiated expression*. So, reverting to our problem of finding the slope at $x = 3$ of our expression $y = 10x - x^2 - 5$, we know we must first differentiate the expression to obtain the slope which gives us $10x^0 - 2x^1 = 10 - 2x$, and then substitute 3 for x. This gives us $10 - 2 \times 3 = 4$. The slope at $x = 3$, therefore, is 4. (Note, incidentally, that the slope at

$x = 8$ is $10 - 2 \times 8 = -6$, *i.e.* a negative result that tells us the slope runs *downwards* from left to right at that point.)

5. Identifying the optimum point. We can now turn to identifying optimum points.

Look again at the curve $y = 10x - x^2 - 5$ in Fig. 5. Here it is easy to identify the value of x that maximises y—it lies under the peak of the curve and is obviously 5. Now consider the slope of the curve at that point. Clearly it must be horizontal—*i.e.* 0, since there will be zero change in y per unit of x.

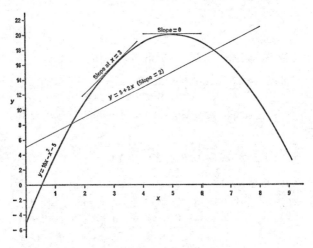

Fig. 5.—*Curves and slopes.*

Therefore at the optimum point dy/dx must equal 0. To find this optimum, then, all we need do is to *set the differentiated expression equal to 0 and solve for x.* Thus we could have found the optimum point of $y = 10x - x^2 - 5$ by writing $10 - 2x$ (*i.e.* the differentiated expression) $= 0$

$$\therefore 2x = 10 \text{ and so } x = 5.$$

which confirms what we observed by eye—that y is at an optimum when $x = 5$.

6. Maxima and minima. An optimum point can be when y is either at a maximum or a minimum depending on the variable y represents—if it is profit we need a maximum while if it represents cost we need a minimum value. Our identification procedure does not, though, tell us whether we have identified a maximum or a minimum. However, in practice this rarely gives us any trouble. Nevertheless, the student is advised always to make a quick sketch of the curve involved. This not only indicates whether our solution is a maximum or a minimum but even more important helps to give the "feel" of the situation that in turn leads to deeper insight into the whole position being investigated.

INTEGRAL CALCULUS

The other situation where calculus is of help is that in which we want to find a cumulative total where the *rate* of accumulation changes throughout the series. The objective is similar to that of finding the sum of a progression. Thus, in a simple situation where a worker produces 7 units in the first hour, 9 in the second, 11 in the third, etc., then in 10 hours he will produce $\sum_{i=1}^{10} (2i + 5) = 160$ units (the sum of a simple arithmetic progression). What, however, if his *rate* of production is 7 per hour at the end of the first hour (after starting at 5 per hour), 9 per hour at the end of the second hour, 11 per hour at the end of the third . . . etc., his rate increasing steadily as he worked. How many units will he produce then in 10 hours?

This is a situation where integral calculus can be used.

7. Integration. Integration is simply the reverse of differentiation. For example, if we differentiate $4x^3$ we obtain $12x^2$. Consequently if we integrate $12x^2$ we obtain $4x^3$. In this latter case mathematicians would say they were "integrating $12x^2$ with respect to x" and symbolise the statement as $\int 12x^2 . dx$. (If at some stage it had been stated that $y = 12x^2$, this latter symbolisation could have taken the form of $\int y . dx$, which is, of course, the same thing.)

Working "reversed differentiation" is certainly a little more complicated than normal straightforward differentiation.

Nevertheless a little thought shows us that essentially it is a matter of observing the following rules:

(a) Since at the time of differentiation the index number is reduced by 1, on integration the index number must be *increased* by 1.

(b) Since also at the time of differentiation the term differentiated will have been multiplied by the *original* index number, on integration the term must be divided by this original pre-differentiation index.

For example $\int 12x^2 \cdot dx = \dfrac{12x^{2+1}}{2+1} = 4x^3$.

Generalising, we can say $\int ax^b \cdot dx = \dfrac{ax^{b+1}}{b+1}$.

8. The indefinite integral. At this point the thoughtful student may have observed that if a non-x term existed in the pre-differentiated expression, then, since it will have vanished in the process of differentiation, it will be impossible to re-establish this term on integration. Thus differentiating $4x^3 + 15$ also gives us $12x^2$—and, as we've seen, integrating $12x^2$ only gives us $4x^3$, the "15" being unknown.

Strictly speaking, then, we cannot really say $\int ax^b \cdot dx = \dfrac{ax^{b+1}}{b+1}$; what we must say is $\int ax^b \cdot dx = \dfrac{ax^{b+1}}{b+1} + c$, where c represents a possible but totally unknown non-x term. This latter formula is known as the *indefinite integral*.

9. Integration and areas. The importance of integration to us at this stage lies in the fact that it enables us to find the area under a curve between any two x-points on the x-axis. To compute such an area we simply adopt the following procedure:

(a) Find the indefinite integral of the expression that relates to the curve in question.

(b) Substitute in turn each of the two x-point values in the indefinite integral.

(c) Find the difference between the two results given by (b).

EXAMPLE:

What is the area below the curve $12x^2$ between the points $x = 2$ and $x = 4$?

Step (a)

$$\int_2^4 12x^2 \cdot dx = \begin{bmatrix} {}^4 \\ 4x^3 + c \\ {}_2 \end{bmatrix}$$

(NOTE: (i) We often write the indefinite integral in square brackets.

(ii) When we are concerned with finding areas we write the relevant x-points as small figures at the top and bottom of the integral sign and the first square bracket.)

Step (b) Substituting 2 and 4 for x gives us respectively:

$$4 \times 2^3 + c = 32 + c$$

and $\qquad 4 \times 4^3 + c = 256 + c.$

Step (c) Finding the difference gives us $(256 + c) - (32 + c) = 224$ (Note the disappearance of c. This always happens when we find areas.)

The area, therefore, is 224.

10. Practical integration. We can now return to the problem formulated at the beginning of this section.

In that situation the worker's production rate was obviously linked to the length of time he had been working, and we can say, then, that at the end of x hours he would be producing at a rate of $5 + 2x$ units per hour—*i.e.* if $y =$ production rate then $y = 5 + 2x$. Graphing this expression we obtain the curve shown in Fig. 6. Now if you know a worker's production rate you can compute his total production by multiplying this by the time he works—*e.g.* if he were to produce at a steady rate of 5 per hour, then in 10 hours he'll produce $5 \times 10 = 50$ units. It so happens that if you multiply a figure on one axis of a graph by a figure on the other axis, the product equals the area formed on the graph. So in our problem we can find the worker's total production by finding the area under the curve between $x = 0$ and $x = 10$.

Stated thus the application of integral calculus is very clear for we can find this area using the procedure given in the previous paragraph, *i.e.*

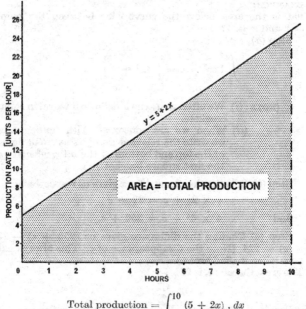

$$\text{Total production} = \int_0^{10} (5 + 2x) \, . \, dx$$

FIG. 6.—*Integration and areas.*

$$\text{Area} = \int_0^{10} (5 + 2x) \, . \, dx$$

$$= \left[5x + x^2 + c \right]_0^{10}$$

$$= (5 \times 10 + 10^2 + c) - (5 \times 0 + 0^2 + c)$$
$$= (150 + c) - c$$
$$= 150$$

So our worker produces 150 units in the 10 hours.

PROGRESS TEST 6

1. (*a*) Differentiate, and (*b*) integrate, the following expressions:
   (*i*) $y = 5x^4 + 15x^2 + 12x + 8$
   (*ii*) $y = 30x^9 - 4x^3 + 18x^{\frac{1}{2}} + 1 + 8x^{-2} - 10x^{-3}$

2. Sketch curve of $y = 12x - 3x^2$ and find:
    (a) Slope at $x = 0$
    (b) Maximum value of y

3. Find values of x that minimise/maximise y below and state whether y is at a maximum or a minimum at these points:
    (a) $y = 120x - 4x^2 - 100$
    (b) $y = x^4 - 32x + 12$

4. Find the area under the curve of the expression in question 2 between the x-points:
    (a) 0 and 1
    (b) 1 and 2
    (c) 2 and 3
    (d) 3 and 4.

CHAPTER VII

INCREMENTAL TECHNIQUES

We have seen how we can find maxima and minima of simple algebraic equations by differential calculus and, as we will see in the chapter on model-building, this is a useful technique for optimising profits. However, there are times when we are not so much interested in the maximum or minimum as the effect of making a minor change in one of the variables. At these times we use an incremental technique which, as the name suggests, tells us what will happen if we make a small incremental change in the situation.

In this chapter we will look at two such techniques—the step-by-step technique and difference equations.

1. Illustrative example. To illustrate our incremental techniques we will examine the following situation:

A company has found from its market research that if a particular product were sold at its marginal cost of £20 1100 units a period would be sold, but for every additional £1 added to the price (this being the smallest practical price "step" in the industry), demand would drop by 200 units. We wish to see how our total product contribution changes with price and at the same time identify the optimum price.

2. The step-by-step technique. Using the step-by-step technique simply involves starting at any logical point, and by altering our variable one unit (increment) at a time ascertaining the incremental effect. In the case of our illustration this involves starting at the most logical point—*i.e.*, where selling price equals marginal cost—and the increasing the selling price £1 at a time. The steps we obtain, then, are as follows:

Selling price £	Contribution £	Sales Units	Total contribution £
20	0	1100	0
21	1	900	900
22	2	700	1400
23	3	500	1500
24	4	300	1200
25	5	100	500

This investigation shows us that the total contribution rises at first but then falls away—the maximum earned being £1500 at a selling price of £23.

Though the step-by-step technique is not a very sophisticated technique it does play a useful part in many quantitative analyses and, indeed, if there is no regular mathematical pattern in the situation it may prove to be the only feasible technique.

3. Difference equations. *Difference equations* are algebraic expressions that are specifically concerned with differences rather than totals. For example, if my earnings increase by 100% every year I can say $E_{t+1} = 2E_t$ where E = earnings and the subscripts t and $t+1$ represent any year and the year after respectively. The virtue of difference equations lies in the fact they can be manipulated—thus $E_{t+2} = 2E_{t+1} = 2 \times 2E_t = 4E_t$ (it probably isn't very long before one realises that since a geometric progression is being formed, then $E_{t+a} = 2^a E_t$).

In the case of our illustration we are concerned with the difference between contribution at one selling price (which we will symbolise as C_s) and the contribution at a price £1 more (C_{s+1}). Now the contribution at C_s = contribution per unit at price $s \times$ units sold at this price = $(s - 20)[1100 - 200(s - 20)]$, since we lose 200 units from our initial 1100 for every £1 the selling price exceeds £20. Similarly, at a price $s + 1$ we have $C_{s+1} = (s + 1 - 20)[1100 - 200(s + 1 - 20)]$. Since it will simplify further work with these expressions if we write x in lieu of $s - 20$, we can re-write the expression so:

$$C_s = x(1100 - 200x) = 1100x - 200x^2;$$
and
$$\begin{aligned}
C_{s+1} &= (x + 1)[1100 - 200(x + 1)] \\
&= (x + 1)(1100 - 200x - 200) \\
&= (x + 1)(900 - 200x) \\
&= 900x - 200x^2 + 900 - 200x \\
&= 700x - 200x^2 + 900
\end{aligned}$$

So the difference between the two contributions is:

$$\begin{aligned}
C_{s+1} - C_s &= (700x - 200x^2 + 900) - (1100x - 200x^2) \\
&= 700x - 200x^2 + 900 - 1100x + 200x^2 \\
&= 900 - 400x
\end{aligned}$$

Replacing $s - 20$ for x:

$$C_{s+1} - C_s = 900 - 400(s - 20) = 900 - 400s + 8000$$
$$= 8900 - 400s$$

Now we are in a position to see the effect of raising the price *at any point* by £1. For example, if we currently have a price of £21, a £1 rise will result in $8900 - 400 \times 21 = 8900 - 8400 = £500$ more contribution (as we can check from the table in the previous paragraph). And if we want to know the selling price that maximises our contribution we simply observe that it pays us to keep on increasing the price until our contribution increase is zero—*i.e.* until

$$C_{s+1} - C_s = 0,$$

i.e.
$$8900 - 400s = 0$$

$$s = \frac{8900}{400} = 22\frac{1}{4}$$

Since, however, we cannot have a fraction of £1, then it is necessary to test if £22 or £23 is the more appropriate number. And all we need to do here is see if going from £22 to £23 gives us an increase or not, *i.e.* find what is $8900 - 400 \times 22$. As this works out positive we gain by going to £23, and so £23 is our optimum price.

4. Step-by-step or difference equations? We have now solved our illustrative problems using both incremental methods, and found the answer to be £23. The question now is which is the best method?

Students at this point no doubt would elect to use the step-by-step technique. In our illustration it gave the answer more quickly and with less chance of error. However, what if in our illustration demand fell by only *5 units* per £1 price increase? It will not take the student long to see the step-by-step method will involve a very lengthy procedure. Using difference equations, however, we can proceed as follows:

$$C_s = (s - 20)[1100 - 5(s - 20)]$$

and

$$C_{s+1} = (s + 1 - 20)[1100 - 5(s + 1 - 20)]$$

Again letting $x = s - 20$ we have:

$$C_s = x(1100 - 5x) = 1100x - 5x^2$$
$$C_{s+1} = (x+1)[1100 - 5(x+1)]$$
$$= (x+1)[1100 - 5x - 5]$$
$$= (x+1)[1095 - 5x] = 1090x - 5x^2 + 1095$$
$$C_{s+1} - C_s = (1090x - 5x^2 + 1095) - (1100x - 5x^2)$$
$$= 1090x - 5x^2 + 1095 - 1100x + 5x^2$$
$$= 1095 - 10x$$

Replacing $s - 20$ for x:

$$C_{s+1} - C_s = 1095 - 10(s - 20) = 1095 - 10s + 200$$
$$= 1295 - 10s$$

So if we want a difference of zero then $1295 - 10s = 0$ and so $s = 129\frac{1}{2}$, *i.e.* the optimum is £129 or £130.

Testing at £129 we have

$$C_{130} - C_{129} = 1295 - 10 \times 129 = 5$$

So it pays to increase to £130, which, therefore, must be the optimum.

By the step-by-step technique this solution would have required over one hundred steps, so we can conclude that the step-by-step technique should be used where the number of steps are likely to be few—otherwise difference equations should be employed.

5. Illustration of the use of difference equations—Application to the Poisson distribution.

In Progress Test 2 we examined the Poisson distribution by allowing x to take a series of discrete values from 0 upwards in the formula $y = e^{-a}\dfrac{a^x}{x!}$. This included a number of relatively complex calculations. Difference equations, however, enable us to find a short cut to the computational work.

First we will write y_x to be the value of y when a specific value of x is employed. We can say, then:

$$y_x = e^{-a}\frac{a^x}{x!} \text{ and } y_{x-1} = e^{-a}\frac{a^{x-1}}{(x-1)!}$$

$$\text{So } y_x - y_{x-1} = e^{-a}\frac{a^x}{x!} - e^{-a}\frac{a^{x-1}}{(x-1)!}$$

Taking e^{-a} out of the brackets, writing a^x as $a^{x-1} \times a^1$ and $x!$ as $x(x-1)!$ (none of which alters any values, of course):

$$y_x - y_{x-1} = e^{-a}\left(\frac{a^{x-1} \cdot a^1}{x(x-1)!} - \frac{a^{x-1}}{(x-1)!}\right)$$

$$= e^{-a}\left(\frac{a^{x-1}}{(x-1)!} \times \frac{a}{x} - \frac{a^{x-1}}{(x-1)!}\right)$$

Now taking $\dfrac{a^{x-1}}{(x-1)!}$ out of the brackets:

$$y_x - y_{x-1} = e^{-a}\,\frac{a^{x-1}}{(x-1)!}\left(\frac{a}{x}-1\right)$$

But $e^{-a}\dfrac{a^{x-1}}{(x-1)!}= y_{x-1}$ as we saw above.

$$\therefore y_x - y_{x-1} = y_{x-1}\left(\frac{a}{x}-1\right) = y_{x-1} \times \frac{a}{x} - y_{x-1}$$

Finally adding y_{x-1} to both sides we have:

$$y_x = y_{x-1} \times \frac{a}{x}$$

In other words each successive term in a Poisson series is the previous term multiplied by $\dfrac{a}{x}$. For example, if the previous term has been 0.4 when x was 6, then when x was 7 y would be $0.4 \times \dfrac{a}{7}$. So a series of simple multiplications gives us our Poisson series (and since when $x = 0$, $y = e^{-a}\dfrac{a^0}{0!} = e^{-a}$, we start by simply looking up our first value directly in the exponential table—*see* Appendix I).

PROGRESS TEST 7

1. A tool costing £120 can be designed to last for (*i.e.* have a capacity of) as many thousand units as may be desired. However, a design that had a 1000-unit capacity would require an average manufacturing cost of 10p per unit over and above the tool depreciation, while for every additional 1000 units the tool was

capable of producing this cost would increase by $\frac{1}{2}$p. Thus a tool with a 2000-units capacity would result in an average unit cost (excluding depreciation) of $10\frac{1}{2}$p, and one of 3000-units capacity, 11p.

Assuming the tool can only be designed to increase its unit capacity in steps of round thousands, find the most economical capacity:

(a) Using the step-by-step method.

(b) Using difference equations.

Which is the most convenient method, and which would be the most convenient method if the tool could be designed to produce any number of units?

CHAPTER VIII

MATRIX ALGEBRA

Practical people rather take for granted the rules embodying normal computations—for example, that $2 + 2 = 4$. But what if we said $2 + 2 = 1$? And that $6 + 2 = 3$, $6 + 3 = 2$, and $6 + 4 = 1\frac{1}{2}$? A moment's study of these odd and unfamiliar results soon shows that really all we've done is substituted a + sign for the more normally correct ÷ sign.

This is a trivial and admittedly useless changing of the rules and has been done merely to show that mathematical "truths" depend very much on how we define our symbols—in this case "+" means "add together the two numbers separated by the symbol +." There are, however, other systems of rules (called algebras) which are neither trivial nor useless. Among these are the matrix and boolean algebras. Boolean algebra is as yet not greatly employed in operational research, but matrix algebra is, and increasingly so.

MATRIX DEFINITIONS

1. Matrices and elements. A *matrix* is simply a layout of numbers in rows and columns. Each number is called an *element* (or sometimes a "cell"). As we saw in II, **17** an element is identified by a suffix detailing its row and column, so that generally element a_{ij} is the element in the ith row and the jth column.

2. Leading and trailing matrices. In ordinary algebra $a \times b$ is the same as $b \times a$. As we will see later, this is not so in matrix algebra—*i.e.* matrix $A \times$ matrix $B \neq$ matrix $B \times$ matrix A. It is, therefore, important that we distinguish which matrix comes first in the expression and to this end we refer to such a matrix as the *leading matrix*, the following matrix being designated the *trailing matrix*.

3. Conformable matrices. Before we can carry out matrix operations (add, subtract or multiply matrices) it is necessary that they should be *conformable*. This means that the number of rows and columns in the matrices are such that the operation called for can be validly performed. How to test for conformity depends upon the operation to be performed, but the student need not really worry too much about making such tests in practice. If the matrices do not conform he'll quickly find the operation can't be done anyway.

4. Other matrix definitions. The following are a few of the commonest terms also used in matrix algebra:

(*a*) *Square matrix.* A matrix in which the number of rows is the same as the number of columns.

(*b*) *Unit matrix.* A matrix in which all the elements are 1's.

(*c*) *Zero matrix.* A matrix in which all the elements are 0's.

(*d*) *Identity matrix.* A square matrix in which:

(*i*) All the elements along the main diagonal (*i.e.* the diagonal that runs from the top left corner to the bottom right corner) are 1's.

(*ii*) All other elements are 0's.

(*e*) *Transpose matrix.* The matrix obtained by re-writing an existing matrix so that the elements in the 1st row become the elements in the 1st column, and those in the 2nd row become those in the 2nd column, etc. (and so that the elements in the 1st column become those in the 1st row, etc. at the same time). Generally, then, so that element a_{ij} in the initial matrix becomes element a_{ji} in the transpose matrix.

(*f*) *Vector.* A matrix with only one row (row vector) or only one column (column vector).

MATRIX MANIPULATIONS

5. Adding and subtracting matrices. Adding or subtracting matrices simply involves adding or subtracting corresponding elements—which is really what one would expect. The answer, naturally, will emerge as a matrix itself. One way of looking at the operation is to imagine one matrix being superimposed on the other—"colliding" elements being added or subtracted according to the nature of the operation (*see* Fig. 7(*a*)).

$$\begin{bmatrix} 3 & 5 \\ 6 & 2 \end{bmatrix} + \begin{bmatrix} 2 & 1 \\ 0 & 8 \end{bmatrix} = \begin{bmatrix} 3_{+2} & 5_{+1} \\ 6_{+0} & 2_{+8} \end{bmatrix}$$

(*a*) Principle.

$$\begin{array}{ll} & \\ J & i \\ O & ii \\ B & iii \\ S & iv \end{array} \quad \overset{\text{MATERIALS}}{\overset{X \quad Y \quad Z}{\begin{pmatrix} 40 & 10 & 15 \\ 15 & 20 & 17 \\ 12 & 25 & 12 \\ 30 & 20 & 50 \end{pmatrix}}} + \overset{\text{MATERIALS}}{\overset{X \quad Y \quad Z}{\begin{pmatrix} 15 & 2 & 9 \\ 0 & 10 & 17 \\ 8 & 0 & 8 \\ 30 & 10 & 20 \end{pmatrix}}} = \overset{\text{MATERIALS}}{\overset{X \quad Y \quad Z}{\begin{pmatrix} 55 & 12 & 24 \\ 15 & 30 & 34 \\ 20 & 25 & 20 \\ 60 & 30 & 70 \end{pmatrix}}}$$

(*b*) Illustration of practical use. In pure matrix algebra the rows and columns have no headings. They have been shown here so the reader can better follow the illustration.

FIG. 7.—*Matrix addition.*

To illustrate the use of matrix addition in a day-to-day context assume we are using three different kinds of materials—X, Y and Z—on four different jobs—*i*, *ii*, *iii*, *iv*. In week 1 we use on job *i* 40 X, 10 Y and 15 Z; on job *ii* 15 X, 20 Y and 17 Z; on job *iii* 12 X, 25 Y and 12 Z; on job *iv* 30 X, 20 Y and 50 Z. This information can be shown in the form of the leading matrix in Fig. 7(*b*). The following week the usage is that shown in the trailing matrix of Fig. 7(*b*), and as can be seen, adding the matrices results in a further matrix which details the total of each material used in each job. Indeed, a whole series of such weekly matrices can be added together to give the cumulative totals over a period of weeks.

In Fig. 8 we demonstrate matrix subtraction by using exactly the same figures but this time assuming that the trailing matrix now relates to *returns* of material to store.

For matrices to be conformable for addition and subtraction it is, of course, necessary that the leading matrix has the *same number of rows and columns* as the trailing matrix.

$$\overset{\text{1st WEEK'S USAGE}}{\begin{pmatrix} 40 & 10 & 15 \\ 15 & 20 & 17 \\ 12 & 25 & 12 \\ 30 & 20 & 50 \end{pmatrix}} - \overset{\text{MATERIAL RETURNED TO STORE}}{\begin{pmatrix} 15 & 2 & 9 \\ 0 & 10 & 17 \\ 8 & 0 & 8 \\ 30 & 10 & 20 \end{pmatrix}} = \begin{pmatrix} 25 & 8 & 6 \\ 15 & 10 & 0 \\ 4 & 25 & 4 \\ 0 & 10 & 30 \end{pmatrix}$$

FIG. 8.—*Illustration of matrix subtraction.*

6. Multiplying matrices. The rules for multiplying matrices are somewhat unexpected. The student should, therefore, study them carefully and at the same time follow their application to the matrix multiplication given in Fig. 9. These rules are as follows:

(*a*) Imagine the *first row* of the leading matrix is a long plank. Push the plank off the top of the matrix and up-end it alongside the *1st column* of the trailing matrix.

(*b*) Multiply together the adjoining elements and then add these products. This sum constitutes one of the elements of the answer matrix.

(*c*) Next lay the up-ended plank against the *next column* of the trailing matrix and repeat step (*b*).

(*d*) Repeat (*c*) until all the columns of the trailing matrix have been involved in the operation.

(*e*) Treat the *next row* of the leading matrix as if that were a plank, too, and up-end it alongside the 1st column of the trailing matrix.

(*f*) Repeat steps (*b*) to (*d*).

(*g*) Repeat steps (*e*) to (*f*) until the last row of the leading matrix and the last row of the trailing matrix have been involved in the operation.

(*h*) It only remains now to locate the answer elements in the answer matrix. The rule here is the answer element is placed in the same numbered row of the answer matrix as the *row number of the leading matrix* used in its computation, and similarly in the same numbered column of the answer matrix as the *column number of the trailing matrix* used in its computation. For example, row 2 (3, 1) times column 1 ($\frac{3}{4}$) gives us 13 which is located in row 2, column 1 of the answer matrix (*see* Fig. 9(*a*) (*vi*)). To be conformable for multiplication, the number of *columns* in the leading matrix must equal the number of *rows* in the trailing matrix.

7. Application of matrix multiplication. Assume we make three products, I, II and III, and these three products have the following standard usage per unit respectively—2W, 5X, 4Y and 3Z; 10W, 1Y and 2Z; 4W and 8X. These standard usages can be shown in the form of a trailing matrix (*see* Fig. 9(*b*)). Assume now the planned production of the three products for the next four weeks is respectively—I: 20, 10, 10 and 30 units;

Problem:

$$\begin{array}{|c|c|} \hline 2 & 5 \\ \hline 3 & 1 \\ \hline \end{array} \quad \times \quad \begin{array}{|c|c|c|} \hline 3 & 1 & 6 \\ \hline 4 & 2 & 0 \\ \hline \end{array}$$

Solution:

i

$$\begin{array}{|c|c|} \hline 2 & 5 \\ \hline 3 & 1 \\ \hline \end{array} \qquad \begin{array}{|c|c|c|} \hline 3 & 1 & 6 \\ \hline 4 & 2 & 0 \\ \hline \end{array}$$

ii

$$\begin{array}{|c|} \hline 3 & 1 \\ \hline \end{array} \quad \begin{array}{|c|} \hline 2 \\ \hline 5 \\ \hline \end{array} \quad \begin{array}{c} \times \\ \times \end{array} \quad \begin{array}{|c|c|c|} \hline 3 & 1 & 6 \\ \hline 4 & 2 & 0 \\ \hline \end{array}$$

Total Row 1, Col. 1

$$= \quad \begin{array}{|c|c|c|} \hline 26 & & \\ \hline & & \\ \hline \end{array}$$

iii

$$\begin{array}{|c|} \hline 3 & 1 \\ \hline \end{array} \quad \begin{array}{|c|} \hline 2 \\ \hline 5 \\ \hline \end{array} \quad \begin{array}{c} \times \\ \times \end{array} \quad \begin{array}{|c|c|} \hline 1 & 6 \\ \hline 2 & 0 \\ \hline \end{array}$$

Total Row 1, Col. 2

$$= \quad \begin{array}{|c|c|c|} \hline 26 & 12 & \\ \hline & & \\ \hline \end{array}$$

iv

$$\begin{array}{|c|} \hline 3 & 1 \\ \hline \end{array} \quad \begin{array}{|c|} \hline 2 \\ \hline 5 \\ \hline \end{array} \quad \begin{array}{c} \times \\ \times \end{array} \quad \begin{array}{|c|} \hline 6 \\ \hline 0 \\ \hline \end{array}$$

Total Row 1, Col. 3

$$= \quad \begin{array}{|c|c|c|} \hline 26 & 12 & 12 \\ \hline & & \\ \hline \end{array}$$

v

$$\begin{array}{|c|c|} \hline 3 & 1 \\ \hline \end{array} \qquad \begin{array}{|c|c|c|} \hline 3 & 1 & 6 \\ \hline 4 & 2 & 0 \\ \hline \end{array}$$

vi

$$\begin{array}{|c|} \hline 3 \\ \hline 1 \\ \hline \end{array} \quad \begin{array}{c} \times \\ \times \end{array} \quad \begin{array}{|c|c|c|} \hline 3 & 1 & 6 \\ \hline 4 & 2 & 0 \\ \hline \end{array}$$

Total Row 2, Col. 1

$$= \quad \begin{array}{|c|c|c|} \hline 26 & 12 & 12 \\ \hline 13 & & \\ \hline \end{array}$$

vii

$$\begin{array}{|c|} \hline 3 \\ \hline 1 \\ \hline \end{array} \quad \begin{array}{c} \times \\ \times \end{array} \quad \begin{array}{|c|c|} \hline 1 & 6 \\ \hline 2 & 0 \\ \hline \end{array}$$

Total Row 2 | Col. 2

$$= \quad \begin{array}{|c|c|c|} \hline 26 & 12 & 12 \\ \hline 13 & 5 & \\ \hline \end{array}$$

viii

$$\begin{array}{|c|} \hline 3 \\ \hline 1 \\ \hline \end{array} \quad \begin{array}{c} \times \\ \times \end{array} \quad \begin{array}{|c|} \hline 6 \\ \hline 0 \\ \hline \end{array}$$

Total Row 2, Col. 3

$$= \quad \begin{array}{|c|c|c|} \hline 26 & 12 & 12 \\ \hline 13 & 5 & 18 \\ \hline \end{array}$$

Complete layout:

$$\begin{pmatrix} 2 & 5 \\ 3 & 1 \end{pmatrix} \quad \times \quad \begin{pmatrix} 3 & 1 & 6 \\ 4 & 2 & 0 \end{pmatrix}$$

$$= \quad \begin{pmatrix} 26 & 12 & 12 \\ 13 & 5 & 18 \end{pmatrix}$$

(*a*) Principle.

	Planned Production				Standard Usage				
Week	I	II	III		W	X	Y	Z	Product
1	20	5	40		2	5	4	3	I
2	10	10	0	×	10	0	1	2	II
3	10	0	0		4	8	0	0	III
4	30	20	40						

	Week	W	X	Y	Z	
	1	250	420	85	70	Planned
=	2	120	50	50	50	Total
	3	20	50	40	30	Material
	4	420	470	140	130	Requirements

(b) Illustration of practical use.

Fig. 9.—*Matrix multiplication.*

II: 5, 10, 0 and 20 units; III: 40, 0, 0 and 40 units. This production plan can be shown in the form of a leading matrix (*see*
Fig. 9(b)).

If these two matrices are now multiplied together the answer
matrix will give us the required quantities of materials needed
week by week to meet our planned production (again *see* Fig.
9(b). The student should check both the correctness of the
multiplication of the matrices and also that the answer matrix
does, in fact, give the required quantities).

8. Multiplication by a scalar. Sometimes we need to multiply
a whole matrix by a single ordinary number—which is, incidentally, called a "scalar" (*e.g.* as would arise in the previous
example if we wanted to know our weekly material requirements should all production be increased by 50%). This involves no problem—all we do is multiply every element by the
scalar (*see* Fig. 10).

$$1\tfrac{1}{2} \times \begin{pmatrix} W & X & Y & Z \\ 250 & 420 & 85 & 70 \\ 120 & 50 & 50 & 50 \\ 20 & 50 & 40 & 30 \\ 420 & 470 & 140 & 130 \end{pmatrix} = \begin{pmatrix} W & X & Y & Z \\ 375 & 630 & 127\tfrac{1}{2} & 105 \\ 180 & 75 & 75 & 75 \\ 30 & 75 & 60 & 45 \\ 630 & 705 & 210 & 195 \end{pmatrix}$$

Fig. 10.—*Multiplication by a scalar. This shows the revised planned
material requirements of Fig. 9(b) on the assumption that production
is to be increased by 50%.*

PROGRESS TEST 8

1. The following are two matrices:

$$\begin{matrix} A \\ \begin{pmatrix} 6 & 8 \\ 1 & 4 \end{pmatrix} \end{matrix} \qquad \begin{matrix} B \\ \begin{pmatrix} 3 & 5 \\ 4 & 0 \end{pmatrix} \end{matrix}$$

Find: (a) A + B; (b) A − B; (c) A × B.

2. The Super-super-store Ltd has a basic 3-grade pay scale—50p (low), 75p (medium) and £1 (high) per hour. It also classifies its stores into three categories, City, Town and Suburban. The staffing requirements for these stores are as follows: City—6 low, 16 medium, 6 high; Town—10 low, 12 medium, 3 high; Suburban—8 low, 4 medium, 1 high. In a particular week it is forecast 3 City, 11 Town and 30 suburban stores will be operating.

(a) Show the above data in matrix form so that the total hourly operating cost for the week in question can be computed simply by performing matrix algebra operations.

(b) Perform these operations and find this hourly operating cost.

PART THREE
PROBABILITY

CHAPTER IX

BASIC PROBABILITY THEORY

Time and again problems in operational research involve probability. This field of mathematics is almost certainly the most baffling of all and unfortunately, as the student will no doubt discover for himself, there is no quick and simple way of being able to handle with certainty problems involving uncertainty. Only careful attention to the detail and a thorough digestion of this Part of the book can give any promise of a future ability to handle probability computations in examinations.

SIMPLE PROBABILITY

We start by looking at the simpler aspects of probability.

1. Defining probability. It seems it is impossible to define probability without including the concept of probability in the definition. Using expressions such as "likelihood," "degree of uncertainty," "toss of a fair coin" only raises the problem of defining "likelihood," "uncertainty" and "fair" themselves without introducing the probability concept. So let us accept that we intuitively understand what is meant by all these terms.

2. Measuring probability. We can measure probability by considering how often an event occurs in relation to how often it could occur. Thus if we toss a coin we would expect a head to occur about half as often as it *could* occur, and if we throw a die we would expect to throw a 6 on about one-sixth of the throws. We have, therefore, probabilities of $\frac{1}{2}$ of tossing a head and $\frac{1}{6}$ of throwing a 6. Putting it in another way, we can say the probability of an event is the long-term average of the number of occurrences of the event relative to the number of attempts —*e.g.* if we toss a coin often enough, the average number of heads will be one-half the number of tosses.

In Fig. 11 we illustrate the full scale of probabilities.

NOTE: No event can have a probability of less than 0 (since an event cannot occur less often than never) nor more than 1 (since an event cannot occur more often than every time).

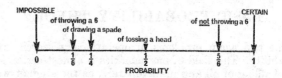

FIG. 11.—*Probability scale.*

3. Events. Crucial to understanding probability theory is appreciating the meanings associated with the word "event." It is vital, then, that the following definititions and explanations are thoroughly grasped:

(*a*) *Event.* An event is simply an occurrence. Tossing a head is, then, an event. An event includes both a single event—where only one thing occurs—and a string-event (which is defined below).

(*b*) *String-event.* A string-event is an event which involves a *string of sub-events.* Thus if we are studying a situation in which a coin is tossed three times the occurrence of three successive heads is a string-event (comprising, obviously, three single sub-events), as is tossing two heads and then a tail. Two points should be noted about string-events:

(*i*) The order of the sub-events is an important feature of a string-event. For example tossing two heads first and then a tail is *not* the same as tossing a tail first and then two heads. Each is a different string-event. Indeed, it may pay the student to envisage string-events as sub-events threaded literally on a string—so that a different order of sub-events gives a different string-event.

(*ii*) The concept of string-event has been specifically created by the author for explanatory purposes. This addition to the terminology of probability theory has been made because a group of sub-events in a specified order can *collectively* be treated just as if it were a *single* event. To simply call it an "event," however, would lead to confusion with the sub-events that comprised it. It was thought preferable to give it a name of its own and "string-event" seemed a reasonable choice. References to string-events, however, are not made in any other literature.

(c) *Exclusive events*. Exclusive events are events that can *never* occur together. Thus a head and a tail with a single toss of a coin are exclusive events since one cannot have both occurring together. On the other hand tossing a head and throwing a 6 with a die are not exclusive events since they can occur together. Note that in a three-tosses situation the string-events head-head-and-tail, and tail-head-and-head are exclusive events since three tosses of a coin cannot give *both* strings of events simultaneously.

(d) *Inclusive events*. Inclusive events are events which can occur together, such as tossing a head while throwing a 6. It should be appreciated that it is irrelevant to consider whether or not simultaneous occurrence is likely—the fact they *can* occur together makes them inclusive. Thus it is unlikely I can run a four-minute mile and be fast asleep at the same time, but since it could just happen these two events are inclusive.

Note that in any situation events are either exclusive or inclusive. And the first thing we need to do in any probability problem is to decide in which category the events in question fall.

4. Success and failure—p and q. In probability theory, if an event we are concerned with occurs, we say we have a *success*. If, then, we are concerned with a die falling a 6, each time it falls 6 we have a success. (Paradoxically, if we are concerned with the number of people who fail an examination, every failure is a success!!) The probability of a success is symbolised p and so we can say that in the case of a die falling a 6 $p = \frac{1}{6}$.

If the event we are concerned with does not occur we have, of course, a *failure*. The probability of a failure is symbolised as q, and a moment's study of Fig. 11 will quickly show that $q = 1 - p$, *i.e.* that the probability of a failure is always 1 minus the probability of a success.

5. Statistical independence. When the probability of one event is in no way affected by the occurrence of another event we say the events are *statistically independent*. Since the probability of a coin falling in a particular way on a given toss is in

no way affected by how it fell previously, we can say such falls
are statistically independent. On the other hand, the probability of a day proving wet to some extent depends on the
previous day's weather, as does the probability of a person
belonging to a particular political party depend to some extent
on his income. Wet days in the course of a week, then, are not
statistically independent and nor are party membership and
income.

In this chapter we are only concerned with statistically independent events—statistically dependent events being dealt
with in the next chapter.

6. Probability situations. In this book we shall refer to
different kinds of *probability situations*. These situations require different computational treatments, which will be
explained in turn. If, therefore, the student can identify the
situation involved in any problem he will appreciate just which
computational treatment he must apply. To make the probability situation immediately clear they will be printed in
BLOCK CAPITALS.

7. The AND situation. The AND probability situation arises
whenever we need to consider the probability of a sequence of
events—*i.e.* 1st event AND 2nd event AND 3rd event . . . etc.
(*e.g.* probability of tossing a head AND throwing a 6). Here the
rule is very simple: in the AND situation *multiply together all
the probabilities of the individual events*. We can show this
symbolically so:

$$P(A \text{ AND } B \text{ AND } C \ldots) = P(A) \times P(B) \times P(C) \ldots$$

where A, B and C are the events and P outside the bracket
refers to the probability of the event shown inside the brackets.

> EXAMPLE: What is the probability of tossing a head, throwing
> a 6 and drawing a spade from a pack of cards?
> Since the separate probabilities of these events are $\frac{1}{2}$, $\frac{1}{6}$ and $\frac{1}{4}$
> respectively, then:
>
> $$P(\text{Head AND } 6 \text{ AND Spade}) = \frac{1}{2} \times \frac{1}{6} \times \frac{1}{4} = \frac{1}{48}.$$

Note, incidentally, the AND situation can relate to *inclusive
events only*. We obviously cannot talk of the probability of this
event AND that event if it is impossible for the two to occur
together (or, more exactly, the probability must be 0).

8. The OR/EXCLUSIVE situation. The OR/EXCLUSIVE situation arises whenever we need to consider the probability of one of a number of exclusive events occurring—*e.g.* 1st event OR 2nd event OR 3rd event . . . etc. (*e.g.* throwing a 4 OR a 5 OR a 6). Again the rule is simple: in the OR/EXCLUSIVE situation *add together all the probabilities of the individual events* —*i.e.*

$$P(A \text{ OR } B \text{ OR } C \ldots) = P(A) + P(B) + P(C) \ldots$$

EXAMPLE: What is the probability of throwing a 4 or a 5 or a 6 with one throw of a die?

Since the separate probabilities are all $\frac{1}{6}$ then:

$$P(4 \text{ OR } 5 \text{ OR } 6) = \tfrac{1}{6} + \tfrac{1}{6} + \tfrac{1}{6} = \tfrac{3}{6} = \tfrac{1}{2}.$$

It is very important to note here this rule *only applies to exclusive events*. We cannot, then, use this rule to find the probability of, say, tossing a head OR throwing a 6 since the events are inclusive—if we both toss the coin and throw the die we can get both a head and a 6. (We can see the rule is inapplicable to inclusive events if we try to apply it to the problem of finding the probability of getting a head OR a head OR a head with three successive tosses of a coin, for applying this rule we get the probability is $\frac{1}{2} + \frac{1}{2} + \frac{1}{2} = 1\frac{1}{2}$—which is clearly ridiculous for not only can we not have a probability greater than certainty, *i.e.* 1, but it isn't even certain that one of the tosses will be a head.)

9. A fourfold classification of probability situations. The probability situations met at this level and their rules can be given by the fourfold classification shown in Fig. 12. Essentially this diagram tells us:

(*a*) The AND/EXCLUSIVE situation can never arise since, by definition, if events are exclusive we cannot talk of them occurring together.

(*b*) In the AND/INCLUSIVE (*i.e.* the AND) situation we *multiply* together the individual probabilities.

(*c*) In the OR/EXCLUSIVE situation we *add* together the individual probabilities.

(*d*) In the OR/INCLUSIVE situation we must think carefully.

We now turn to considering the OR/INCLUSIVE situation.

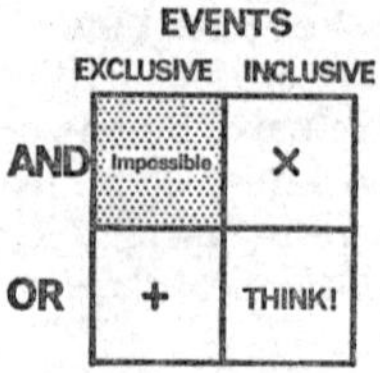

FIG. 12.—*Basic probability situations.*

THE OR/INCLUSIVE SITUATION

Although the OR/INCLUSIVE situation needs careful study it appears and reappears in so many operational research contexts that such study is well rewarded.

10. The or-both/but-not-both ambiguity. First, however, we must note an ambiguity in our language. If we ask, "What is the probability of this or that?" it is not clear if we are asking "What is the probability of this or that or both?" or "What is the probability of this or that but not both?" Normally the former question is implied and in our discussion we will assume we mean "this or that or both." The ambiguity, incidentally, in no way complicates the probability theory—as long as we are clear in our own minds just what we mean there is no problem.

11. Creating string-events. Let us look at a simple kind of OR/INCLUSIVE situation. Assume we ask ourselves, what is the probability if we take a card from each of two packs that we find we have a spade? In other words, what is the probability the first card is a spade OR the second card a spade, or both?

Now the key to handling OR/INCLUSIVE situations lies in *creating a series of string-events which collectively cover every possible permutation of a successful outcome to our problem.* In this case each string-event will include two sub-events—the suits of the first and second cards respectively—and the permutations which will all rank as successes can be shown as follows:

SUB-EVENTS

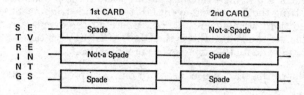

As can be seen, each string-event would count as a success. (Actually only one further permutation is possible, and that is the string-event:

—which clearly is a failure.)

One important point must be very carefully noted and that is that in every single string-event there must be a box for every sub-event—even if the sub-event doesn't give us what we are looking for. In other words, it is as important to put in the "Not-a-Spade" sub-events as the "Spade" sub-events.

12. Computing OR/INCLUSIVE probabilities. Having created string-events in this way, a moment's thought will show the student that there are two important features to such strings— *i.e.*:

(*a*) Each string-event comprises a number of sub-events *in the AND situation.* For example, in our illustration we have Spade AND Not-a-Spade, Not-a-Spade AND Spade, Spade AND Spade.

(*b*) The string-events are *all exclusive events*—we cannot have a "Spade and Not-a-Spade" and, at the same time, "Not-a-Spade and a Spade"—or a "Spade and a Spade."

So we can see that the creation of string-events enables us to tackle the problem of finding OR/INCLUSIVE probabilities as follows:

(*a*) By first finding the probability of each string-event using the AND situation rule—*i.e.* multiplying the probabilities of the sub-events.

(b) By then finding the probability of actually obtaining one of the string-events by asking what is the probability of getting the first string-event OR the second string-event OR the third string-event ... etc. where all the events are exclusive. And since this is the OR/EXCLUSIVE situation we simply add all the string-event probabilities.

Illustrating this procedure with our card problem we have:

STRING-EVENT	PROBABILITY OF STRING-EVENT
Spade—Not-a-Spade	$\frac{1}{4} \times \frac{3}{4} = \frac{3}{16}$
Not-a-Spade—Spade	$\frac{3}{4} \times \frac{1}{4} = \frac{3}{16}$
Spade—Spade	$\frac{1}{4} \times \frac{1}{4} = \frac{1}{16}$
SUM OF STRING-EVENT PROBABILITIES	$\frac{7}{16}$

So the probability of taking two cards and having a spade is $\frac{7}{16}$.

NOTE: If we only want the probability of the first card a Spade OR the second card a Spade, but not both, we add only the probabilities of the first two string-events—i.e. $\frac{3}{16} + \frac{3}{16} = \frac{6}{16} = \frac{3}{8}$.

13. Cross-check to string-events probabilities.

It should be appreciated that if we list *all* the possible string-events permutations in a situation then, since it is certain that one of them must occur, the sum of their probabilities must come to 1. This, then, enables us to make a cross check for if we total the probabilities of all the possible string-events and obtain 1 as a result then we know that we have:

(a) Ensured that all our string-events are genuinely exclusive.

(b) Computed correctly the probabilities of the individual string-events.

For example, in our card illustration only one possible string-event remains to be listed—the "Not-a-Spade—Not-a-Spade" event. The probability of this event is $\frac{3}{4} \times \frac{3}{4} = \frac{9}{16}$, and adding this to our previous probability total of $\frac{7}{16}$ gives us $\frac{9}{16} + \frac{7}{16} = 1$. This proves the accuracy of our earlier work.

14. Probability-trees. Where there are only two or three sub-events in the string-events the complete listing of all the permutations is a simple enough task. Where, however, the number of sub-events increases so does the difficulty of ensuring each and every permutation is correct. The probability-tree is a technique designed to overcome this difficulty, and is best explained by means of an illustration.

Assume a die has four red and two yellow faces. We throw the die four times. What is the probability we will obtain a total of two red and two yellow faces?

To construct the appropriate probability-tree for this problem we start on the left-hand side of the tree (*see* Fig. 13) and ask ourselves, where is the first point we can have alternative results? The answer, of course, is at the first throw of the die, so we place a circle at this point and then draw from it "branches" leading to other circles—there being one circle for each possible result we can obtain (two in this illustration—a red face or a yellow face). The probabilities of each result is then written alongside the branch leading to that result. Then considering *each new circle in turn* we again draw branches with the appropriate probabilities shown to each possible alternative at the next step of our experiment (in the illustration this involves considering what can happen at the *second* throw of our die). And this procedure continues until we reach the end of the experiment—*e.g.* after the fourth throw of our die.

The tree is now constructed and all that remains is to list the string-events and compute their probabilities. The string-events are read *backwards* (though written forwards) by starting at the right-hand tips of the branches and tracing back to the beginning of the tree, recording the results marked in the circles as one does so. And the string-event probabilities are found by multiplying together the probabilities marked against each branch traversed. Finding the probability of obtaining two red and two yellow faces with our die, then, simply involves identifying the string-events that count as successes and adding their probabilities. As can be seen from Fig. 13, this gives us

$$(4 + 4 + 4 + 4 + 4 + 4) \div 81 = \tfrac{8}{27}.$$

15. Stochastic processes. A *stochastic process* arises whenever we have a series of events in which *each event is determined by chance*. The probability-tree situation just examined, then, is an example of a stochastic process.

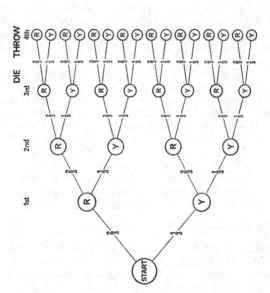

* Successful string-events (see text).

FIG. 13.—*Probability-tree—independent events.*

16. The AT LEAST situation. We sometimes need to know not so much the probability of having a given number of successes in a string-event (*e.g.* adapting the background of the previous illustration, finding the probability of 1 yellow) as the probability of having *at least* a given number of successes (*e.g.* probability of at least 1 yellow). This we can call the AT LEAST situation.

Obviously an AT LEAST problem can be solved by constructing a probability-tree, identifying all string-events which contain the given number of successes or more and adding their probabilities. Sometimes, however, we can take a short cut for since it is certain that a string-event will contain either at least the required number of successes (x) or less then we can say:

$$P(\text{AT LEAST } x \text{ successes}) + P(\text{Less than } x \text{ successes}) = 1$$
$$\therefore P(\text{AT LEAST } x \text{ successes}) = 1 - P(\text{Less than } x \text{ successes})$$

EXAMPLE: What is the probability of at least one yellow in previous illustration?

$$P(\text{AT LEAST 1 yellow}) = 1 - P(\text{Less than 1 yellow})$$
$$= 1 - P(\text{0 yellow})$$

And $P(0 \text{ yellow})$ is, of course, the probability of 1st throw not yellow AND 2nd throw not yellow AND 3rd throw not yellow AND 4th throw not yellow $= \frac{2}{3} \times \frac{2}{3} \times \frac{2}{3} \times \frac{2}{3} = \frac{16}{81}$

$$\therefore P(\text{AT LEAST 1 yellow}) = 1 - \frac{16}{81} = \frac{65}{81}$$

—which the student may check if he wishes against the probability-tree figures in Fig. 13.

PROGRESS TEST 9

1. What is the probability of:
    (*a*) (*i*) Tossing two heads
        (*ii*) Throwing a double six
    (*b*) Throwing a die and scoring a 5 or a 6
    (*c*) Drawing an ace from a pack of cards
    (*d*) Tossing a head and a tail
    (*e*) Throwing two dice and scoring a total of 11
    (*f*) Throwing two dice and scoring 7
    (*g*) Backing at least one winner when laying bets on four horses having winning probabilities of $\frac{1}{3}$, $\frac{2}{5}$, $\frac{13}{40}$ and $\frac{4}{9}$.

2. Prepare a probability-tree to find the probability of throwing three dice and then tossing two coins and obtaining a final result of

a score of 4 or less and 1 head. (Terminate any branches that cannot lead to a success with a //.)

3. A market-survey worker is required to interview a quota of two retailers per day. Unfortunately retailers are not always prepared to be interviewed—in fact, there is a 0·4 probability a given retailer will refuse. If the worker can approach a maximum of four different retailers in a day, what is the probability:

(a) He will have completed his quota after visiting:
  (i) 2 retailers
  (ii) 3 retailers
  (iii) 4 retailers
(b) He will fail to achieve his quota.

4. Looking at her diary Angela finds she arranged to go out for the evening with two different boyfriends, Tom, who is to take her dancing, and Jerry, who is to take her to the cinema. It is Angela's policy in this sort of situation to go out with the first to arrive. In this particular instance both Tom and Jerry will be coming by train, so the probability that they both arrive together exists—in which case all three will almost certainly go for a drink. There are four possible trains the boys could arrive by and the probabilities of being on the respective trains are:

Train	Tom	Jerry
1st	0·1	0·1
2nd	0·1	0·2
3rd	0·4	0·2
4th	0·3	0·4

If neither boy turns up she'll wash her hair, of course. What is Angela more likely to do?

CHAPTER X

CONDITIONAL PROBABILITY

In the last chapter we looked at the probability theory that related to statistically independent events. In this chapter we consider the theory where events are not statistically independent.

FUNDAMENTAL CONDITIONAL PROBABILITY THEORY

1. Conditional probability. Imagine an urn that contains 10 marbles—4 red, 6 yellow.

NOTE: By tradition urns are regarded as indispensable to the study of probability.

If we draw out a marble, what is the probability it will be red? No problem here—if 4 out of 10 marbles are red the probability of a red marble is $\frac{4}{10}$.

What, however, having drawn one marble we now draw a *second* marble? What is the probability that marble will be red? Here we clearly have to think, for although we know there are 9 marbles left in the urn, unless we know whether the first marble drawn was red or not we cannot know the probability of the second being red. If the first marble *was* red, the probability of the second marble being red, then, is $\frac{3}{9}$ (3 reds in a total of 9 marbles), but if the first marble *wasn't* red, the probability is $\frac{4}{9}$. So clearly the probability of the second marble being red *depends upon the colour of the first marble.* When the probability of one event depends upon an earlier event we refer to it as a *conditional probability, i.e.* it is conditional upon the earlier event.

2. Prior and subsequent events. Conditional probability, then, requires us to distinguish between the earlier event and the later event whose probability depends upon the earlier event. Logically the earlier event is referred to as the *prior event*, and the later event as the *subsequent event*. Symbolically a conditional probability is written as "$P(\textit{subsequent event} \mid \textit{prior event})$" which should be read as "the conditional probability of the subsequent event *given the prior event*." We would, then, write the conditional probabilities discussed in the previous paragraph as:

$P(\text{Red} \mid \text{Red}) = \frac{3}{9}$, *i.e.* probability of drawing a red second marble given the first marble was red $= \frac{3}{9}$.

$P(\text{Red} \mid \text{Yellow}) = \frac{4}{9}$, *i.e.* probability of drawing a red second marble given the first marble was yellow $= \frac{4}{9}$.

3. Conditional probability computations. The only difference between conditional probability computations and those discussed in the last chapter is in the changing probabilities as one moves from one sub-event to the next. Thus the probability of drawing a red AND a red AND a red from our urn is still found by multiplying the individual probabilities together—but this time the probabilities are conditional probabilities and are, in fact, $\frac{4}{10}$, $\frac{3}{9}$ and $\frac{2}{8}$ respectively giving the overall probability of three successive reds as $\frac{4}{10} \times \frac{3}{9} \times \frac{2}{8}$.

To illustrate a more detailed conditional probability computation we will ask the same question that we asked in paragraph **14** in the previous chapter—only this time pose it in terms of our urn and marbles situation. In other words, we will find the probability of obtaining a total of 2 red and 2 yellow marbles when we take 4 marbles at random from an urn containing 4 red and 6 yellow.

The string-event computations to this problem are given in Fig. 14. As will be seen we have there just the same probability-tree that we had in Fig. 13—except that the probabilities along the branches are now the conditional probabilities and not the previous unchanging probabilities that arose when the events were statistically independent. The branch conditional probabilities are, of course, found by dividing the number of marbles of the relevant colour still left in the urn at that point on the tree by the total number left in the urn.

Again, our solution simply requires us to identify the successful string-events and add their probabilities—which gives us $(360 + 360 + 360 + 360 + 360 + 360) \div 5040 = \frac{3}{7}$.

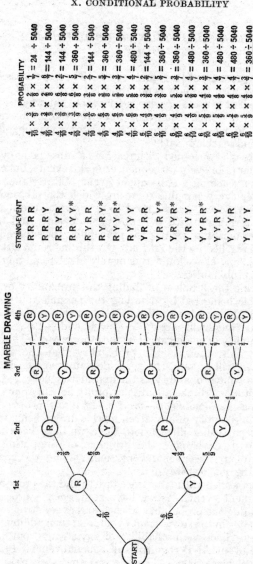

* Successful string-events (see text).

Fig. 14.—*Probability-tree—conditional probability.*

FURTHER CONDITIONAL PROBABILITY THEORY

4. P(subsequent event | any prior event). There are occasions when what we wish to know is not what is the probability of a subsequent event given a specific prior event, but what is the probability of a subsequent event whatever the prior event. For example, in our current illustration what is the probability that our second marble is red?

Here we are not concerned with reaching a subsequent event via a particular prior event (or sequence of prior events) but only on ultimately reaching a subsequent event. Clearly then we must consider every possible route by which the subsequent event can be reached, *i.e.* we need to set down all the string-events that terminate with the subsequent event. And then we simply ask ourselves what is the probability the subsequent event will be reached by the 1st route OR the 2nd route OR the 3rd route . . ., and as we know this merely involves adding the string-event probabilities.

So we tackle the problem of finding the probability of our second marble being red by detailing the possible routes—in this case red AND red, and yellow AND red. The probabilities of these two string-events are $\frac{4}{10} \times \frac{3}{9} = \frac{12}{90}$ and $\frac{6}{10} \times \frac{4}{9} = \frac{24}{90}$, so the probability of getting one OR the other is $\frac{12}{90} + \frac{24}{90} = \frac{36}{90} = \frac{4}{10}$. And this, then, is the probability that the second marble drawn will be red. (It is, incidentally, no coincidence that it is the same probability as the first marble being red. In fact, if the student thinks about it carefully he will appreciate that as long as *we do not know—or care—what colours are drawn earlier*, the probability of any given marble drawn being red is $\frac{4}{10}$. In this particular illustration, then, we have been more concerned with developing the principle of computing the probability of a subsequent event than solving the specific problem in the quickest way.)

Finally, let us generalise the procedure to find the probability of a subsequent event. As we have seen, such a procedure involves finding the probability of each and every string-event that terminates in the subsequent event, and then adding these probabilities. Since the probability of any string-event of the form (prior event AND required subsequent event) is $P(Prior\ event) \times P(Subsequent\ event \mid prior\ event)$, then we can say that the probability of a string-event involving prior event i is:

$P(Prior\ event\ i) \times P(Subsequent\ event \mid prior\ event\ i)$

where i identifies the route by which the subsequent event is reached. So adding all these string-events leads to the general formula:

$$P(Subsequent\ event) = \sum_{i=1}^{n} [P(Prior\ event_i) \times P(Subsequent\ event \mid Prior\ event_i)]$$

where: n = the total number of prior events that can lead to the subsequent event.

5. The probability square. A useful visual device for grasping conditional probabilities is what we can call the *probability square*. This is simply a square with sides one unit long (*e.g.* one inch). The bottom side is divided into sections equal to the probabilities of all the possible prior events, and verticals drawn to divide the square into a series of adjoining rectangles. Across each rectangle a horizontal line is drawn at a height equal to the conditional probability of the subsequent event given the prior event associated with the rectangle. The total area, then, lying below all the horizontal lines is the total probability of the subsequent event—*i.e.* $P(Subsequent\ event)$.

Let us illustrate the use of the probability square in dealing with the following problem:

There are three urns A, B and C each containing a total of 10 marbles of which 2, 4 and 8 respectively are red. A pack of cards is cut and a marble is taken from one of the urns depending on the suit shown—a black suit indicating A urn, a diamond B urn, and a heart C urn. What is the probability a red marble is finally drawn?

The probability square for this problem is built up as follows (*see* Fig. 15). First the base is divided in $\frac{1}{2}$, $\frac{1}{4}$ and $\frac{1}{4}$ to represent the probabilities of each prior event—*i.e.* of a black, diamond and heart suit—and verticals erected. If a black suit is shown a marble will be drawn from urn A where the conditional probability of obtaining a red is 0·2—so a horizontal line is drawn 0·2 of the way up the black rectangle. Similarly horizontal lines are drawn 0·4 and 0·8 of the way up the diamond and heart rectangles. Now at this point the areas of each of the shaded rectangles is found by multiplying the base by the height—*i.e.* P(*Prior event*) × P(*Subsequent event | prior event*). So clearly the probability of the subsequent event (*i.e.* drawing a red marble) given any prior event is the sum of those areas— 0·4.

6. Bayes' Theorem. Finally in our study of conditional probability let us see if it is possible to deduce *the probability that a prior event had occurred given only the occurrence of the subsequent event.* For example, if in the previous situation somebody else secretly cut the cards and drew out a marble and then announced to us a red marble had in fact been drawn, could we compute the probability of the *card cut* being, say, a heart (or, more generally, can we compute the probability of a specified prior event *given* the subsequent event did occur)?

By looking at our probability square in Fig. 15 a clue to our method can be observed. As we see on average 4 times out of 10 a red marble will be drawn (*i.e.* probability of a red marble is 0·4). Out of these 4 times just once a red marble will be drawn after a black suit has been cut (probability 0·1) and just once after a diamond has been cut (probability again

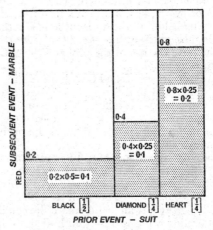

As can be seen, the probability of drawing a red marble is 0·1 + 0·1 + 0·2 = 0·4.

FIG. 15.—*The probability square used to find the probability of a subsequent event.*

0·1), but twice after a heart has been cut (probability 0·2). So half the times a red marble is drawn, a heart preceded the draw. Therefore if we know a red marble has in fact been drawn the probability a heart was cut is 0·5.

> NOTE: Without the knowledge of the result of the draw we could have only assessed the probability of a heart as $\frac{1}{4}$—but the information that a red was, in fact, drawn, coupled with our knowledge of the distribution of red marbles in the urns, enabled us to state a more accurate probability that the card was a heart.

Thinking back over our logic we see our probability figure was derived by comparing the probability of arriving at the given subsequent event via the required prior event with the probability of arriving at the subsequent event via *any* prior event. And we can show this procedure symbolically as follows (where p stands for "Required prior event" and s stands for "Subsequent event"):

$$P(p \mid s) = P(p) \times P(s \mid p) \div P(s).$$

And since

$$P(s) = \sum_{i=1}^{n} [P(p_i) \times P(s \mid p_i)]$$

then

$$P(p \mid s) = P(p) \times P(s \mid p) \div \sum_{i=1}^{n} [P(p_i) \times P(s \mid p_i)]$$

This formula is known as Bayes' Theorem, and although it looks rather complex it simply states generally what we have seen to be a relatively straightforward piece of logical thinking.

PROGRESS TEST 10

1. There are two urns, A and B. In A are 2 black and 1 white marble and in B 1 black and 2 white. A marble is chosen at random from A and placed in urn B. A marble is then chosen at random from urn B. What is the probability this last marble is white?

2. Poorkwality Ltd. manufacture poorkwality units on three machines, A, B and C. A can handle 300 units an hour and produces 10% substandard, B can handle 200 units an hour and produces 15% substandard while C can only handle 100 an hour and produces 24% substandard. Incoming parts are allocated to machines on a basis of machine availability. What is the probability:

(*a*) an individual unit is produced on machine A and emerges substandard?

(*b*) an individual unit selected at random from the finished output proves substandard?

(*c*) a substandard unit found by chance in the finished output was made on machine A?

CHAPTER XI

PROBABILITY DISTRIBUTIONS

INTRODUCTION

It frequently happens that in the sort of work we are considering we need to know the probability that a given number of items in a sample will have a specified characteristic—*e.g.* number of marbles that are red, components that are defective, employees who are absent, customers requiring service at a particular moment, people who prefer brand X. Because we are continually meeting these sorts of situations it pays us to see if we cannot classify them and make generalisations about such classes—ideally in the form of a general formula so that our answers can be found simply by slotting the relevant figures of the problem into the appropriate formula.

To be of value such formulae must be able to answer the question, "What is the probability of x successes (*i.e.* x items having the required characteristic)?," where x is any number we may happen to be interested in. And if our interest extends to letting x equal a whole range of values in turn (*e.g.* 0, 1, 2, 3, 4, etc.), then we will obtain answers which will tell us how the probabilities are distributed over our range of x values. Such a series of probabilities is called a *probability distribution*, and in this chapter we look at four of the most common of these kinds of distributions.

1. Definition and symbols. Throughout this chapter we will be using the following terms and symbols and these, then, should be carefully noted:

Term	Symbol	Definition
Population	N	The total number of items from which we draw our sample.
—	r	The total number of items in the population having the required characteristic.
Sample	n	The number of items drawn from the population for investigation.
—	x	The number of items in the sample having the required characteristic.

Term	Symbol	Definition
Success	p	The probability an *item* has the required characteristic.
—	$P(x)$	The probability that a *sample* contains *exactly* x items.
Cumulative probability	$P(<x)$	The probability that a sample contains *less than* x items.

2. Cumulative probabilities. It should be appreciated that a complete list of the samples that collectively contain all the possible values x can take in a given situation form a list of mutually exclusive events—*i.e.* a sample can contain either 0 or 1 or 2 or 3, etc. items with the required characteristic but cannot simultaneously contain, say, 0 and 1, or 3 and 6, such items. This means the probability of a sample having 0 OR 1 OR 2 OR 3 ... such items can be found by adding the individual probabilities (since we have the OR/EXCLUSIVE situation). Generally, then, we can say:

$$P(< x) = P(0) + P(1) + P(2) + \ldots P(x - 1),$$

i.e. the cumulative probabilities up to, but excluding, the probability of exactly x items.

3. The progressive development of probability distributions. As the chapter unfolds it will be seen that we cope with progressively more complicated probability situations by adopting a series of approximations. This progression and the approximations we adopt is diagrammatically shown in Fig. 16 and it

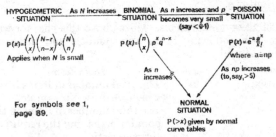

*The nearer p is to 0·5 the sooner the normal distribution can be used as an approximation to the binomial. When np is greater than 5 the normal distribution can be used regardless of p.

FIG. 16.—*Probability situations showing the succession of approximations that can be made in estimating $P(x)$.*

is to this diagram the student should continually refer in order to keep himself orientated in our development of probability distributions.

HYPOGEOMETRIC DISTRIBUTION

We start with the hypogeometric distribution. Although rarely featured in examinations, this distribution is an integral part of our development of probability distributions. It warrants, therefore, a brief mention, though not a detailed study.

4. The HYPOGEOMETRIC situation. In the previous chapter we considered what would happen if we drew 4 marbles from an urn containing 4 red and 6 yellow marbles. The dominating feature of that situation was that as the marbles were drawn one by one from the urn the probability of selecting a marble of a given colour changed. Where this feature is distinctive we have a HYPOGEOMETRIC situation. In other words a HYPOGEOMETRIC situation is one in which *the probability that an item will be a success (i.e. have a specified characteristic) changes as one proceeds with the drawing of the sample.*

5. The hypogeometric distribution. In **3** of the previous chapter we considered the probability of obtaining 2 red marbles in a sample of 4 from an urn containing 4 red and 6 yellow marbles. Now let us prepare the whole probability distribution that emerges from this particular set of circumstances—*i.e.* consider the probabilities of 0, 1, 2, 3 and 4 reds. This procedure leads to the following distribution:

x (*No. of red marbles*)	Probability (*hypogeometric*) *distribution* (see Fig. 14)
0	$\frac{360}{5040} = \frac{15}{210}$
1	$\frac{1920}{5040} = \frac{80}{210}$
2	$\frac{2160}{5040} = \frac{90}{210}$
3	$\frac{576}{5040} = \frac{24}{210}$
4	$\frac{24}{5040} = \frac{1}{210}$
	$\overline{1}$

NOTE: The distribution must total 1 since it is certain a sample of 4 will contain 0 OR 1 OR 2 OR 3 OR 4 reds.

6. The hypogeometric distribution formula. Whilst a probability-tree can always be used to solve a HYPOGEOMETRIC situation problem it is often simpler to use the following formula which can be given (without proof) as follows:

$$P(x) = \binom{r}{x} \binom{N-r}{n-x} \div \binom{N}{n}$$

EXAMPLE: Check the distribution given in the previous paragraph using the hypogeometric formula. Here $N = 10$, $n = 4$, r (number of red marbles) $= 4$, so the distribution is:

$$
\begin{array}{cl}
x & \qquad\qquad\qquad P(x) \\
0 & \binom{4}{0} \binom{10-4}{4-0} \div \binom{10}{4} = \dfrac{4!}{0!4!} \times \dfrac{6!}{4!2!} \div \dfrac{10!}{4!6!} = \dfrac{15}{210} \\[2mm]
1 & \binom{4}{1} \binom{10-4}{4-1} \div \binom{10}{4} = \dfrac{4!}{1!3!} \times \dfrac{6!}{3!3!} \div \dfrac{10!}{4!6!} = \dfrac{80}{210} \\[2mm]
2 & \binom{4}{2} \binom{10-4}{4-2} \div \binom{10}{4} = \dfrac{4!}{2!2!} \times \dfrac{6!}{2!4!} \div \dfrac{10!}{4!6!} = \dfrac{90}{210} \\[2mm]
3 & \binom{4}{3} \binom{10-4}{4-3} \div \binom{10}{4} = \dfrac{4!}{3!1!} \times \dfrac{6!}{1!5!} \div \dfrac{10!}{4!6!} = \dfrac{24}{210} \\[2mm]
4 & \binom{4}{4} \binom{10-4}{4-4} \div \binom{10}{4} = \dfrac{4!}{4!0!} \times \dfrac{6!}{0!6!} \div \dfrac{10!}{4!6!} = \dfrac{1}{210}
\end{array}
$$

BINOMIAL DISTRIBUTION

We can now progress to the more important binomial distribution.

7. Limitations of the hypogeometric distribution. Obviously the hypogeometric distribution can give us quite involved computations and the larger the population N becomes the more onerous the calculations (imagine, for example, our urn contained 400 red marbles in a total of 1000 instead of 4 red in 10). It would be useful, then, if we could find a simpler distribution for use when N was large that would at the same time give us an acceptable approximation to the true hypogeometric distribution. Such a distribution fortunately exists. It is the binomial distribution.

8. The BINOMIAL situation. Let us now take up the situation imagined in the previous paragraph and consider what would happen if our urn contained 400 red marbles in 1000, and we again took a sample of 4. Clearly the probability our 1st marble will be red, *i.e.* a success, is $\frac{400}{1000} = 0.4$, *i.e.* just as before. However, when we take the 2nd marble our conditional probability theory gives us two probabilities that this will be red depending on the colour of the 1st marble, *i.e.*:

P(2nd marble red | 1st marble red) $= \frac{399}{999} = 0.3994$
P(2nd marble red | 1st marble not red) $= \frac{400}{999} = 0.4004$

As can be seen, these probabilities are virtually the same as the 0.4 of the 1st marble—and, indeed, a quite insignificant error will be introduced if it is assumed the probability for the 2nd marble remains at 0.4.

When this situation applies, that is to say *where the probability of a success (i.e. of drawing an item with a given characteristic) does not significantly change as the sample is drawn* we say we have a BINOMIAL situation.

9. The binomial distribution. If we have a BINOMIAL situation then the binomial probability distribution can be computed from the following formula:

$$P(x) = \binom{n}{x} p^x q^{n-x}$$

EXAMPLE: A random sample of 4 marbles is drawn from an urn containing 1000 marbles, 400 of which are red. What is the probability distribution?

First note $p = \frac{400}{1000} = 0.4$ and $q = 1 - 0.4 = 0.6$. The required distribution, then, is as follows:

x				$P(x)$
0	$\binom{4}{0} \times 0.4^0 \times 0.6^{4-0} =$	$\frac{4!}{0!4!}$	$\times 1 \times 0.6^4$	$= 0.1296$
1	$\binom{4}{1} \times 0.4^1 \times 0.6^{4-1} =$	$\frac{4!}{1!3!}$	$\times 0.4 \times 0.6^3$	$= 0.3456$
2	$\binom{4}{2} \times 0.4^2 \times 0.6^{4-2} =$	$\frac{4!}{2!2!}$	$\times 0.4^2 \times 0.6^2$	$= 0.3456$
3	$\binom{4}{3} \times 0.4^3 \times 0.6^{4-3} =$	$\frac{4!}{3!1!}$	$\times 0.4^3 \times 0.6$	$= 0.1536$
4	$\binom{4}{4} \times 0.4^4 \times 0.6^{4-4} =$	$\frac{4!}{4!0!}$	$\times 0.4^4 \times 1$	$= 0.0256$
				$\overline{1.0000}$

10. The derivation of the binomial formula. Although the formula for the binomial distribution can be taken as given it is not difficult to see how it is derived. The logical reasoning can, in fact, be made in the following manner:

(*a*) The first thing to note is that if one constructs a probability-tree for the problem one ends with a list of string-events each of which has as many sub-events as items in the sample—*i.e.* *n* (*e.g.* if we take a sample of 4 marbles each string-event comprises 4 sub-events—*see* Fig. 13, page 78).

(*b*) The next thing to note is that since in each string-event the probabilities of all the sub-events are multiplied together, we will:

(*i*) Multiply together as many *p*'s as there are successes in the sample—*i.e.* if we are concerned with *x* such successes we multiply *x* *p*'s together—which will give us p^x (*e.g.* if *x* is 3 reds, then we have $0 \cdot 4^3$).

(*ii*) Multiply together as many *q*'s as there are items in the sample *without* the required characteristic (failures)—*i.e.* $(n - x)$ *q*'s = q^{n-x} (*e.g.* $0 \cdot 6^{4-3} = 0 \cdot 6^1$).

(*iii*) Multiply together the results from (*i*) and (*ii*) to obtain the probability of getting a *single* string-event containing *x* successes, *i.e.* $p^x q^{n-x}$.

(*c*) The final thing to note is that since we add all the probabilities of the string-events containing *x* successes, and since each such string-event has the same probability, we can find this total by multiplying the probability of a single string-event by the number of such events. And the number of such events is found by considering how many combinations we can form from a sample of *n* items taking *x* at a time—which as we know from Chapter V is $\binom{n}{x}$. So by multiplying (*b*) (*iii*) by $\binom{n}{x}$ we obtain the required prob-

ability, *i.e.* $P(x) = \binom{n}{x} p^x q^{n-x}$.

If in any BINOMIAL context you desire to work out $P(x)$ by logic rather than formulae, remember all you need to do is to write out one single string-event containing the required number of successes (*e.g.* red, red, red, not-red), find its probability, and then multiply this by the number of string-events that have an identical number of successes.

11. Samples from an infinite population.

It is worth noting at this point that if we take a sample from an infinite population (*e.g.* a sample of three tosses of a coin from the infinity of tosses that could be made) then the probability of a success will remain *absolutely* unaltered from item to item and not just approximately unaltered. In such a situation, then, the binomial formula gives the exact, and not just the approximate, probability distribution.

In this context it should be appreciated that if after each time we draw an item for our sample we *return it to the population* (*i.e.* sample with replacement) we create an infinite population (since no amount of sampling will ever reduce it). In such a case even our earlier 10 marbles in an urn becomes an infinite population, and what was a HYPOGEOMETRIC situation becomes a pure BINOMIAL situation (for a moment's thought will show the probability of drawing a red remains at 0·4 no matter how often a draw is made).

12. Mean and standard deviation of a binomial distribution.

For students with an interest in statistics we give here the mean and standard deviation of a binomial distribution:

Mean $= np$ (*i.e.* sample size $\times$ probability of a success)
Standard deviation $= \sqrt{npq}$

EXAMPLE: 60 dice are all rolled at once a large number of times. What will be the average number of 6's thrown per time and what will be the standard deviation?

$$\text{Mean} = 60 \times \tfrac{1}{6} = 10.$$

so an average of 10 6's per throw will be obtained.

$$\text{Standard deviation} = \sqrt{60 \times \tfrac{1}{6} \times \tfrac{5}{6}} = 2\cdot89$$

NOTE: There is a link here between the binomial distribution and the standard error of a proportion (see the M. & E. *Statistics* HANDBOOK). In statistics, taking a random sample of items where each item selected has a virtually constant probability of having a required characteristic is, of course, a BINOMIAL situation—and the standard deviation of the sampling distribution that results is, then, $\sqrt{npq}$. If we now aim to find what *proportion* this standard deviation is of the original sample we must divide it by n—*i.e.* we get:

$\dfrac{\sqrt{npq}}{n}$—and this simplifies to:

$$\sqrt{\dfrac{pq}{n}}$$

$\left(\text{since } \dfrac{\sqrt{npq}}{n} = \dfrac{\sqrt{n} \times \sqrt{pq}}{\sqrt{n} \times \sqrt{n}} = \dfrac{\sqrt{pq}}{\sqrt{n}} = \sqrt{\dfrac{pq}{n}}\right)$

which, of course, is the formula for the standard error of a proportion.

13. Bernoulli trials. Students should be warned that the BINOMIAL situation is sometimes referred to as an *independent Bernoulli trial*, a Bernoulli trial being a trial (string-event) in which there can be only two outcomes for each sub-event. The "independent," of course, refers to statistical independence so as to exclude a conditional probability situation.

POISSON DISTRIBUTION

We now turn to another equally important distribution—the Poisson distribution.

14. Limitations of the binomial distribution. Like the hypogeometric distribution for which it can be substituted, the binomial distribution, too, becomes computationally onerous in certain circumstances and needs itself to be succeeded by a simpler distribution. For example, what if our urn now contains 100,000 marbles, 120 of which are red, and from which we draw a sample of 1000? Our p here is obviously $\dfrac{120}{100,000}$ $= 0.0012$ and so applying the binomial formula we obtain the following expression:

$$P(x) = \binom{1000}{x} \times 0.0012^x \times (1 - 0.0012)^{1000 - x}$$
$$= \dfrac{1000!}{(1000 - x)!\,x!} \times 0.0012^x \times 0.9988^{1000 - x}.$$

and since x takes all the values from 0 to 1000 we have clearly a discouraging series of calculations ahead of us.

15. The POISSON situation. A POISSON situation can be defined as *a BINOMIAL situation in which* (a) *the sample size is very large and* (b) *the probability of a success is very small—i.e.* where n is large and p is small.

The above situation is clearly a POISSON situation and in a POISSON situation the Poisson distribution gives an acceptable approximation to the strictly more accurate binomial distribution.

16. The Poisson formula. We have already met the Poisson formula (*see* Progress Test 2). Using our probability symbol $P(x)$ it can be written:

$$P(x) = e^{-a} \frac{a^x}{x!}$$

where a = average number of successes per sample.

Only the symbol "a," and the thought of computing a^x and $x!$ where x is a large number, may possibly give the student some concern at this point. However, no concern is needed for we know from **12** that the average of a binomial distribution is np, so $a = np$, and, as will soon be seen, $P(x)$ so quickly becomes insignificant as x increases that we rarely take x even to double figures.

Let us then prepare the probability distribution of our 100,000 marble urn using the Poisson formula. In this instance $n = 1000$ and $p = 0 \cdot 0012$ so $a = 1000 \times 0 \cdot 0012 = 1 \cdot 2$. The formula, then, becomes $P(x) = e^{-1 \cdot 2} \dfrac{1 \cdot 2^x}{x!}$ and the distribution is as follows:

x		$P(x)$
0	$e^{-1 \cdot 2} \times \dfrac{1 \cdot 2^0}{0!} = 0 \cdot 3012 \times \dfrac{1}{1}$	$= 0 \cdot 3012$
1	$e^{-1 \cdot 2} \times \dfrac{1 \cdot 2^1}{1!} = 0 \cdot 3012 \times \dfrac{1 \cdot 2}{1}$	$= 0 \cdot 3614$
2	$e^{-1 \cdot 2} \times \dfrac{1 \cdot 2^2}{2!} = 0 \cdot 3012 \times \dfrac{1 \cdot 44}{2 \times 1}$	$= 0 \cdot 2169$
3	$e^{-1 \cdot 2} \times \dfrac{1 \cdot 2^3}{3!} = 0 \cdot 3012 \times \dfrac{1 \cdot 728}{3 \times 2 \times 1}$	$= 0 \cdot 0867$

$$4 \quad e^{-1\cdot2} \times \frac{1\cdot2^4}{4!} = 0\cdot3012 \times \frac{2\cdot0736}{4 \times 3 \times 2 \times 1} = 0\cdot0260$$

$$5 \quad e^{-1\cdot2} \times \frac{1\cdot2^5}{5!} = 0\cdot3012 \times \frac{2\cdot48832}{5 \times 4 \times 3 \times 2 \times 1} = 0\cdot0062$$

$$\left.\begin{array}{l} \cdot \\ \cdot \\ \cdot \\ 1000 \end{array}\right\} \begin{array}{l} \text{Since we know the whole probability distri-} \\ \text{bution must add to 1, all these } P(x)\text{'s must} \\ \textit{collectively} \text{ be just sufficient to enable this} \\ \text{result to be achieved—\textit{i.e.} they must} \end{array} \quad = 0\cdot0016$$

$$\overline{1\cdot0000}$$

As we can see, the probabilities drop rapidly once x passes 2, and indeed, the probability of a sample of 1000 containing more than 5 reds is a mere 0·0016.

17. The mean and standard deviation of the Poisson distribution.
Since the Poisson distribution is simply an approximation to the binomial distribution its mean and standard deviation are the same as the binomial distribution. However a slight simplification can be made as follows:

$$\text{Mean} = np = a.$$
$$\text{Standard deviation} = \sqrt{npq},$$
and since when p is very small $q \simeq 1$,
$$\sqrt{npq} = \sqrt{np \times 1} = \sqrt{np} = \sqrt{a}.$$

In other words the standard deviation of the Poisson distribution is the square root of its mean.

18. The POISSON situation with an unknown sample size.
The Poisson distribution has one very valuable feature—it can be employed even though the sample size is not known. This is because the Poisson formula only requires the *average* number of successes to be known, and we can know the average without knowing either p or n. For example, to take the classical case, assume we are studying thunderstorms and have been counting the number of lightning flashes. We find over a total period of 1000 minutes there were 1200 flashes—*i.e.* an *average* of 1·2 flashes a minute. Now if we regard a particular minute as a

very large sample of many very small moments of time, and if there is a very small but constant probability of a single lightning flash occurring during each moment of time, then we have a POISSON situation with $a = 1 \cdot 2$. So we can prepare our Poisson distribution which will tell us the probability of having in a given minute, 0, 1, 2, 3, 4, etc. lightning flashes.

NOTE: Since the a here is the same as the a in paragraph **16** the distribution will be *exactly the same*—i.e. the probability of **0** flashes will be $0 \cdot 3012$, 1 flash $0 \cdot 3614$, 2 flashes $0 \cdot 2169$, etc. It is an interesting fact that no matter how diverse phenomena are, if they have the same average rate of successes and providing events are random they will have identical Poisson distributions. Thus, *if* (and note this "if") there is an average of $1 \cdot 2$ defects per square yard of cloth, or $1 \cdot 2$ goals scored per game of football, or $1 \cdot 2$ deaths from accidents per day, or $1 \cdot 2$ air-crashes per week, then the probabilities of 0, 1, 2, 3, etc. "successes" per square yard of cloth, per game of football, per day and per week respectively, will be given in every case by the distribution in **16**.

NORMAL DISTRIBUTION

We turn finally to the normal distribution—which will no doubt be familiar to students of statistics.

19. Limitations of the Poisson distribution. As we have seen, where n is large and p small the Poisson distribution is relatively far easier to handle than the binomial. Even so it, too, has its limitations. Consider, for example, in our 100,000-marble urn situation if we took a 7500 sample—and wished to know the probability of having 12 reds. In this instance $a = np = 7500 \times 0 \cdot 0012 = 9$ so the probability of having 12 reds will not be insignificant. Nevertheless, the thought of computing $e^{-9} \dfrac{9^{12}}{12!}$ is not very appealing.

20. Further limitations of the binomial distribution. We have seen the binomial distribution becomes unwieldy where n is large and p small (and that the Poisson distribution can be used as an approximation in such a situation), but a moment's thought will show it becomes unwieldy in *any* situation where n is large—only if p is *not* small we cannot turn to the Poisson distribution for help. For example, take our illustration where we have 400 red marbles in an urn of 1000. What would be the probability there of, say, 13 red in a sample of 20? Here we have the problem of computing

$$\frac{20!}{13!7!} \times 0 \cdot 4^{13} \times 0 \cdot 6^7.$$

Again, not an appealing prospect.

21. The NORMAL situation. Needless to say, in both these unpleasant-looking situations there is again a simpler distribution that gives us acceptable approximations and that is the normal distribution. In other words we can use the normal distribution wherever we have a NORMAL situation. Whether a situation can be classed as NORMAL or not depends very much on n and p, but for practical purposes we can say that if np (or nq, whichever is the smaller) is greater than 5 a NORMAL situation exists. In our examples above, for instance, np is 9 and $20 \times 0 \cdot 4 = 8$ respectively, so both these are NORMAL situations.

22. The NORMAL situation and cumulative probabilities. It is very common in NORMAL situations to have large sample sizes so the probability of getting any *exact* number of successes is inevitably extremely low. Imagine, for example, tossing 1000 pennies. How often, do you think, you would get exactly 500 heads, neither one more nor one less? Not often, obviously, even though 500 is the average. Clearly, then, in these situations it is more useful to know the probability of there being *more* (or less) than a specified number of successes.

At this point the student (who, it is assumed, knows his statistics) should begin to appreciate the role of normal curve tables in the NORMAL situation, since, for example, $\frac{1}{3}$ of the area of the normal curve lies outside the 1σ-either-side-mean boundaries, then $\frac{1}{6}$ of the area lies above the upper of these two boundaries. This, in turn, means $\frac{1}{6}$th of all occurrences lie beyond this point, so the probability of obtaining an occurrence above that point is $\frac{1}{6}$ (*see* Fig. 17). In other words, the area to the right of a given point measures the probability of obtaining a value above that point (and vice versa).

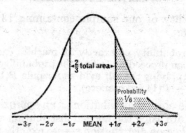

FIG. 17.—*Probability x will exceed mean + 1σ in a normal distribution.*

23. The continuity correction. One minor point in connection with using normal curve tables in the current context needs explaining. The normal curve is a *continuous* curve, but we wish to use it where *discrete* data is involved (*i.e.* we can only have whole successes and cannot talk of half or quarter of a success—*e.g.* we cannot draw out $\frac{1}{2}$ a red marble). This means on a continuous scale the discrete value, say 13, extends $\frac{1}{2}$ a unit on either side, *i.e.* from $12\frac{1}{2}$ to $13\frac{1}{2}$ (*see* Fig. 18). In all normal curve table applications, therefore, we must make *continuity corrections of $\frac{1}{2}$ a unit* to all our discrete values.

24. Using the normal distribution as an approximation to the binomial. We are now in a position to solve the problem of finding probabilities when we take a sample of 20 marbles from an urn containing 400 red marbles in 1000. This is basically a BINOMIAL situation and we know the mean and standard deviation of the resulting distribution is np and $\sqrt{npq}$—*i.e.* $20 \times 0.4 = 8$ and $\sqrt{20 \times 0.4 \times 0.6} = 2.2$ respectively in this case. But since the normal distribution here approximates to the binomial distribution we can use a normal curve with a mean of 8 and standard deviation of 2·2 in lieu.

Assume now we wish to know the probability of obtaining 13 red marbles or more. All we need to do here is first find how many standard deviations we need to be above the mean—which is given simply by (Required number — mean — $\frac{1}{2}$) ÷ standard deviation = $(13 - 8 - \frac{1}{2}) \div 2.2 = 4\frac{1}{2} \div 2.2 \approx 2$. So we need to know the area lying 2 or more standard deviations above the mean—and normal curve tables (if not our memory) will tell us this is some $2\frac{1}{2}\%$ of the total curve area.

So the probability of our sample containing 13 or more red marbles is 0·025.

> NOTE: The probability of exactly 13 marbles can be found, if desired, by then proceeding to find the probability of 14 or more marbles and applying the self-evident formula $P(13\ \text{red}) = P(13\ \text{red or more}) - P(14\ \text{red or more})$.

25. Using the normal distribution as an approximation to the Poisson. If we are using the normal distribution as an approximation to the Poisson distribution we use exactly the same procedure as above. For example, if we take a sample of 7500 marbles from an urn containing 120 reds in 100,000 marbles then the mean and standard deviation of the underlying Poisson distribution are a and $\sqrt{a}$, i.e. $7500 \times 0\cdot0012 = 9$, and $\sqrt{9} = 3$ respectively. Our normal curve, then, will have a mean of 9 and a standard deviation of 3, so the value 13 lies

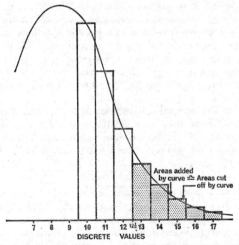

If we want the probability $x \geqslant 13$ we need to add the areas of all the rectangles from 13 onwards—i.e. the shaded part of the diagram. It will be noticed that (i) all the tiny pieces cut off and those added to the rectangles by the curve tend to cancel out; and (ii) the area above and to the right of the *discrete* value 13 is given by the area to the right of the continuous value $12\frac{1}{2}$. We must, then, always make a continuity correction of $\frac{1}{2}$ when using a continuous curve in connection with discrete data.

FIG. 18.—*Continuity correction.*

$(13 - 9 - \frac{1}{2}) \div 3$ standard deviations above the mean, *i.e.*
$3\frac{1}{2} \div 3 = 1.17$ standard deviations. And normal curve tables
show the area above this point is 0.1210. So the probability of
our sample containing 13 reds or more is 0.121.

26. Summary. We can summarise the chapter on probability
distributions as follows:

(*a*) When we have a very small population we are in the
HYPOGEOMETRIC situation and can use the hypogeometric distribution to compute the probability of *x* successes.

(*b*) When the population becomes so large that the probability of a success, *p*, remains virtually unchanged throughout the drawing of the sample we are in the BINOMIAL
situation and can use the binomial distribution as an approximation to the hypogeometric to compute the probability of *x* successes. And the larger the population the
better the approximation.

(*c*) When the sample size *n* becomes very large and *p* very
small we are in the POISSON situation and can use the
Poisson distribution as an approximation to the binomial to
compute the probability of *x* successes (for this *p* should
ideally be less than 0.1). Note the Poisson distribution can
be used where neither *n* nor *p* are known but the average
number of successes is ascertainable.

(*d*) When *np* becomes greater than 5 then we are in a
NORMAL situation and the normal distribution can be used
as an approximation to either the binomial or the Poisson to
compute the probability of *x* or more successes.

PROGRESS TEST 11

1. Identify the situations (as categorised in the chapter) which
exist when a study is being made of the number of people who are
blue-eyed and a random sample of 12 is taken in each of the
following cases:

(*a*) The population is a large city in which 25% of the people
are blue-eyed.

(*b*) The population is a large city in which 50% of the people
are blue-eyed.

(*c*) The population is a large city in which 5% of the people
are blue-eyed.

(*d*) The population is the combined 1st and 2nd elevens of a
football club in which a total of 13 players are blue-eyed.

2. If exactly half the population in a city were male what would be the probabilities that a random sample of 8 people would contain 0, 1, 2, 3, 4, 5, 6, 7 and 8 males?

3. A particularly delicate electronic component is known to have a 30% probability of failure during the 1st year of its life. A user of electronic equipment purchases a unit that contains 4 of the components. What is the probability none of the components will fail, 1 will fail, 2 will fail, 3 will fail, all 4 will fail, during the course of the 1st year?

4. A cloth manufacturer has established that his rolls of cloth have, on average, 3 blemishes per roll. If the blemishes occur as a result of purely random causes, what are the probabilities that a given roll contains 0, 1, 2, 3, 4, 5, or 6 or more, blemishes?

5. If the electronic equipment user in question 3 purchased a unit containing 2100 components, what is the approximate probability that more than 650 will fail in the first year?

PART FOUR

OPERATIONAL RESEARCH TECHNIQUES

CHAPTER XII

MODEL BUILDING

As we saw in Chapter I, the most basic technique in operational research is modelling the situation to be investigated. In this chapter we consider how a real world business situation can be depicted in the form of a model.

INTRODUCTION

1. Models. A *model* is essentially *a device that reflects the workings of the real world*. There can be various kinds of models. Some are simply scaled-down versions of a real three-dimensional engineering entity such as a model car, others model the technical operations as well such as a model railway, and yet others model the *way* a thing works rather than the thing itself—and these we call working models.

The type of model we are most frequently building in operational research is, however, a *mathematical model*, that is, a model that reflects the workings of the real world by means of *mathematical symbols and formulae*. We could, for instance, model the "workings" of our bank account by letting $a =$ opening balance, $b =$ deposits, $c =$ withdrawals, $d =$ closing balance and then saying $d = a + b - c$.

2. Advantages and limitations of models. If we wish to gain insight into the workings of the real world it is usually better to use models than conduct real-life experiments since model manipulation is quicker, more practical and less dangerous than using the real world. One can easily see the truth of this by considering whether it is better to use a model railway layout of a complex junction or the real thing when experimenting to check if proposed operating plans are feasible.

Models do, however, have a serious limitation—namely, they may provide the wrong answers. The validity of any answer depends very much on the accuracy of the model in reflecting real-life events. To ensure a model is valid it is important that:

(a) All *relevant real-world variables* are included in the model. In so much that bank charges are not included in our bank account model in **1**, that model is invalid and will give the wrong answer.

Note the emphasis on "relevant." Including irrelevant variables does not *per se* invalidate the model but may result in confusing the issue to some extent or even result in an inoperable model if their values are not known. We would not, then, include the colour of the bank cashier's eyes in our model.

(b) The *relationships between variables* are correctly expressed in the model. For example, it requires little imagination to appreciate the consequences of writing "$+c$" instead of "$-c$" in our bank account model.

Although these principles are crucial to valid model-building, there is, unfortunately, no fool-proof way of ensuring they are fully observed. This must always depend upon the skill of the model-builder.

3. Model building as an art. Since model-building is more of a skill than a procedure and an art than a science, it cannot be taught in the form of a series of "steps." All we can do, then, is illustrate model-building in a few common contexts and in this way hope the student obtains the "feel" of the technique.

MODEL BUILDING ILLUSTRATIONS

In this section we illustrate the building and manipulation of models in three contexts—that of profit maximisation, break-even points and working capital.

4. A profit maximisation model. The market research department of Simpelasticity Ltd, has established that the link between demand and selling price for their product, which has a marginal cost of £6, is such that the number of units demanded is equal to 20,000 minus 1000 times the selling price. The company is interested to know what selling price will maximise profit.

Since we maximise profit by maximising contribution, we can effectively model this situation as follows:

Let x = selling price.
Then demand (in units) = $20,000 - 1000x$.
And contribution per unit = $x - 6$.
$$\therefore \text{ Total contribution} = (20,000 - 1000x)(x - 6)$$
$$= 20,000x - 120,000 - 1000x^2$$
$$+ 6000x$$
$$= 26,000x - 1000x^2 - 120,000$$

We know from Chapter VI that we can find the value of x that maximises the total contribution by differentiating and setting the result equal to 0, *i.e.*:

$$\frac{d(\text{Total contribution})}{dx} = 26,000 - 2000x = 0$$
$$\therefore x = 13$$

So a selling price of £13 maximises the profit.

5. A break-even model. The Sales Manager of Tiny Turnover Ltd. maintains he could increase the sales turnover (in units) of any of the company's products by 50% if he was authorised to give a 10% price discount and place appropriate additional advertising matter. The Board wish to know the maximum additional advertising expense they can incur without the Manager's proposal resulting in a smaller profit.

This situation can be modelled as follows:

Let s = current product selling price;
m = product marginal cost; and
t = current turnover (in units).

The current product contribution = $t(s - m)$ and the new product contribution, net of additional advertising

$$= 1 \cdot 5t \,(0 \cdot 9s - m) - \text{Cost of additional advertising.}$$

Since at the worst these two contributions must equal each other, then:

$$t(s - m) = 1 \cdot 5t \,(0 \cdot 9s - m) - \text{Cost of additional advertising}$$

$\therefore$ Cost of additional advertising
$$= 1 \cdot 5t \,(0 \cdot 9s - m) - t(s - m)$$
$$= 1 \cdot 35ts - 1 \cdot 5tm - ts + tm$$
$$= 0 \cdot 35ts - 0 \cdot 5tm$$
$$= t(0 \cdot 35s - 0 \cdot 5m)$$

Since we can put this expression in a more useful form by taking $\frac{1}{2}$ out of the brackets we have:

$$\text{Maximum additional advertising cost} = \frac{t}{2}(0{\cdot}7s - m)$$

The Board now have a useful model, for if one of their products has a marginal cost of £4 and sells 10,000 units at £10, then:

$$\text{Maximum additional product advertising cost}$$
$$= \frac{10,000}{2}(0{\cdot}7 \times 10 - 4) = \underline{\underline{£15,000}}$$

The model, however, goes further than this, for it also tells the Board that any product with a marginal cost of 70% or more of the selling price must never be subjected to the Sales Manager's proposal. This follows from the fact that if $m > 0{\cdot}7s$, then $(0{\cdot}7s - m) = (0{\cdot}7s -$ a value exceeding $0{\cdot}7s) =$ a negative result, i.e. the additional advertising would need to be negative. It would, then, be impossible to allow the Manager any additional advertising expenditure.

6. A working capital model. Flyboys have negotiated a very profitable new deal under which they forecast that sales will be £1000 in month 1, £2000 in month 2, £3000 in month 3, i.e. increase by £1000 each month. They have no additional costs other than the product cost-of-sales which will be 90% of sales, nor will they need to carry any stock. They must, however, give two months' credit to customers while receiving no credit themselves. They wish to know the maximum working capital they will ultimately be called upon to provide and when this will be.

Here we will use difference equations (see Chapter VII) and our model is as follows:

$$\text{Let } t = \text{month under consideration}$$
$$\text{Then } S_t = \text{sales in month } t = 1000t$$
$$\text{And } F_t = \text{cash flow for month } t$$
$$\therefore F_t = S_{t-2} - 0{\cdot}9S_t$$

(i.e. cash flows in from customers who bought two months earlier and flows out to pay the cost-of-sales for the current month).

Now F_t will start negative and finance will be increasingly required until F_t becomes positive—*i.e.* the turning-point will be when $F_t = 0$.

If $F_t = 0$, then:

$$S_{t-2} - 0 \cdot 9 S_t = 0$$
$$\therefore S_{t-2} = 0 \cdot 9 S_t$$
$$\therefore 1000(t-2) = 0 \cdot 9 \times 1000t$$
$$\therefore 1000t - 2000 = 900t$$
$$\therefore 100t = 2000$$
$$\therefore t = 20,$$

i.e. month 20 is our turning-point. Now the "balance sheet" of this operation at the end of month 20 will only contain debtors equal to the sales of months 19 and 20, ploughed-back profits from months 1 to 20 at 10% of sales, and a cash deficit equal to the required working capital finance. And these figures are:

Debtors $= 19,000 + 20,000 = £39,000$
Ploughed-back profits $= 100 + 200 + 300 + \ldots + 2000*$

$$= \left(\frac{100 + 2000}{2} \right) \times 20$$

$$= £21,000$$
$$\therefore \text{Cash deficit} = 39,000 - 21,000 = £18,000$$

So Flyboys will need £18,000 finance by month 20.

MARKOV CHAINS

We close this chapter by discussing a form of modelling that can often be employed where *probabilities* enter the model. Such modelling involves the concept of Markov chains.

7. MARKOV CHAIN situations. A MARKOV CHAIN situation is a probability situation in which the object under investigation *can only move between a number of limited states*—the move from one state to another being governed by constant probabilities. For example, the weather can only move day-by-day between the states of being wet and being dry, and if the

---

* NOTE: The ploughed-back profits form an arithmetical progression (*see* Chapter IV).

probabilities of a wet day being followed by a dry day, and a dry day being followed by a wet day remain constants, then, we have a MARKOV CHAIN situation—the Markov chain being the chain of sequential states actually occurring. (Note, incidentally, that if, say, a wet day is followed by a wet day we regard this as a "move" from a wet state to a wet state.) In another context a machine can, minute-by-minute, move between the states of "good repair," "broken down," "being repaired" (though, of course, there will be long sequences of minutes when the move will simply be from one state to the same state). A Markov chain is in many ways identical to a probability-tree—except for the fact that sooner or later the object under investigation will return to a previously experienced state.

8. Diagrammatic representation of a MARKOV CHAIN situation.
Assume there are only two suppliers, A and B, of a weekly household necessity, and market research has shown that there is a 0·75 probability that a customer who bought A one week will buy A the next, but only a 0·5 probability that a customer who bought B one week will again buy B the next.

This information can be shown in the form of a diagram (see Fig. 19(a)) where arrows show the possible transitions (moves) from one state to another (the case where, in fact, there is no real change in state being depicted by a circular arrow returning back to the state it left), the probabilities of the transitions being shown alongside the arrows.

9. Matrix representation of a MARKOV CHAIN situation.
A MARKOV CHAIN situation can also be represented by means of a matrix—the initial states being listed in rows and the transitional states in columns (it is very important to get the matrix the right way round). Such a matrix is called a transitional matrix and each element is, of course, the probability of moving from the initial state to the transitional state (see Fig. 19(b)). Note, incidentally, that since it is certain that there will be a move from any given initial state to one of the transitional states, the sum of the probabilities in each and every row will be 1.

10. Computing future state probabilities.
Let us take our illustration one step further and assume that in a given area in

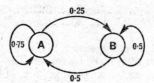

(a) Diagrammatic representation.

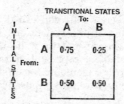

(b) Transitional matrix.

FIG. 19.—*Markov chain.*

the first week of the year the total market of 6400 customers is equally shared between A and B (*i.e.* 3200 each). What will be the position one week later? Clearly, with a 0·75 probability that an A customer will re-buy A, then 2400 old A customers will buy A. In addition, 0·5 of the old B customers—*i.e.* 1600 will now turn to A, so a total of 4000 customers will buy A (the other 2400 buying B, of course).

Consideration of this result may well lead the student to notice that matrix multiplication (Chapter VIII) in which the initial market numbers form the leading matrix and the transitional matrix the trailing matrix, gives the very same result—*i.e.*:

Initial Customers   *Transitional Matrix*   *Subsequent Share of Market*

| A | B | | | A | B |

$$(3200 \quad 3200) \times \begin{pmatrix} 0·75 & 0·25 \\ 0·50 & 0·50 \end{pmatrix} = (4000 \quad 2400)$$

If we wish to see the position a further week later then all we have to do is repeat the matrix multiplication using the previous answer matrix as the new leading matrix, so:

$$(4000 \qquad 2400) \times \begin{pmatrix} 0·75 & 0·25 \\ 0·50 & 0·50 \end{pmatrix} = (4200 \qquad 2200)$$

And A now has 4200 customers.

The process can obviously be repeated indefinitely, and so we can generalise and say that in any MARKOV CHAIN situation the position after n transitions is given by:

$$(\text{INITIAL POSITION MATRIX}) \times (\text{TRANSITIONAL MATRIX})^n$$

If rather than numbers we are concerned with the *probability* of a given state existing after n transitions, all we need to do is proceed in the same way except we write the "initial position matrix" so that the element representing the *current* state has a value 1 and all the other elements are 0 (since it is certain we have the actual current state and impossible that we have any of the others).

11. The steady state. In our illustration it may appear at first sight as though A will continually win customers from B until finally he is selling to the whole market. A few additional transitional calculations, however, will show that A's gain of customers progressively decreases, and, in fact, a point will ultimately be reached where the market shares of A and B will remain unaltered week by week. This position is known as the *steady state* and to compute the steady state in any MARKOV CHAIN situation it is only necessary to appreciate that when in the steady state then by definition the *position before the transitions is identical to the position afterwards.* Thus in our illustration A customers will be the same 1 week later. If, then, A has x customers (and B $6400 - x$) then using our transitional probabilities we can say A has $0·75x + 0·5(6400 - x) = 0·25x + 3200$ customers one week later. But, by definition, this must equal x, so $0·25x + 3200 = x$, and therefore $x = 4266\frac{2}{3}$ or, more usefully, $\frac{2}{3}$ of the total market.

If we wish to use matrix algebra the steady state is found by allocating a, b, c, etc. to the elements of the initial position matrix *and* the answer matrix. The matrix multiplication, then, results in a series of simultaneous equations which, together with the fact that $a + b + c$ etc. equals the total in the situation, enables unique values to be given to these algebraic symbols.

PROGRESS TEST 12

1. Simpelasticity Ltd. (the company mentioned in **4**), have just discovered that owing to very exceptional circumstances the marginal cost of their product has risen to £11. What is the optimal selling price now?

2. In a particular one-product company it has been noted that the total *value* of sales per day is given by the expression £(10,000 ÷ Selling price per unit in £s). If daily fixed costs amount to £1000 and the variable cost per unit is £2, then:

(*a*) Prepare a profit model.

(*b*) Find the price at which the product must be sold to maximise profits.

3. Under the Rowan incentive scheme a shop-floor worker is given a time allowance to complete a job. If he does the job in less time than the allowance then he is paid a percentage bonus on the wages earned during the time spent on the job—this bonus percentage being equal to the percentage the time *saved* on the job bears to the time allowed.

(*a*) Build a model of wages earned on a given job.

(*b*) If a worker is given two jobs with time allowances of 10 and 8 hours respectively, and completes both in the course of an 8-hour day, how should he book his time to the two jobs if the maximisation of his wages was the sole consideration?

4. A foundry uses the following price-fixing formula:

	£
Cost of metal	
Direct labour	
0'h'ds (200% Direct Labour)	
Total cost	
Profit (10% on cost)	
Selling price	

Foundry costs are as follows: Metal £6 per ton; Direct labour £5000 per week; Variable overheads £1 per ton; Fixed costs £8000 per week.

Labour responds to work load by speeding-up in busy time and slowing down in slack so that total hours booked to production remains a constant.

Prepare a profit model based on tons of metal poured in a week. What anomaly does the model bring to light?

5. A tool costs £50 to buy. Parts produced by the tool must then be "finished." The cost of "finishing" depends on the age of the

tool—the first part produced by the tool costs £0·01, the second £0·02, the third £0·03 and so on, the "finishing" cost increasing by £0·01 per unit.

How many units should be produced by the tool before the tool is thrown away?

CHAPTER XIII

DECISION THEORY

When faced with a number of alternatives and the need to make a decision between them mathematics can often be used to help us—particularly in probability situations. The basic principles of applying mathematical probabilities to decision-making is called *decision theory*.

EXPECTATION

Almost certainly the most important concept in decision theory is *expectation*. Although so important it is fortunately not a difficult concept—it is, in fact, nothing more than an average and can be regarded simply as the average result obtained if a particular situation arose time and time again. Thus, if we toss 10 coins all at once on average we'd expect 5 heads—so 5 heads is our expectation.

1. Monetary expectation. In decision-making it is usually more informative if we express our expectation in monetary terms. For example, if in our 10-coin tossing illustration we won £4 every time a head fell but lost £2 every time a tail fell we would win on average $5 \times £4 + 5 \times -£2 = £10$. Our expectation, then, would be £10 per time, or £1 per coin tossed.

2. Computation of expectation. To compute expectation all one does is:

    (*a*) List all the possible *exclusive* events.
    (*b*) Value each event.
    (*c*) Calculate PROBABILITY OF EVENT × VALUE OF EVENT.
    (*d*) Add the products.

We could, therefore, have computed the expectation per coin tossed found in **1** as follows:

117

Event	Probability	Value	Expectation
Head	$\frac{1}{2}$	$+£4$	$+£2$
Tail	$\frac{1}{2}$	$-£2$	$-£1$
			$+£1$

The emphasis given above on the need for events to be exclusive doubtless has warned the student the usual care on this aspect of probability needs to be taken. For example, considering yet again our 10-marble urn with 4 reds and 6 yellows, assume we can draw 1 marble at a time until we draw either a red marble or have drawn a total of 3 marbles. At the end of our drawing we are paid £120 per red marble drawn and £30 per yellow. What is our expectation?

Using our conditional probability theory we can solve this problem as follows:

Event	Probability	Value	Expectation (£)
Red	$\frac{4}{10} = \frac{2}{5}$	£120	48
Yellow, Red	$\frac{6}{10} \times \frac{4}{9} = \frac{4}{15}$	£150	40
Yellow, Yellow, Red	$\frac{6}{10} \times \frac{5}{9} \times \frac{4}{8} = \frac{1}{6}$	£180	30
Yellow, Yellow, Yellow	$\frac{6}{10} \times \frac{5}{9} \times \frac{4}{8} = \frac{1}{6}$	£90	15
	1		£133

We can interpret this result by saying that if we carried out this exercise a sufficient number of times we would "win" £133 on average.

3. Expectation $\neq$ actual winnings. It should be appreciated that very often expectation does *not* equal any possible actual result. In the above exercise, for example, it is impossible ever to win £133 at one time.

4. Expectation and decisions—Bayes' Rule. Next assume one has the choice of either the above exercise or one in which you took exactly 2 marbles. What should your choice be?

The first step is clearly to find the expectation of the second alternative. This is:

Event	Probability	Value	Expectation (£)
Red, Red	$\frac{4}{10} \times \frac{3}{9} = \frac{2}{15}$	£240	32
Red, Yellow	$\frac{4}{10} \times \frac{6}{9} = \frac{4}{15}$	£150	40
Yellow, Red	$\frac{6}{10} \times \frac{4}{9} = \frac{4}{15}$	£150	40
Yellow, Yellow	$\frac{6}{10} \times \frac{5}{9} = \frac{1}{3}$	£60	20
	1		£132

Since it is better to be in a situation where one wins £133 on average than one in which one wins £132, the former alternative is the more profitable.

In this approach to decision-making we are employing what is termed *Bayes' Rule* which in effect lays down that when deciding between two or more alternatives one should select the alternative with the highest expectation.

5. Alternative-expectation and decision-expectation. Although not part of the normal terminology it will pay us in decision theory discussion to distinguish between what we can call:

(a) *alternative-expectation*, which is the expectation from a given alternative; and

(b) *decision-expectation*, which is the expectation from the alternative decided upon.

Thus in our previous illustration our alternative-expectations were £133 and £132 respectively, and our decision-expectation was £133.

DECISION RULES

In decision-making we can adopt one of a number of decision rules, and these we now consider. To illustrate these rules we will use the following illustrative figures:

A retailer trades in a particular product having a cost price of £4 and a selling price of £7. Daily demand is variable, though the probabilities are known to be as follows:

Demand (Units)	Probability of Demand
0	0·1
1	0·4
2	0·3
3	0·2

6. Procedure where units can be stocked. If units can be stocked then the retailer has no decisions to make (other than stock level decisions, which are looked at in Chapter XVII)—all he needs to do is draw on his stocks according to demand. In this situation his profit expectation is:

Event	Probability	Value (Profit)	Expectation (£)
Demand = 0 units	0·1	£0	0
,, = 1 ,,	0·4	£3	1·2
,, = 2 ,,	0·3	£6	1·8
,, = 3 ,,	0·2	£9	1·8
	1·0		£4·8

So on average the retailer will make £4·8 profit per day.

7. Procedure where units cannot be stocked. Where units cannot be stocked the retailer is faced with the problem of deciding how many should be delivered each day. If we assume, then, in our example that units unsold at the end of the day must be sold off cheaply for a mere £2 a unit, we can examine all the different ways in which the retailer can view the problem and reach a decision as to his required daily delivery.

8. Pay-off table. To aid our analysis of this situation we will first construct a *pay-off table*, which is simply a table detailing the profit (or loss) made in respect of every combination of decision and event. Conventionally the decisions are shown in columns and the events in rows, and so our pay-off table for our illustration will take the form given in Fig. 20.

9. Maximax rule. Under the maximax rule the retailer selects the alternative that can give him his *maximum possible profit*. Our pay-off table shows the maximum profit is £9, and this is obtained by ordering 3 units. The retailer, then, decides to order 3 units.

The obvious disadvantage of this rule is that it totally ignores possible losses—up to £6 with this decision. It is, then, a rule more suitable for a gambler whose philosophy is all or nothing than a responsible businessman.

(a) Basic data: Product cost price: £4

	Product Selling Price	Profit
If sold during day	£7	£3
If not sold during day	£2	−£2

(b) Pay-off table.

Pay-off in profit (£s):

Possible decisions
No. Units ordered for delivery

			0*	1†	2‡	3‡
		0	0	−2	−4	−6
Possible	Units	1	0	+3	+1	−1
Events	Demanded	2	0	+3	+6	+4
		3	0	+3	+6	+9

* If 0 units ordered, then £0 profit in all events.
† If 1 unit ordered, maximum profit is £3.
‡ Profit = units sold × £3 − units unsold × £2.

Fig. 20.—*Illustrative pay-off table.*

10. Minimax rule. Under the minimax rule the retailer selects the alternative that *minimises the maximum possible loss.* Since the pay-off table shows orders of 0, 1, 2 and 3 units have maximum losses of £0, £2, £4 and £6 respectively, the retailer will identify the minimum of these, £0, and place his order accordingly—*i.e.* order 0 units.

Clearly the minimax rule is one very biased towards caution and since caution and opportunity rarely go together, the rule rarely gives worthwhile results. In our example, for instance, while following the rule limits the retailer's loss to £0, it also limits his profit to £0. Nevertheless the minimax rule may be a very suitable one in a situation where the stakes are of a very high order. For example, an ordinary person would be wise to accept the alternative of paying £1 for a toss of a coin where he would win £3 if he tossed a head, rather than the alternative of paying £10,000 for a toss where he would win £50,000 if he tossed a head—even though limiting his loss to £1 means passing up the more financially attractive big prize offer.

11. Maximum likelihood rule. Under the maximum likelihood rule the retailer selects the *most likely alternative*. Since our basic figures on page 119 show the most likely event is a demand of 1 unit then this is the number ordered.

The disadvantage of this rule is that no consideration is given to less likely but more consequential results. To take an extreme example, assume that we are offered the chance of one throw of a die for £1 and will be paid £1000 if we throw a six. Clearly, although we are more likely to lose £1 than win £1000 we would be making the wrong decision if we refused the offer.

12. Bayes' rule. As we have seen under Bayes' rule one selects the alternative with the highest expectation. This involves finding all the alternative-expectations which in our example can be done as follows:

POSSIBLE DEMAND		NUMBER OF UNITS ORDERED FOR DELIVERY							
UNITS	PROBAB- ILITY	0		1		2		3	
		PROFIT	EXPECT	PROFIT	EXPECT	PROFIT	EXPECT	PROFIT	EXPECT
0	.1	0	0	−2	−0.2	−4	−0.4	−6	−0.6
1	.4	0	0	+3	+1.2	+1	+0.4	−1	−0.4
2	.3	0	0	+3	+0.9	+6	+1.8	+4	+1.2
3	.2	0	0	+3	+0.6	+6	+1.2	+9	+1.8
TOTAL			0		+2.5		+3.0		+2.0

As can be seen the alternative-expectations are £0, £2·5, £3 and £2 respectively. Selecting the maximum of these, then, indicates 2 units should be ordered.

Generally speaking, Bayes' rule is the best of the decision rules.

13. The value of perfect information. If our retailer adopted Bayes' rule and always ordered 2 units, we know from the decision-expectation he would make an average profit of £3 per day.

Although maximising his expectation, the retailer would doubtless be concerned that he is not making his *potential* profit, since on days when demand is over 2 units he will lose sales and on days when it is less he will be selling his left-overs at a loss. Indeed he will very likely say to himself, "If only I knew tomorrow's demand today then I could run a more profitable business. I can accept the demand will vary—all I want is to know twenty-four hours in advance what it will be." What if his wish could be granted? How much extra profit could he make?

The answer to these questions is not difficult, for if he were always able to order the exact number of units actually demanded, then he would be in an identical position to the retailer who can stock his units—indeed, all he would be doing, in effect, would be withdrawing from the wholesaler's stock just enough units to meet demand. And in **6** we saw that the expectation in that situation was £4·8.

So with *perfect information*—*i.e.* knowing in advance exactly what will occur—he can make £4·8 per day. Since his decision-expectation is only £3 a day then we can say the *value of perfect information* is 4·8 − 3·0 = £1·8 per day. In other words, having perfect information will enable him to make £1·8 per day more profit.

The importance of knowing the value of perfect information lies in the fact that it measures the maximum we would pay for such information. Our retailer, for instance, may be offered a service which would enable him to predict to a greater or lesser extent his next day's demand, and the better such a prediction were the more profitable it would be, of course, for our retailer to buy the service. Nevertheless, even though such predictions were perfect, he should never pay more than the value of perfect information—*i.e.* £1·8 per day in this case.

DECISION-TREES

Decisions are rarely as simple as the one we have just examined and so we must now consider a technique we can use in more complex situations.

14. Decisions and probability-trees. Just as the more complex probability problems could, as we've seen, often be solved

using a probability-tree, so the more complex decision problems can be solved using a *decision-tree*. A decision-tree is, in
fact a probability-tree that incorporates branches leading to
alternatives we can select (decision-branches) among the usual
branches leading to events that depend on probabilities (probability-branches), and the object of a decision-tree is, of course,
to decide which of the available alternatives should in fact be
selected.

NOTE: To distinguish between the two kinds of branches we will
adopt the convention in this book of showing probability-
branches as *unbroken* lines and decision-branches as *dotted* lines.

15. A decision-tree problem. Assume a salesman has two
customers he can visit, Retailer Ltd and Manufacturer Ltd, on
a given day. His probabilities of catching the people he wants
depend upon whether he makes a morning or afternoon visit—
the probabilities of catching the Buyer at Retailer Ltd. being
0·8 in the morning and 0·7 in the afternoon while the probabilities of catching the Buyer at Manufacturer Ltd. is 0·5 in the
morning and 0·4 in the afternoon. He has the choice of making
a morning visit to either customer. If he catches the appropriate Buyer in he will not have time to make any further visits,
but if he fails he has the option of waiting until the afternoon
and trying again or driving over to the other customer for an
afternoon visit there. He considers that catching the Buyer of
Retailer Ltd. will be worth £800 of business while catching the
Buyer of Manufacturer Ltd. will be worth £1000. What should
the salesman do?

16. The forward pass. To construct the appropriate decision-
tree for this decision we first make what is called the *forward
pass*. We begin by drawing a circle on the left-hand side of the
tree and writing START inside it. As we know, at the start the
salesman has a choice of going to Retailer Ltd. or to Manufacturer Ltd. so we show these alternatives as circles with VR and
VM in them and dotted decision-branches leading to them
(*see* Fig. 21). Taking the VR alternative we see from the problem the salesman has a 0·8 chance of catching Retailer's Buyer,
so we draw the two probability-branches ending with circles
for catching the Buyer (BI) and not catching him (BO), the
latter event, of course, having a probability of $1 - 0·8 = 0·2$.

If the salesman fails to catch the Buyer then he must decide whether to wait until the afternoon and re-visit Retailer or drive over to Manufacturer. This choice is shown by appropriate dotted decision-branches. The possible results of each decision are then shown at the ends of probability-branches.

We now return to the START alternative shown on the tree as a VM circle and, following virtually the same procedure as that just discussed, complete the lower half of the tree.

17. The backward pass. Our next step is to make the *backward pass*. To do this we write against every *final* event on the tree the *value* of that event. Obviously in this case BI events are worth £800 and £1000 respectively, and a BO event £0.

This done we then work backwards along the branches complying with the following rules:

(*a*) If the branches are *probability-branches*, write the expectation alongside the junction of the branches.

(*b*) If the branches are *decision-branches*, select the branch with the highest expectation as the branch to be chosen in the event of a decision being needed, and write this expectation alongside the junction of the branches. This selection should be recorded by ticking the decision-branch.

Contemplation of these rules will show that what we are doing is selecting the alternatives with the highest expectations (as per Bayes' rule) and then marking the decision-expectation at the point the decision is made. In our illustration this junction figure, of course, gives us the average sale we can expect from that point onwards along the tree. Thus, in the top half of our tree (Fig. 21) we see that if the salesman waits at Retailer until the afternoon he will average £560 sales, while if he drives to Manufacturer he will only average £400. So his correct decision is to wait. Similarly at the very beginning, if he goes first to Retailer he'll average £752, but if he goes first to Manufacturer he'll average £780. So he should go first to Manufacturer.

18. Reading the completed tree. To read the completed tree, then, we begin at START and simply follow the ticked decision-branches. Thus in our illustration we will say:

The salesman should first visit Manufacturer Ltd. If he fails

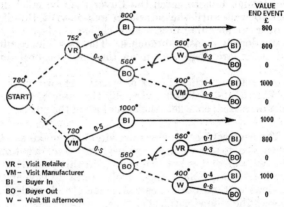

Ticks and figures with ● inserted during backward pass.

FIG. 21.—*Decision-tree.*

to catch the Buyer there he should drive to Retailer Ltd. for an afternoon visit.

NOTE:
(*i*) The overall expectation is given by the figure at START. Our salesman, then, will on average make sales of £780 in this situation.
(*ii*) Once a decision-branch has been eliminated all the subsequent part of the tree becomes irrelevant. The top half and bottom right-hand quarter of our tree, then, is now irrelevant.

19. Decision-trees and costs of alternatives. In more complex (and realistic) decision-tree situations not only do the pay-offs differ but also the costs of the various alternatives. One way of handling this additional factor is to write the cost of each alternative against its branch in the decision-tree when making the forward pass, and then, when making the backward pass, to write the alternative-expectations *net of the alternative costs* in appropriate places alongside the junction of the decision-branches. Once the decision is made on the basis of the highest net expectation the other expectations are simply crossed out.

To illustrate this procedure let us assume a trader has the choice of stocking a "Big" or a "Little". A Big costs £200 and there is a 0·4 probability of selling it at £300. If it remains unsold it can only be remaindered at £150. On the other hand a Little costs £100, sells with a 0·8 probability for £150, and has a remainder value of £50. Which should the trader stock?

We begin our forward pass by drawing the two decision-branches of the tree and inserting the alternative costs of £200 and £100 (*see* Fig. 22). We complete the tree in the normal way with two sets of probability-branches. On the backward pass we first compute the expectation at the first probability junctions in the normal way, to obtain £210 and £130 respectively. We then write at the START junction the net expectations of 210 − 200 = £10 and 130 − 100 = £30 respectively. Since a £30 expectation is better than one of £10 we take the Little decision-branch and cross out the £10 Big expectation.

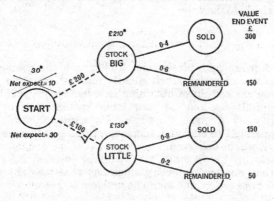

Ticks and figures with ● inserted during backward pass.

FIG. 22.—*Decision-tree with alternative costs.*

REDUNDANCY

We close this chapter by briefly looking at the probability concept of redundancy.

20. The REDUNDANCY situation. A REDUNDANCY situation is one in which more units are provided in an operation than are strictly necessary—the additional units being included in case any of the initial units fail to operate. In a communications satellite, for example, if the electronic circuit included only one critical component and this failed then a very expensive satellite would immediately become a piece of use-less space junk. If, however, a number of such components were wired into the circuit in such a way that if one failed an-other took over its function then the probability of *satellite* (as against component) failure would be very much reduced.

21. Solving redundancy problems. The principle underlying the solution of a REDUNDANCY situation problem is to in-clude the extra units one at a time and at each step to compare the cost of the unit with the *increase in the pay-off expectancy*. As long as this cost is below the expectancy increase it is profit-able to include the unit.

22. A redundancy illustration. To illustrate this principle let us take a commercial, albeit slightly unusual, example. Sup-pose you are certain of obtaining an overseas contract worth £1000 profit—as long as your tender reaches the overseas authority by a given dead-line. Unfortunately the bulky tender costs £1 to mail and, moreover, there is only a 0·8 prob-ability it will be delivered.

Clearly in this situation we would be justified in sending more than one tender, even though any that are delivered in excess of one are redundant. The problem is, how many should one mail?

First we note that we will obtain the contract if at least one tender arrives. We have, then, an AT LEAST situation and as we indicate in Chapter IX, **16** we can say:

Probability of AT LEAST 1 tender arriving = $1 - P(0$ tenders arriving)

And, of course, the probability "0 tenders arriving" is the probability all fail to arrive

$$= P(Failure) \times P(Failure) \times P(Failure) \ldots$$
$$= P(Failure)^n, \text{ where } n = \text{number of tenders.}$$

We can, therefore, make the following analysis:

No. of Tenders	Probability of Contract	Expectation*	Increase in Expectation
1	$1 - 0.2^1 = 0.8$	£800	—
2	$1 - 0.2^2 = 0.96$	£960	£160
3	$1 - 0.2^3 = 0.992$	£992	£32
4	$1 - 0.2^4 = 0.9984$	£998·4	£6·4
5	$1 - 0.2^5 = 0.99968$	£999·68	£1·28
6	$1 - 0.2^6 = 0.999936$	£999·936	£0·256

* £1000 × probability of contract.

Clearly the cost of the 6th tender (£1) exceeds the increase in our expectation and therefore does not warrant sending.

PROGRESS TEST 13

1. The probability of the demand for lorries for hiring on any day in a given district is as follows:

No. of lorries demanded	Probability
0	0·1
1	0·2
2	0·3
3	0·2
4	0·2

Lorries have a fixed cost of £9 each a day to keep and the daily hire charge (net of variable costs of running) is £20.

(a) If the lorry-hire company owns 4 lorries, what is its daily expectation?

(b) If the company is about to go into business and currently has no lorries, how many lorries should it buy?

2. A company markets a particular machine for £1000. There is a certain demand for at least 1 machine per period and a 0·4 probability of the demand being for 2 units in any period (this being the maximum number that can be demanded). The machine is supplied to the company at a list price of £600, but the supplier agrees to supply 3 machines for a total of £1700 or 4 for £1900. For technical reasons any machines held by the company at the end of the next but one period will be valueless, while for commercial reasons it is necessary to place a firm order *now* for all machine requirements for these forthcoming two periods.

(a) How many machines should the company order?

(b) What would be the value of perfect information?

3. You wish to invent and market a new kind of revolutionary

product. You have a choice of two different research and development plans, A and B. A costs £1m and has a 0·4 chance of success while B costs £½m but only has a 0·3 chance of success. In the event of a success you then have to decide whether or not to advertise the product heavily or lightly. Heavy advertising will cost £400,000 but give a 0·7 probability of full acceptance (as against partial acceptance) by the market while light advertising will cost £100,000 and give a 0·5 probability of full acceptance. Full market acceptance of the product developed via plan A would be worth £4m and via plan B £3m. Partial market acceptance in either case will be worth £2m. Which plan, if either, should you adopt and what level of advertising should be undertaken in the event of marketing the product?

CHAPTER XIV

SIMULATION

Simulating is essentially no more than experimenting with a model and observing the consequences. It is a kind of try-it-and-see technique. Thus pilots can be trained on the ground by allowing them to experiment with a working model that "simulates" an aircraft's flight. In operational research the models involved, of course, are usually mathematical models.

Strictly speaking, experimenting with *any* model by inserting selected values is a simulation, so if we have the model "Unit contribution = S − M" where "S" and "M" are the selling price and marginal cost respectively, then inserting £3 for "S" and £2 for "M" and observing the unit contribution is £1 can be referred to as "running a simulation." However we usually reserve the term for much more involved situations where the model is too complex to give us easily the answer we seek. For example, a profit model may contain some twenty variables and the only way we can discover which combination of values will maximise the profit is by experimenting with one combination after another and observing the resulting profit in each case. Operational research simulations, then, are normally experiments that involve relatively complex models.

PROBABILITY SIMULATIONS

The commonest form of operational research simulations are those relating to probability situations. So often in real-life probability situations the number of possible combinations of events is astronomical (the relatively short probability-trees previously discussed give some indication of the rate at which branches can multiply) and unless there is a fortuitous mathematical short cut it is just not possible to compute all the required answers. Imagine, for example, we wish to know the probability of a man obtaining a specified book by visiting not more than 30 bookshops at random where only 1 shop in 36 actually stocks the book. In principle this is easily solved—it is simply a matter of computing the probability of finding the book in the 1st shop OR not in the 1st but in the 2nd OR not in the 1st and 2nd but in the 3rd OR . . ., and then adding. In other words we would compute:

$$\tfrac{1}{36} + \tfrac{35}{36} \times \tfrac{1}{36} + (\tfrac{35}{36})^2 \times \tfrac{1}{36} \cdots (\tfrac{35}{36})^{29} \times \tfrac{1}{36}$$

Clearly, what may be simple in principle may be quite complicated in application (it is, as a matter of interest, approximately 0·57).

NOTE: Actually there are two different short cuts here as the student may have spotted for one can either argue that the probability of getting the book is 1—the probability of not getting it $= 1 - (\tfrac{35}{36})^{30}$ or simply note we need the sum of a geometric progression where the first term is $\tfrac{1}{36}$ and the constant $\tfrac{35}{36}$. In real life we rarely have such mathematical good luck.

1. Monte Carlo simulation.

Let us assume we neither spot the short cuts nor relish the idea of making the longer computation, and that we are prepared to accept a close approximation if we can forgo the arduous work (and in real life there are so many imponderables that a close approximation is often as useful as a mathematically exact answer). In this situation we can see that the probability of the man finding the book in a given shop is exactly the same as the probability of throwing a double six. We can, therefore, simulate the man's success in a given shop by throwing two dice—if a double six results, he's found his book. And we can simulate the whole search by throwing the two dice up to 30 times and seeing if we ever get a double six.

Of course, simulating just one search will tell us nothing about the probability of a search of 30 shops being successful. To do this we have to simulate a large number of searches—after which the required probability can be found by dividing the total searches made into the number of successful searches. And, of course, the more searches we simulate, the closer our approximate probability will be to the exact probability.

A simulation that employs a random device for determining what happens at a given point in the situation is called a *Monte Carlo simulation*. Such simulations, though simple enough to run, do tend to be lengthy and tedious—unless, of course, a computer is available. However, they may well prove to be the only way an answer can be economically obtained in a given practical situation.

2. Random numbers. Throwing dice in a serious simulation is not, of course, practical since it is time-consuming, the dice may be weighted, and above all, it would be very complicated to apply where the probabilities were expressed in decimals rather than multiples of $\frac{1}{6}$.

All these difficulties are overcome by using a table of *random numbers*. Such a table is prepared on a computer and is essentially the sort of results you would obtain if you threw an unbiased ten-sided die (with faces numbered 0 to 9) and recorded each throw. Random number tables are usually written in blocks five or six digits wide and as many deep. To use a random number table one simply regards the digits as dice-throwing results. Thus if our book-hunting friend had a 0·1 probability of finding this book in a given shop we could simulate his 30-shop search by designating a given digit (say "9") a "find" and running our eye along a row of 30 random number digits. If there is a "9" anywhere among them he finds his book—otherwise he doesn't.

In using a table of random numbers (an example of which is given in Appendix II) the following points should be noted:

(*a*) Choose the starting-place in the table at random. Do *not* always start at the same point.

(*b*) The numbers may be read in any order—horizontally, vertically, diagonally or backwards if desired.

(*c*) If the probabilities are not single-digit probabilities (*e.g.* the probability of finding a book is 0·163) then read the random numbers in appropriate-sized digit groups (*e.g.* in 3-digit groups) and allocate an appropriate range as signifying the specific event being considered (*e.g.* allocate 000 to 162 as signifying "book found" and 163 to 999 as signifying "no book found").

(*d*) If the probability is not a decimal (*e.g.* it is, say, $\frac{5}{36}$), work only with random numbers within the required range and treat all other numbers as if they didn't exist (*e.g.* work only with digits 00 to 35—designating 00 to 04 "success" numbers and 05 to 35 as "failures"—and ignore all numbers in the 36 to 99 range).

MONTE CARLO SIMULATION ILLUSTRATION

The rest of the chapter will be devoted to a short but comprehensive illustration of a Monte Carlo simulation.

3. The problem. A retailer has found from experience that the daily demand for a particular product is equally likely to be for 1, 2, 3, 4 or 5 units. He obtains his supplies from a wholesaler's delivery vehicle which, while coming frequently, seems to have no systematic delivery schedule other than to arrive last thing in the afternoon on the day it comes. An analysis of the last 100 deliveries show the following:

Days after Previous Delivery	No. of Deliveries
1	4
2	12
3	21
4	36
5	18
6	9
	100

At each delivery time the retailer has to decide how many units to buy. He notes his average daily sales are $(1 + 2 + 3 + 4 + 5)/5 = 3$ units and that deliveries are usually made on the 4th day. He argues, therefore, that he will require on average $3 \times 4 = 12$ units and if he allows himself a buffer stock of, say, 2 units he will need to purchase at each delivery sufficient units to bring his total stock up to 14.

Before he makes a final decision, however, he would like to know how often (as a percentage of days) under this policy:

    (a) he will be unable to meet demand; and

    (b) he will have an over-night stock of 10 or more units (this information being needed for insurance purposes).

4. The solution approach. We will use a Monte Carlo simulation to solve this problem by arbitrarily selecting a total of 50 deliveries and using random numbers first to simulate the dates of these deliveries and then to simulate the demand day by day. Analysis of the results will then enable us to give the retailer the information he desires.

This simulation will be recorded in a working table, and the completed table is shown in Fig. 23. Explanations relating to the procedures used and the build-up of the table are given in the subsequent paragraphs.

Random numbers for "Demand" simulation						Overnight stock, day 0 : 14
Random number	0, 1	2, 3	4, 5	6, 7	8, 9	
Units demanded	1	2	3	4	5	

Days after previous delivery	1	2	3	4	5	6	Days	Nights
Random numbers allocation:	00–03	04–15	16–36	37–72	73–90	91–99	No supply	10 or more units
Delivery No: 1	5 9	1 8	5 3A				0	1
2	4 10	3 7	4 3	2 1	4 *A		1	2
3	5 9	2 7	1 6	3 3A			0	1
4	5 9	1 8	5 3A				0	1
5	2 12	1 11	3 8	1 7	3 4A		0	3
6	1 13	5 8	2 6	1 5	2 3	5 *A	1	2
7	2 12	4 8	5 3	5 *	5 *A		2	2
8	1 13	3 10A					0	2
9	5 9	3 6	3 3A				0	1
10	1 13	1 12	1 11A				0	3
11	4 10	3 7	1 6	1 5A			0	2
12	2 12	5 7A					0	2
13	1 13	1 12A					0	2
14	1 13	1 12	2 10A				0	3
15	3 11	4 7	2 5	2 3A			0	2
16	2 12	2 10	1 9	3 6A			0	3
17	3 11	3 8	4 4	3 1A			0	2
18	2 12	4 8	5 3A				0	2
19	2 12	1 11	1 10	4 6A			0	4
20	2 12	3 9	2 7	5 2	5 *	1 *A	2	2
21	4 10	4 6	5 1	3 *	1 *	5 *A	3	2
22	4 10	2 8	3 5A				0	2
23	3 11	5 6	5 1	2 *A			1	2
24	1 13	1 12	4 8A				0	3
25	2 12	1 11A					0	2
26	5 9	3 6A					0	1
27	4 10	3 7	5 2	1 1A			0	2
28	2 12	5 7	1 6	4 2	1 1	3 *A	1	2
29	1 13A						0	1
30	1 13	3 10A					0	2
31	1 13	2 11	4 7	4 3A			0	3
32	5 9	4 5	5 0A				0	1
33	4 10	5 5	5 0A				0	2
34	3 11	3 8	3 5	5 0A			0	2
35	2 12	3 9	3 6	1 5A			0	2
36	1 13	3 10	4 6	2 4A			0	3
37	2 12	3 9	2 7	2 5	3 2	3 *A	1	2
38	1 13A						0	1
39	1 13	3 10	1 9	5 4A			0	3
40	5 9	3 6	1 5	4 1	3 *A		1	1
41	5 9	3 6	3 3	1 2A			0	1
42	3 11	5 6	2 4	4 0	5 *A		1	2
43	2 12	5 7	2 5	3 2A			0	2
44	4 10	5 5	1 4	5 *A			1	2
45	3 11	2 9	1 8A				0	2
46	1 13	3 10	3 7	5 2	5 *	2 *A	2	3
47	4 10	2 8	5 3	2 1	3 *	4 *A	2	2
48	3 11	5 6	1 5A				0	2
49	5 9	1 8	1 7A				0	1
50	2 12	1 11	3 8	1 7	3 4A		0	3
Total days/nights	50	48	42	29	13	7	19	101

Total days in simulation 189

∴ Time out of stock = 19/189 × 100 ≃ 10%   * Out of stock

∴ Time over-night 10 units or more = 101/189 × 100 ≃ 53%

FIG. 23.—*Illustrative simulation.*

5. Simulating arrival dates. Our first task, then, is to simulate the arrival dates. This is done by taking the following two steps:

(a) Ranges of 2-digit numbers are allocated to each "Days after previous delivery"—there being as many 2-digit numbers in a given range as there were deliveries during the previous 100-delivery period. Thus the four numbers 00 to 03 relate to "1 day after previous delivery," and the twelve numbers 04 to 15 to "2 days after previous delivery" (*see* Fig. 23). The probability, then, of selecting a 2-digit number at random that lies within a given range is exactly equal to the probability of a delivery being made on the day that relates to that range.

(b) Fifty 2-digit random numbers are next read from a table of random numbers and the delivery days so identified are shown on our working table by a small "A" on the right-hand side of the "day" column. (In Fig. 23 the delivery days were found by arbitrarily selecting the sixth block in the table in Appendix II as our starting-point and reading vertically, for ease, the first two digits in each line of this column of blocks—moving to the first two digits in each line of the next *column* of blocks, again for ease of reading, after the 40th reading.)

6. Simulating demand. Our next task is to simulate the day-by-day demand. Again we can allocate ranges of numbers to each of the five possible demand levels—in this case 0 and 1 to 1 unit demand, 2 and 3 to 2 units demand, etc. (or, if desired, 1, 2, 3, 4 and 5 to a demand for 1, 2, 3, 4 and 5 units respectively, the digits 6, 7, 8, 9 and 0 being ignored)—the full allocation being shown in Fig. 23. And once again we read off sufficient random numbers (1-digit, this time) to give us the demand day-by-day for all the appropriate days in the period—the demand being shown at the left-hand side of the "day" column. (For Fig. 23 our random numbers were read horizontally from the table arbitrarily starting at the beginning of the 6th line.)

7. Computing stock balances. As the daily demands were recorded in the working table it was a simple matter to compute at the same time the over-night stock balances day-by-day by deducting the 1st day's demand from 14 and subsequent demands from subsequent stock balances. These stock balances

are shown in the centre of the "day" column in Fig. 23, an *
marking those days on which the demand exceeded the available stock.

8. Days when demand could not be met. We are now able to
answer the retailer's first question and tell him how often he
will be unable to meet demand. All we need to do is count the
number of days with an * and find what percentage this is of
the total days covered by the simulation. Since Fig. 23 shows
there are 19 *'s and a total of 189 days the simulation indicates
demand will exceed supply approximately 10% of the time.

9. Over-night stock 10 units or more. In much the same way
we can answer the retailer's second question and tell him how
often he will have an overnight stock of 10 units or more. Since
there will always be 14 units in stock on the first night we need
to add 1 to the total days having an over-night stock of 10 or
more shown in each line of our table (but be careful not to
double-count nights when a delivery was made and the *old*
stock balance was 10 or more). Adding all these figures in the
table we find there were 101 such nights—*i.e.* the simulation
indicates an over-night stock of 10 or more units will be carried
on $\frac{101}{189}$ = just over half the total number of nights.

10. Abnormal run cross-check. After making any Monte
Carlo simulation it always pays to check if the run was an
abnormal one or not by checking where possible the simulation
results against any model constants. For example, in our
illustration our model (the original data) gives us the delivery
distribution of the simulation as follows:

DAYS AFTER PREVIOUS DELIVERY	SIMULATION		MODEL
	No. OF DELIVERIES	% OF DELIVERIES	% OF DELIVERIES
1	2	4	4
2	6	12	12
3	13	26	21
4	16	32	36
5	6	12	18
6	7	14	9
TOTAL	50	100	100

As can be seen, the run is not too bad, though we have been a little unlucky in having a bigger percentage of "6 days" and a smaller percentage of "5 days" than we should have done. This implies, of course, that in reality we will not run out of stock quite as often as the simulation suggests. On the other hand a check (not illustrated) on the frequency of demand levels shows that smaller demand quantities occurred just a fraction more often than they should, which, to some extent, counterbalances this possibility.

11. Conclusion. We have now solved a problem by means of a simulation that would otherwise have involved a rather formidable mathematical exercise (the student may like to *try* and sketch the probability-tree needed to represent this situation). It should, however, be appreciated that 50 deliveries is a rather small sample—5000 deliveries would have been a better choice. Such a simulation run manually would, of course, prove very tedious, but a computer could easily be programmed to make a run of this size quickly and accurately.

PROGRESS TEST 14

Since it is often found that many simulations involve queues, the Progress Test for this Chapter is combined with that of the next, where a queue/simulation problem is given. In this way, the student is able to kill the two "birds" of simulation and queues with one stone.

CHAPTER XV

QUEUES

INTRODUCTION

Queueing is a common phenomenon in the business world, and all queues display a number of basic features which we will examine in this chapter.

1. Queue formation. A queue forms at any time when *the demand for a service exceeds the capacity of the service facility.* Queues are usually composed of people but objects, too, can form queues—*e.g.* machines out of order awaiting maintenance attention. A queue, in fact, does not have to contain discrete units—liquid entering in a sudden large volume into a tank having only a small outlet pipe can be said to be "queueing" in the tank. It should be appreciated, incidentally, that a queue need not involve a physical line-up. Any group of people or items awaiting their turn for service constitutes a queue (*e.g.* patients waiting at home for a visit from the doctor).

2. Queueing situations. As the previous paragraph implied there is a diversity of queueing situations of which the following are but a short list of examples:

(*a*) Customers queueing for service in a shop or garage forecourt.

(*b*) Employees queueing at materials, components or tool store.

(*c*) Passengers queueing for a bus.

(*d*) Cars queueing to pass a road bottleneck.

(*e*) Semi-processed parts queueing for the next process.

(*f*) Broken-down cars awaiting A.A. or R.A.C. service patrols.

(*g*) Ships queueing for berths or locks; and trains queueing for platforms.

(*h*) People on a Council housing list.

(*i*) People on remand awaiting trial.

(*j*) Company accounts awaiting audit.

(*k*) Income tax returns awaiting the Inspector's attention.

As this list indicates, queues clearly differ one from the other. Some form rapidly and disperse slowly (*e.g.* at the ticket-barrier after a train has pulled in), some form slowly and disperse rapidly (*e.g.* a bus queue), some form and disperse at the same rate (*e.g.* units arriving one a minute at a machine having a process rate of one a minute), and some form and disperse erratically (*e.g.* queues at a Post Office counter).

3. Queues and economics. Virtually all queueing situations have economic implications. In general there are two opposing economic aspects to queues:

(*a*) It can cost money for an item to be idle in a queue. An employee has to be paid while queueing at the tool store, valuable production is lost while a machine stands out of order, tax receipts are delayed while documents remain in the Inspector's in-tray. And, of course, the smaller the service facility the longer the queues and the higher the costs.

(*b*) On the other hand it costs money to increase the service facility—even if it is only interest on the capital sunk in providing it. Moreover, the larger the service facility the quicker it will disperse queues and, therefore, the more often it will stand idle.

Clearly one reason for studying queues is to enable the optimum service facility size to be selected so that the overall cost of a service is minimised.

BASIC QUEUE FEATURES

All queueing situations reveal five basic features each of which is discussed in its own paragraph below. These features are:

(*a*) The arrival pattern.

(*b*) The service pattern.

(*c*) The traffic intensity.

(*d*) The number of service channels.

(*e*) The queue discipline.

4. The arrival pattern. Queue components can arrive at the queue in a variety of patterns. They can arrive in large groups, regularly or irregularly (*e.g.* passengers disembarking from trains), or steadily (*e.g.* if they leave a previous service such as a prior production process at a constant rate), or at random (*e.g.* customers at a supermarket check-out point). The latter is both the commonest and the most complex, though a moment's thought will indicate it can often be handled using the Poisson distribution (since in a given tiny fraction of time there is a very small probability of a customer joining the queue, but there are a great many tiny fractions of time involved).

A crucial figure in queueing theory is the *average arrival rate* (symbolised as a). This is simply the average number of queue components arriving per minute, hour, day, etc., and is found, of course, by dividing the total number of arrivals by the total units of time.

5. The service pattern. Servicing similarly takes a variety of patterns and can be regular (*e.g.* machining identical parts), or virtually instant but with periods of no service at all (*e.g.* passengers boarding a bus at a bus stop), or again random. The latter pattern can often be handled using a negative exponential distribution (*see* Progress Test 3, question 1(*d*)).

NOTE: Arrivals normally involve discrete distributions but service time involves continuous distributions. Consequently we cannot talk of the probability of the service time being an exact period, but only the probability of the service being completed during a given period. This probability is obtained by finding the area below the distribution curve that relates to the period given. The mathematics of this, however, is not pursued in this book.

A further crucial figure in queueing theory is the *average service rate* (symbolised as s). This is simply the average number of queue components that can be serviced per minute, hour, day, etc.

6. The traffic intensity. *Traffic intensity* (symbolised as i) is the ratio of the average arrival rate to the average service rate, *i.e.* $i = a/s$.

The traffic intensity indicates the likelihood and the extent of queueing. For example, if it is 0·1 then queue components can be serviced ten times faster than the average arrival rate, so if arrivals are random queues will be rare. If on the other hand, the traffic intensity is 1 then queue components will be arriving as fast as they can be serviced, while if it is greater than 1 then, since they are arriving faster than they can be serviced, the queue will always grow longer.

7. The number of service channels. Arrival and service patterns are often beyond our immediate control, but one thing we usually have full control over is the number of service channels (check-out counters, maintenance men, bus schedules, etc.). Indeed, the object of most queue analyses is to determine the optimum number of service channels.

In this book we will look only at 1-channel situations. The student should, however, be warned that although doubling the number of channels doubles the average service rate a 2-channel system does *not* operate in quite the same way as a 1-channel system with double the capacity.

8. The queue discipline. Although most queues are based on a first-come first-served (F.I.F.O.) system, this isn't always so. Sometimes certain queue components have priorities (*e.g.* ambulances at traffic lights), sometimes a L.I.F.O. system works (as when a tax inspector always takes the top document from his in-tray), and sometimes components are served at random (as when a number of people persist in trying to get through to the same telephone number and the successful caller is the one who is lucky enough to dial just at the moment the receiver is replaced after the previous call).

There are, therefore, different methods of determining the order of service. The method appertaining to any situation is known as the *queue discipline*.

9. Queues and systems. The terms "queue" and "system" are often used in queueing literature and it is important the student knows the difference, which can be seen by comparing the two definitions:

A *queue* is the group of components *waiting* to be serviced.
A *system* is the group of components that includes both those waiting to be serviced and also those *in the process of being serviced*.

SIMPLE QUEUES

A simple queue is defined as one that has the following features:

(*a*) The arrival pattern is Poisson.

(*b*) The service pattern is negative exponential (*i.e.* where the probability of the service time extending to one more unit of time decreases exponentially).

(*c*) The traffic intensity is less than 1.

(*d*) There is only one service channel.

(*e*) The queue discipline is F.I.F.O.

10. Formulae relating to a simple queue. Once a simple queue has reached a steady state (*see* p. 114) the following formulae apply:

(*a*) Probability that a given component has to wait for service = i. (And, therefore, probability of immediate service = $1 - i$.)

(*b*) Average number of components in:

(*i*) system = $\dfrac{i}{1 - i}$

(*ii*) queue = $\dfrac{i^2}{1 - i}$

(*iii*) queue, when a queue actually exists = $\dfrac{1}{1 - i}$

(*c*) Average time a component is in:

(*i*) system = $\dfrac{1}{s - a}$

(*ii*) queue = $\dfrac{i}{s - a}$

EXAMPLE: A simple queue of people has an arrival rate of 8 people a minute and a service rate of 10 people a minute.

In this example $i = \tfrac{8}{10} = 0\cdot8$

Then:

(*a*) Probability a person has to wait in the queue = $0\cdot8$

(*b*) Average number of people in:

(i)   system $= \dfrac{0 \cdot 8}{(1 - 0 \cdot 8)} = 4$

(ii) queue $= \dfrac{0 \cdot 8^2}{(1 - 0 \cdot 8)} = 3 \cdot 2$

(iii) queue, when a queue actually exists

$$= \dfrac{1}{(1 - 0 \cdot 8)} = 5$$

NOTE: The average number of people in the queue is *not* (average-number-in-system − 1) as one might expect. This is because there are times when there is no one at all in the system. That subtracting 1 from the average-number-in-system is invalid can be seen if one considers a traffic intensity of $0 \cdot 1$, in which case the average-number-in-system is $\dfrac{0 \cdot 1}{(1 - 0 \cdot 1)} = \frac{1}{9}$ — this low average being due to the frequent occasions no one is in the system. Now obviously we cannot say that the average queue $= \frac{1}{9} - 1$ since this will give us a *negative* average.

(i)   system $= \dfrac{1}{(10 - 8)} = 0 \cdot 5$ minutes

(ii)   queue $= \dfrac{0 \cdot 8}{(10 - 8)} = 0 \cdot 4$ minutes

NOTE: This is as one would expect. If you wait on average $0 \cdot 4$ minutes to reach a service point that serves you on average in $0 \cdot 1$ minutes your total time in the system is, on average, $0 \cdot 5$.

11. Queueing and simulations. Many queueing situations in practice are so complex that they cannot be handled by formulae and mathematical methods. Such situations, of course, lend themselves ideally to the simulation technique discussed in the previous chapter.

PROGRESS TEST 15

1. A retailer finds that during a 15-minute lunch-time peak a certain counter opened specifically to cover this period is approached by customers at random at an average rate of 3 per minute. If

there are as many as 6 people already in the system the approaching customers turn away and the sale is lost. The retailer estimates such a lost sale costs him 20p a time.

The retailer can employ as many girls as he wants on the counter, but during this period he has to pay £1 per girl for the 15 minutes. Each girl takes 1 minute to serve a customer (and for the purpose of this exercise it can be assumed that exactly at the end of each and every minute 1 customer per girl leaves the system). How many girls should be employed on the counter?

NOTE: Use the Poisson distribution developed in the answer to question 4, Progress Test 11. To obtain the same simulation as given in the suggested answers use the first 3 figures in each line of the final 5-digit column of figures in the Random number table shown in Appendix II.

2. Plot queue length against traffic intensity from $i = 0$ to $i = 1$ for a simple queue that has reached a steady state.

CHAPTER XVI

REPLACEMENT THEORY

A common type of management dilemma is deciding whether a part or item should be replaced or not. The theoretical study of this kind of dilemma is called *replacement theory*, and there are essentially two distinct replacement theory situations:

(*a*) When it is necessary to determine the *optimum age* for replacing a relatively expensive item that is gradually deteriorating (*e.g.* a vehicle).

(*b*) When it is necessary to decide whether to replace an adequately functioning but gradually deteriorating item *at a convenient moment or wait until it actually fails*—when such a failure may prove expensive (*e.g.* ageing control switches in a vital bottle-neck process).

In this chapter we will examine these two situations in turn.

OPTIMUM REPLACEMENT AGE

Assume we have a vehicle which will perform its task adequately for 20 years—if we are prepared to keep it and maintain it that long. At what point is it most economical to replace it?

1. Opposing cost curves. In this kind of replacement situation it will be found there are two opposing costs. In this particular case they are depreciation, which reduces year by year, and maintenance, which increases year by year. (Note, incidentally, in operational research contexts depreciation is *always* measured by the *loss in market value* over the operating period.) Let us assume we have the following data relating to our vehicle:

Purchase price of vehicle – £1,600

YEAR:	1	2	3	4	5	6	7	8	9
2nd HAND VALUE AT YEAR END £'s	1200	900	700	550	450	375	300	250	225
MAINTENANCE COSTS £'s	50	100	150	200	250	300	400	500	700

2. Average cost per unit of time. To find the optimum replacement date it is important to appreciate that this moment in time can be identified as the point of *minimum average annual cost*, and not the point of minimum annual cost. Clearly, if we minimise our average cost per year we will minimise our total cost over an indefinite number of replacements (marginal or differential costing, then, plays no part in this decision).

In our vehicle illustration, therefore, all we need to do is:

(*a*) Find the annual cost year by year of keeping the vehicle;

(*b*) Find the *cumulative* cost year by year of keeping the vehicle;

(*c*) Find the average annual cost year by year of keeping the vehicle;

(*d*) Identify the year with the minimum average annual cost and adopt the policy of replacing the vehicle at this point in time.

Following this procedure gives us these calculations:

YEAR	DEPRECI—ATION *	MAINT—ENANCE COST	(a) TOTAL ANNUAL COST	(b) CUMU—LATIVE COST	(c) AVERAGE ANNUAL COST	IDENTIFI—CATION MINIMUM AVERAGE
	£	£	£	£	£	
1	400	50	450	450	450	
2	300	100	400	850	425	
3	200	150	350	1200	400	
4	150	200	350	1550	387½	
5	100	250	350	1900	380	
6	75	300	375	2275	379$\frac{1}{6}$	←
7	75	400	475	2750	392$\frac{6}{7}$	
8	50	500	550	3300	412½	
9	25	700	725	4025	447$\frac{2}{9}$	

* Depreciation = value at beginning of year — value at end of year

As the table shows, £379$\frac{1}{6}$ is the minimum average cost and this minimisation is obtained by replacing the vehicle at the end of the sixth year.

3. Non-critical optimum replacement ages. The observant student may well have noticed in this illustration that the averages around the optimum replacement age are very much the same—indeed replacements in years 4, 5, 6 and 7 giving averages all within a £14 range. This relatively trivial change in the average around the optimum age is a very common phenomenon in practice and indicates that for all practical purposes the exact replacement date is not critical and the actual date of replacement selected, therefore, would depend on other factors such as convenience, cash flow position, etc.

4. Buying second-hand equipment. Another thing the student may have observed is that in years 3, 4, 5 and 6 the total annual cost is actually *less* than the optimum average cost, and he may wonder if it might be better for the company to buy second-hand vehicles rather than brand-new ones. For instance, if a 2-year-old vehicle could be bought for £900 and were sold one year later for £700 after incurring maintenance costs of £150 (all figures from the table in **1**) then the "average" annual cost would be only £350, so if this policy were followed year after year a considerable saving over the previous optimum cost would be achieved.

Clearly, in this case, it is better to buy second-hand than new. Of course, in practice, it would be unlikely that you could buy a vehicle for the same price that you could sell it—a £40 differential, for example, would raise our new average of £350 to £390, *i.e.* over our previous optimum. Nevertheless our figures do show that it is worthwhile investigating a policy of buying second-hand vehicles only. Such an investigation would, however, be rather lengthy and would involve preparing a series of matrices (one for each step of the previous procedure) showing the costs for each "age at purchase/age at disposal" combination, and identifying the minimum average cost in the final matrix to give the optimum combination.

5. Step-by-step and calculus methods. The above illustration used a step-by-step method in its solution. If, however, there had been a mathematical pattern in the original data then differential calculus could, of course, have been used as an alternative method.

For example, assume that a piece of equipment has a total depreciation charge of £1000 no matter how long it is used, but the cumulative maintenance to the end of year n is £$4n^3$. Here the total cumulative cost to the end of year n is $1000 + 4n^3$, and the average cost per year, then, $(1000 + 4n^3) \div n = 1000/n + 4n^2$. Differentiating and setting to zero, then, we have:

$$\frac{d(\text{Av. cost})}{dn} = \frac{d(1000n^{-1} + 4n^2)}{dn}$$
$$= -1000n^{-2} + 8n$$

$$\therefore 8n - \frac{1000}{n^2} = 0$$

$$\therefore 8n^3 - 1000 = 0$$

$$\therefore n^3 = 1000/8 = 125$$

$$\therefore n = \sqrt[3]{125} = 5$$

So the equipment is replaced after 5 years.

REPLACING AT CONVENIENT MOMENT

There are many replacement problems that revolve around the need to decide whether to replace an adequately functioning item at a convenient moment or accept the cost of breakdown when it occurs. We will illustrate this situation by means of three increasingly complex examples.

6. Avoidance of breakdown v. acceptance of breakdown. A company's vehicles go for service every month. A vehicle can be given a basic service for £20 after which there is a 0·05 probability of it breaking down before the next service, or an extended service where all vulnerable parts are replaced for £35 after which the service department guarantee there will be no breakdowns. If a breakdown occurs the company suffers a loss of £200. Which service should be requested?

Here we note that if there is a 0·05 probability of breakdown, then such a breakdown will occur on average once in 20 months. Our costs over an average 20-month period, then, will be as follows:

Service	*Service Cost*	*Breakdown Cost*	*Total Cost*
Basic	£20 × 20 = £400	1 × £200 = £200	£600
Extended	£35 × 20 = £700	0	£700

In this case it is cheaper to request the basic service and accept the breakdown cost.

7. Total *v.* selective replacement. A unit has 100 identical components costing £1 each which have unfortunately very short lives. Using the principle of redundancy (*see* XIII, **20**) the unit has been designed so that it functions satisfactorily until 25 units have failed, when it stops. There is a basic cost of £20 incurred each time the unit stops for maintenance. Unfortunately it is not easy to identify the failed units and management have the choice between inspecting every component at a cost of 20p to see if it has failed or not, and then replacing the failed ones (selective replacement), or replacing all 100 components and dispensing with the inspection process (total replacement). Past records show the unit breaks down twice a month using selective replacement but only once a month using total replacement. Which is the more economical replacement method?

This problem can be solved as follows:

METHOD	COST PER BREAKDOWN			AVERAGE COST PER MONTH
	BASIC	INSPECTION	REPLACEMENTS	
Total	£20	—	£1 × 100 = £100	1 × £120 = £120
Selective	£20	20p × 100 = £20	£1 × 25 = £25	2 × £65 = £130

Here it is cheaper to adopt a total replacement policy than one of selective replacement.

8. "When to make replacements" problem. For the remainder of the chapter we will examine a somewhat more complicated problem which can be stated as follows:

An electronic device used in controlling a manufacturing process relies upon the correct functioning of 10 identical components costing £4 each. Experience has shown that if all the components are new then on average 1 will fail during the 2nd week, 2 during the 3rd week, 5 during the 4th week and the remaining 2 during the 5th week. If a breakdown occurs while the process is operating, production worth £30 is lost, and in addition a cost of £10 is incurred in simply removing and replacing the device. However, once the device has been removed the failed component can be identified and replaced immediately, and, indeed, it costs no more to replace all 10 components than just 1 (other than the £4 cost per component already mentioned). If maintenance work is carried out at the week-end when the process is not operating, then the cost of lost production is nil. What replacement policy should be adopted?

9. The possible replacement policies. Management have a choice of any one of the following replacement policies:

(a) Replace individual components as they fail.
(b) Replace all components each week-end.
(c) Replace all components every:
  (i) second week-end;
  (ii) third week-end;
  (iii) fourth week-end,
      replacing components that fail in the meantime at the time of failure.

(d) Await first breakdown and then replace all components.

10. Replacement policy costs. These replacement policies have the following costs:

Policy (a) To find the cost of the policy of replacing components as they fail it is necessary to first find the life expectation of a component. If we assume components on average fail in the middle of their week of failure we can calculate the life expectation as follows:

Life (Weeks)	No. Failing	Total Life (Weeks)
$1\frac{1}{2}$	1	$1\frac{1}{2}$
$2\frac{1}{2}$	2	5
$3\frac{1}{2}$	5	$17\frac{1}{2}$
$4\frac{1}{2}$	2	9
	——	——
	10	33

$\therefore$ Average life $= \frac{33}{10} = 3\cdot3$ weeks.

This means a component will fail on average once every 3·3 weeks and when it does so it will cost £30 + £10 + £4 = £44 to replace. Since there are 10 components in the unit there will be a total cost of £44 × 10 = £440 every 3·3 weeks, *i.e.* a total average maintenance cost of $\frac{440}{3\cdot3}$ = £133⅓ per week.

Policy (b) Under the policy of replacing all components every week-end there are no costs of lost production, but every week there are costs of £10 + £4 × 10 = £50 per week.

Policy (c)

(*i*) Under the policy of replacing all components every second week-end we have the week-end cost of £10 + £4 × 10 = £50 *and* the cost of replacing the component that will fail during the second week. This additional cost is £30 + £10 + £4 = £44, so the total bi-weekly cost is £50 + £44 = £94, *i.e.* $\frac{94}{2}$ = £47 per week.

(*ii*) Under the policy of replacing all components every third week-end we again have our week-end maintenance cost of £50. This time *ad hoc* repairs need to be made in respect to the 1 component which fails during the second week and the 2 components that fail during the third week. In addition there is *the possibility that the component replaced during the second week will fail* before the third week-end. This possibility arises because there is a 0·1 probability of replacing the component which failed after an average 1½ weeks by another component which fails after an average 1½ weeks—*i.e.* after an average 3 weeks from the start of the cycle. Now this 3-week average coincides with the third week-end, so we would expect that half the time the second unit would last until the maintenance week-end and the other half the time it would fail before that week-end. This probability of failure, then, is 0·1 × ½ = 0·05. So the expected *ad hoc* maintenance cost will be (1 + 2 + 0·05) × (£30 + £10 + £4) = 3·05 × £44 = £134·2. The total maintenance cost for 3 weeks, then, is £50 + £134·2 = £184·2, *i.e.* $\frac{£184\cdot2}{3}$ = £61·4 per week.

(*iii*) The policy of replacing all components every fourth week-end is mathematically the most complex of all. We will, therefore, find the cost by the technique discussed in **12**. For the moment we will merely argue that if policy (*c*) (*ii*) is dearer than (*c*) (*i*), then intuitively (*c*) (*iii*) will be dearer than (*c*) (*ii*). As we shall see later, this is a correct conclusion.

Policy (*d*) If we adopt the policy of awaiting the first failure and then replacing all the components we will wait on average $1\frac{1}{2}$ weeks—at which point the replacement cost will be £30 + £10 + £4 × 10 = £80, *i.e.* $\dfrac{80}{1\frac{1}{2}} = \underline{\underline{£53\frac{1}{3} \text{ per week.}}}$

11. Illustration summary. As can be seen policy (*c*) (*i*), replacing the components every second week-end, has the lowest weekly cost and should, therefore, be adopted.

It is, perhaps, a little surprising that a policy that requires us to replace just one component around the middle of the second week and then open up the device and replace all the components (including the one put in a day or so earlier) should be cheaper than the policy of replacing all the components at the time of the first failure. The reason is, of course, that the only additional cycle cost of the cheaper policy is the £10 opening up cost and the £4 for the component put in only just previously— but accepting this cost buys us $\frac{1}{2}$ a week more cycle time. And the weekly cost of this exchange is only $\dfrac{10 + 4}{\frac{1}{2}} = £28$ per week. Since this is less than the weekly cost of policy (*d*) it reduces the total average weekly cost—from £53$\frac{1}{3}$ to £47 per week as we have seen.

12. Failure-trees. In order to analyse the complex policy of (*c*) (*iii*), replacing all components every fourth week-end, we need to use a *failure-tree* which is simply a tree diagram with horizontal branches showing how many components survive and how many fail over a period of time—the surviving components remaining on their initial horizontal branches and the failing components "falling" to the next lower branch.

To analyse policy (*c*) (*iii*) we will (merely to avoid odd-looking fractions) imagine we have 100 devices and trace the component failures in these devices over a 4-week cycle (*see* Fig. 24).

First we obviously start with 100 × 10 = 1000 components. All these survive the first week, but 1 in 10, *i.e.* 100, fail in the middle (on average) of the second week. There are, therefore, 900 survivors at the end of week 2, but another 200 fail in the middle of this week leaving 700 at the end of week 3. Week 4 is a very poor week, 500 units failing and only 200 surviving to

the end of the cycle. Of course, the replacements of the 500
that fail all survive the remaining half-week.

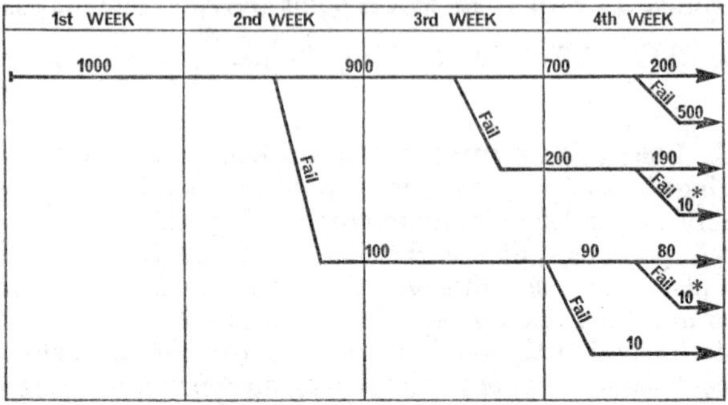

1st WEEK	2nd WEEK	3rd WEEK	4th WEEK

* One-half of the number of units that in theory would fail exactly
at the end of week 4.

FIG. 24.—*Failure-tree.*

Going back to the 200 that fail mid-week 3 all their replacements survive to mid-week 4, and in theory the 20 that fail half
a week later fail exactly at the end of the cycle. In practice of
course, half, *i.e.* 10 would fail before that since our theoretical
result is based on an average.

Finally going back to the first 100 that fail all the replacements would survive to mid-week 3 but then 10 would fail at
the end of that week (their replacements surviving to the end
of the cycle). Of the 90 reaching week 4 in theory 20 would fail
at the end of the week—so in practice 10 would fail before then.

13. The cost of policy (c)(iii). With the failure-tree completed finding the cost is simple enough. Single replacement
maintenance takes place 500 + 200 + 10 + 100 + 10 + 10
= 830 times at a cost each time of £30 + £10 + £4 = £44,
i.e. a total cost of £36,520. The maintenance during the fourth
week-end involves replacing all the components in 100 devices
at a cost of £10 + £4 × 10 = £50 a device, *i.e.* a total cost of
£5000.

Altogether, then, a grand total of 36,520 + 5000 = £41,520
is spent. This is the cost of 100 devices all on a 4-week cycle,
i.e. the cost of 400 weeks' operations. The average cost, then, is
$\frac{41,520}{400}$ = £103·8 per week.

14. Conclusion. If the student has grasped all the ideas involved in these replacement illustrations he should be able to handle most of the replacement problems that he is likely to meet in examinations.

PROGRESS TEST 16

1. An earthmoving contractor has an arrangement with the supplier of his earthmoving equipment whereby the supplier provides a particular piece of equipment for £3000 and gives a trade-in allowance of £1750, £1250 or £1000 if traded in at the end of 1, 2 or 3 years respectively. The contractor has established from past records that he need only spend £100 maintenance on such equipment during the year it is to be traded in—otherwise such maintenance costs are £200 and £300 for the first and second years respectively.

A deciding factor influencing the contractor is the possibility of a breakdown since such an occurrence in repairs and lost work will cost £2000 a time. Again, records show the probability of a breakdown during a piece of equipment's first year is 0·05, second year is 0·25 and third year is 0·65. A breakdown in any year, incidentally, in no way affects the probability of a breakdown in a future year, though it reduces the probability of a breakdown later in the *same* year to a negligible figure.

When should the contractor replace his equipment?

2. Your company has a purpose-built computer with 5000 special components which have a random failure rate of, on average, one every 2 weeks. The computer functions satisfactorily as long as no more than 1 component has failed, but if more than one fails it breaks down.

A computer maintenance company has offered to provide you with maintenance. They have a very flexible scheme under which they provide week-end inspection and maintenance at £120 per time—the price to cover the replacement of any failed units. You have the option of selecting the inspection periods—either weekly, bi-weekly, every third week-end, or any other periods of weeks you may desire. A feature of the maintenance company's scheme is that it guarantees to take over all your computer work in the event of your computer breaking down until your next inspection week-end. The charge for this service depends solely on the inspection period you have selected and is £100 per week. Thus if you had selected a bi-weekly inspection period then in the event of a breakdown you would pay 2 × £100 for the service, and if you selected a 5-week inspection period it would, of course, be 5 × £100. This charge is quite independent of the actual breakdown period.

Under a quite different scheme the maintenance company is prepared to make immediate repairs on breakdown for a charge of £350.

What should your company do to minimise maintenance costs?

CHAPTER XVII

STOCK CONTROL

It costs money to hold stock. It costs money in terms of storage space, equipment, personnel, insurance, deterioration and obsolescence, and, above all, the cost of capital involved in financing stocks. On the other hand it costs money to run out of stock—placing orders, lost production, lost profits, loss of goodwill, and the disorganisation that follows a stock shortage.

This chapter is concerned with finding the point of balance between these costs. Our study will be made in two parts—firstly examining the situation where usage and delivery times are known with certainty and secondly where they are not. First, however, we must cover a few introductory points.

1. Graphing stock levels. It often helps to obtain insight into a stock-control situation if a graph is drawn showing levels of stock against time (*see* Fig. 25). Such a graph usually takes a saw-tooth pattern as periods in which units are steadily drawn from stock are followed by moments in time when new deliveries are made, the degree of slope reflecting the usage rate and the sudden vertical rise the delivery quantity.

2. Stock-control terms. The following terms are often used in stock control (and are illustrated in Fig. 25):

(a) *Re-order level* (*ROL*). The level of stock at which an order for new stock is placed.

(b) *Re-order quantity.* The quantity ordered when the re-order level is reached.

(c) *Lead time.* The time between stock reaching the re-order level and the subsequent delivery of new stock.

(d) *Stockout.* Being out of stock when a unit is required.

(e) *Buffer stock.* The reserve stock held to guard against a stockout due to usage or lead time exceeding the average.

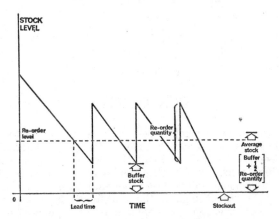

Fig. 25.—*Stock levels—typical graph.*

STOCK CONTROL UNDER CERTAINTY

We start by looking at situations where the usage and lead time are known with certainty.

3. Economic order quantity. Placing a stock order costs money in terms of purchasing and delivery costs—which may well be the same no matter how many units are ordered. We can, therefore, keep these costs down over the year by making only a few orders of large quantities. On the other hand, the larger the order quantity the larger our stockholding and therefore the higher the stockholding costs.

Clearly, there must be an order quantity that minimises the total annual cost of these two opposing costs. Such a quantity is called the *economic order quantity* (often abbreviated to EOQ) and can be found by the following model-building exercise:

Let: N = Total units required per annum
n = Order quantity
P = Cost specifically incurred in making a single order
S = Cost of holding 1 unit in stock for one year
B = Buffer stock

Then:

(i) annual purchase cost $= P \times \dfrac{N}{n}$ (since $\dfrac{N}{n}$ = number

of orders required per year)

(ii) the average stock held $= B + \frac{1}{2}n$ (since under certainty the buffer stock should remain untouched and, with steady withdrawals from stock, we will also have *on average* half the order quantity—*see* Fig. 25).

$$\therefore \text{ annual stockholding cost} = S(B + \tfrac{1}{2}n)$$
$$= SB + \tfrac{1}{2}Sn$$

So total annual cost = Purchase + stockholding cost

$$= \frac{P\,N}{n} + SB + \tfrac{1}{2}Sn$$

and to minimise this total cost we differentiate with respect to n and set equal to 0:

$$\frac{d(\text{total annual cost})}{dn} = \frac{d(PNn^{-1} + SB + \tfrac{1}{2}Sn)}{dn}$$

$$= -PNn^{-2} + \tfrac{1}{2}S \text{ (Note elimination}$$
of buffer stock element)

$$\therefore -\frac{PN}{n^2} + \frac{S}{2} = 0$$

Multiply both sides by $2n^2$

$$\therefore -2PN + Sn^2 = 0$$
$$Sn^2 = 2PN$$
$$n^2 = \frac{2PN}{S}$$
$$\therefore \text{EOQ} = \sqrt{\frac{2PN}{S}}$$

EXAMPLE: Usage is 1000 units a year, which cost £1 per unit per annum to store. It costs £5 to make an order and a buffer stock of 20 is carried. What is the EOQ?

$$\text{EOQ} = \sqrt{\frac{2 \times 5 \times 1000}{1}} = 100$$

(This situation is graphed in Fig. 26.)

4. Limitations of EOQ theory. Although we have seen how to find the theoretical EOQ the student should be warned there are a number of practical objections to its uncritical adoption. It frequently happens (as can be seen in Fig. 26) that the total cost curve is relatively flat in the EOQ region, and so adopting any order quantity in this region makes little difference to the overall cost. The actual order quantity, therefore, is often made in consideration of other factors such as storage space, risks of obsolescence and deterioration, purchase office work load (*see* **6**), etc.

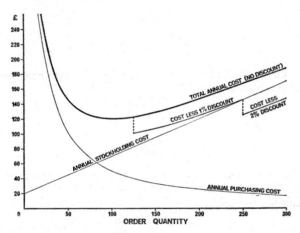

FIG. 26.—*Illustrative stock cost curves.*

5. EOQ and quantity discounts. If a quantity discount is offered then naturally the EOQ may be affected. To allow for this factor:

(*a*) Find the EOQ in the normal way.

(*b*) Find the total annual cost if EOQ adopted from the formula developed in **3**.

(*c*) Find the total annual costs of buying minimum quantities that qualify for discounts, and deduct from these costs the value of the discounts.

(d) Compare these net costs with each other and the EOQ cost and select the order quantity that gives the minimum cost.

EXAMPLE: Using the figures of the example in **3** and assuming the supplier now offers a 1% discount on orders of 125 or more, a 2% discount on orders of 250 or more and 5% on orders of 500 or more, and that the unit list price is £2, find the EOQ.

(a) Normal EOQ as in **3**, *i.e.* 100 units.

(b) Total annual cost of this EOQ

$$= 5 \times \frac{1000}{100} + 1 \times 20 + \frac{1 \times 100}{2} = £120.$$

(c) Annual costs at quantity discount levels:

ORDER QUANTITY	125	250	500
ANNUAL COST	$5 \times \frac{1000}{125} + 1 \times 20 + \frac{1 \times 125}{2}$	$5 \times \frac{1000}{250} + 1 \times 20 + \frac{1 \times 250}{2}$	$5 \times \frac{1000}{500} + 1 \times 20 + \frac{1 \times 500}{2}$
	$= 122\frac{1}{2}$	$= £165$	$= £280$
ANNUAL VALUE OF DISCOUNT	$1000 \times £2 \times \frac{1}{100}$	$1000 \times £2 \times \frac{2}{100}$	$1000 \times £2 \times \frac{5}{100}$
	$= £20$	$= £40$	$= £100$
NET ANNUAL COST	$122\frac{1}{2} - 20 = £102\frac{1}{2}$	$165 - 40 = £125$	$280 - 100 = £180$

Comparing these three costs with each other and that of the normal EOQ cost of £120 it is clear that an order quantity of 125 units should be adopted. (*See* also Fig. 26).

6. Two-bin and periodic review systems. There are two systems under which the re-ordering of units can be initiated—the two-bin and the periodic review.

(a) *The two-bin system.* Under this system the balance of stock on hand is checked after every issue, and as soon as the balance falls below the re-order level an order is placed.

(b) *The periodic review system.* Under this system the balance of stock on hand is checked periodically, and if the stock is found to be below the re-order level an order is placed.

The relative advantage of the two-bin system is that stocks are kept at a lower level. Clearly the re-order level under the periodic review system needs to be higher (since if, say, a month passes between reviews, the re-order level has to be high enough to ensure the stock cannot fall to an unacceptably low level before the next review a month later) and so stock levels generally are higher.

The advantage of the periodic review system is that the purchase office work load is more evenly spread. Under the two-bin system it is possible for an abnormally large group of stock items to fall below the re-order level on the same day—an event that is much less likely to happen under the periodic review system.

7. Re-order levels. Setting re-order levels under certainty (or, at least, near certainty) is not complicated. The procedures under the two systems are as follows:

(a) *Two-bin system.* Under this system simply multiply lead time by usage per unit of time and add the buffer stock. If, for example, the lead time is 15 days, the daily usage 200 units a day and a 500 unit buffer stock is held, then the ROL is $15 \times 200 + 500 = 3500$ units.

(b) *Periodic review system.* Under this system it would be necessary to ensure that the stock could not fall between reviews to a level less than the usage during the lead time— *e.g.* taking the example just given, less than $15 \times 200 = 3000$ units. If we assume the stock is reviewed every 20 days this means it must be above $3000 + 20 \times 200 = 7000$ units. So adding on our buffer stock of 500 we have a 7500 ROL.

NOTE: (i) It will only be very rarely that an order will be placed when stock is in the vicinity of 7500 units. In fact, since stock to be re-ordered will be between 7500 and 3500 at the time it is reviewed, the average level will be the mid-point of this range— *i.e.* 5500. This, nevertheless, is 2000 units above the level of stock at which the two-bin system stock is ordered.

(ii) More sophisticated control techniques not discussed here can reduce this high ROL figure.

8. Economic batch quantity. When units for stock are manufactured in batches a similar situation arises to that in purchasing. Preparing machines (setting-up) to manufacture a batch of units involves a once-and-for-all cost, like the purchasing cost, for that batch, so the larger the batches the lower the total annual setting-up cost. On the other hand, the larger the batch the larger the cost of subsequent stockholding of the units.

At first glance it may appear that the EOQ formula developed in **3** can be applied unchanged—the batch set-up cost simply replacing the purchase cost in that formula. Unfortunately the situation is a little more complex, for whereas a purchase order can be placed on a supplier at any time a manufacturing order cannot be similarly placed on a production department since it may well have *only just started making the economic batch quantity for some other product.* For example, assume A and B are made on the same machine which can produce 200 units of either per day and the demand for these units is 100 each per day. Assume also that using the formula in **3** the economic batch quantities have been found to be: A 200 units; B 800 units. What if we start by producing 200 A (1 day's production) and then turn to producing 800 B (4 days' production)? Obviously by the time we are only half-way through the B batch we will be out of stock of A (and starting off with an A buffer stock only defers the impasse as a moment's thought will show).

Clearly we need a modified formula to allow for this situation. And the key to this new formula lies in using *cycles of batches,* each product batch in the cycle involving sufficient units to ensure no stockout occurs before the product's turn in the cycle comes round again.

Let us investigate this approach in a situation where three products, 1, 2 and 3 are all made in batches on the same machine. Now:

Let n = Number of cycles per year.

Let N_1, N_2, N_3 = Annual requirements of the respective products.

Let F_1, F_2, F_3 = Fixed set-up costs per batch of the respective products.

Let S_1, S_2, S_3 = Stockholding cost per unit per annum of the respective products.

Then:

	PRODUCT 1	PRODUCT 2	PRODUCT 3
Number of units per batch if year's requirements are to be made in n cycles	N_1/n	N_2/n	N_3/n
Average stockholding cost per annum	$\frac{1}{2} \times N_1 S_1/n$	$\frac{1}{2} \times N_2 S_2/n$	$\frac{1}{2} \times N_3 S_3/n$
Set-up costs p.a.	nF_1	nF_2	nF_3

$\therefore$ Total annual cost

$$= \frac{N_1 S_1}{2n} + nF_1 + \frac{N_2 S_2}{2n} + nF_2 + \frac{N_3 S_3}{2n} + nF_3$$

$$= n(F_1 + F_2 + F_3) + \frac{1}{2n}(N_1 S_1 + N_2 S_2 + N_3 S_3)$$

$\therefore \dfrac{d(\text{Total annual cost})}{dn}$

$$= (F_1 + F_2 + F_3) - \frac{n^{-2}}{2}(N_1 S_1 + N_2 S_2 + N_3 S_3)$$

Setting equal to 0 to minimise total cost:

$$(F_1 + F_2 + F_3) - \frac{1}{2n^2}(N_1 S_1 + N_2 S_2 + N_3 S_3) = 0$$

$$\therefore (F_1 + F_2 + F_3) = \frac{1}{2n^2}(N_1 S_1 + N_2 S_2 + N_3 S_3)$$

Multiplying both sides by $2n^2$:

$$2n^2(F_1 + F_2 + F_3) = (N_1 S_1 + N_2 S_2 + N_3 S_3)$$
$$\therefore n = \sqrt{(N_1 S_1 + N_2 S_2 + N_3 S_3) \div 2(F_1 + F_2 + F_3)}$$

i.e.

$$n = \sqrt{\sum_{i=1}^{3} N_i S_i \div 2\sum_{i=1}^{3} F_i}$$

Generalising we can say:

Economic number of batch cycles (where p = no. of products)

$$= \sqrt{\sum_{i=1}^{p} N_i S_i \div 2\sum_{i=1}^{p} F_i}$$

(the economic batch quantity of product i being, of course, $N_i \div$ economic number of cycles).

EXAMPLES: The following data relate to two products made on the same machine:

	Product A	Product B
Required annual quantity	8000	2000
Set-up cost per batch	£70	£30
Stockholding cost per unit p.a.	£1·2	£1·6

Find the economic batch quantities.

Now economic batch cycles

$$= \sqrt{(8000 \times 1·2 + 2000 \times 1·6) \div 2(70 + 30)}$$
$$= \sqrt{12800 \div 200}$$
$$= 8$$

∴ Economic number of cycles is 8 per year.

∴ Economic batch quantities are: A 8000/8 = 1000;
  B 2000/8 = 250.

STOCK CONTROL UNDER UNCERTAINTY

We now look at stock control where there is uncertainty—though for simplicity the uncertainty will be restricted to usage during the lead time.

9. Basic illustrative figures. In this section the following illustrative figures will be used:

A retailer places orders for a particular unit on average 10 times a year. The unit costs him £60 and sells for £100. An analysis of the demand during the lead time (which is constant) of the last 20 deliveries gave the following distribution:

Demand During Lead Times (Units)	Occasions	Demand Probability	Reverse Cumulative Probability*
20	1	0·05	1·00
21	2	0·10	0·95
22	3	0·15	0·85
23	4	0·20	0·70
24	4	0·20	0·50
25	3	0·15	0·30
26	2	0·10	0·15
27	1	0·05	0·05
	20	1·00	

* Probability of demand of at least the level shown in the left-hand column.

10. Re-order level where units are perishable. Now let us assume in our illustrative figure that the units are such that:

(a) the goods are perishable, and any remaining unsold at the end of the lead time must be thrown away; and

(b) the cost of a stockout is considered to be trivial.

In this situation what re-order level should the retailer set?

This problem could, of course, be solved using Bayes' rule (see XIII, **12**) but it would involve a rather large analysis table. Instead we will approach the problem via an incremental technique, and ascertain for each possible ROL the *additional* profit expectation we will have by increasing the ROL by *one unit*. Such an approach gives the following analysis:

ROL	PROBABILITY OF DEMAND BEING AT LEAST 1 UNIT MORE (i.e. P(Demand > ROL))	COST OF ADDITIONAL UNIT	ADDITIONAL INCOME EXPECTATION	ADDITIONAL PROFIT EXPECTATION (See note)
20	0.95	£60	£100 × 0.95 = £95	+£35
21	0.85	£60	£100 × 0.85 = £85	+£25
22	0.70	£60	£100 × 0.70 = £70	+£10
23	0.50	£60	£100 × 0.50 = £50	−£10
24	0.30	£60	£100 × 0.30 = £30	−£30
25	0.15	£60	£100 × 0.15 = £15	−£45
26	0.05	£60	£100 × 0.05 = £5	−£55
27	0	£60	£100 × 0.00 = £0	−£60

NOTE: Additional income expectation—cost of additional unit.

As can be seen, this table shows the additional income we can expect by having 1 more unit in stock and since the cost of the additional unit is a certain £60, the additional profit expectation is easily found. This profit expectation, it will be observed, is positive up to an ROL of 22—and negative thereafter. Therefore at an ROL of 22 it pays to have 1 more unit, but no more. The ROL, therefore, that should be set is $22 + 1 = 23$ units.

This problem can also be solved in model terms, for we can say that as long as $[£100 \times \text{P(Demand} > \text{ROL)}] - £60 > 0$ (i.e. [additional expected income—£60 certain cost] is positive), then it pays us to stock the additional unit, i.e. as long as:

$$[100 \times \text{P(Demand} > \text{ROL)}] - 60 > 0$$
i.e. $\qquad 100 \times \text{P(Demand} > \text{ROL)} \qquad > 60$
i.e. $\qquad \text{P(Demand} > \text{ROL)} \qquad > 60 \div 100$
i.e. $\qquad \text{P(Demand} > \text{ROL)} \qquad > 0.6$

Running our eye down the second column of our table we see this situation holds up to ROL of 22. So $22 + 1 = 23$ is the optimum ROL. Note that this technique avoids the need for the three right-hand columns.

11. Re-order level where stockout penalty is high. We will now consider the situation that arises where our illustrative figures in **9** relate to units having a stockout penalty of £500 (for simplicity we will assume this figure includes all lost profits on unsuppliable units).

The difference between this situation and the previous one lies in the fact that before we were critically concerned with the probability of the demand being for *at least* one more unit, since a high probability implied we should stock one extra unit. This time, however, the probability of a demand of at least one more unit is of no help, since *if the demand is for two or more units* buying just one additional unit will not enable the retailer to avoid a stockout. For example, with an ROL of 22 units there is a probability of a demand of 23 or more units of 0·70, but buying the 23rd unit won't help the retailer if the demand turns out to be 24 or more.

To adjust for this new aspect, though, it is only necessary to specify the probability of *exactly* one more unit being demanded. Our incremental analysis, then, will look like this:

ROL	PROBABILITY OF SELLING EXACTLY 1 MORE UNIT (a)	SAVING STOCKOUT EXPECTATION (b)	COST OF ADDITIONAL UNIT	EXPECTED SAVING
19	0.05	£500 × 0.05 = £25	£60	25 − 60 = −£35
20	0.10	£500 × 0.10 = £50	£60	50 − 60 = −£10
21	0.15	£500 × 0.15 = £75	£60	75 − 60 = +£15
22	0.20	£500 × 0.20 = £100	£60	100 − 60 = +£40
23	0.20	£500 × 0.20 = £100	£60	100 − 60 = +£40
24	0.15	£500 × 0.15 = £75	£60	75 − 60 = +£15
25	0.10	£500 × 0.10 = £50	£60	50 − 60 = −£10
26	0.05	£500 × 0.05 = £25	£60	25 − 60 = −£35
27	0	£500 × 0.00 = £0	£60	0 − 60 = −£60

(a) This is simply the probability that the demand will be for the next ROL quantity.

(b) By stocking 1 more unit, the occasions a stockout will be avoided (as a proportion of all occasions) will be the same as the probability of the demand being for just that extra unit—so the average saving is £500 × Probability (1 extra unit demanded).

Using inspection once more we see at an ROL of 24 units it just pays to have one more unit, but no more. The ROL figure therefore, that should be set is 24 + 1 = 25 units.

> NOTE: The two minus values at the beginning of the "Expected saving" column are a little confusing. Intuitively one feels, correctly, that it *does* pay to have an ROL of over 20. Strictly speaking we should have an additional column headed "Cumulative expected saving" when we would see the later savings wipe out the earlier minuses and where the optimum ROL would be given by the next ROL level to the maximum cumulative expected saving ROL. Common sense, however, usually saves us the trouble of creating this extra column.

Again we can use a model to solve this problem, for as long as the saving stockout expectation is greater than the certain £60 cost it is worth having 1 more unit, *i.e.* as long as:

$$£500 \times P(\text{Demand} = 1 \text{ more unit}) > £60$$

i.e. $$P(\text{Demand} = 1 \text{ more unit}) > \frac{60}{500}$$

i.e. $$P(\text{Demand} = 1 \text{ more unit}) > 0 \cdot 12$$

Examining the second column of our table we see this is so up to 24 units—so 25 units is the optimum ROL.

12. Generalising the incremental technique. The above two stock-control situations can be generalised in terms of the incremental technique as follows:

(a) *Where the stockout penalty is insignificant.* Where we are essentially only concerned as to whether or not the demand will be for *at least* 1 more unit we can use the test:

If P(At least 1 more unit) >

Additional cost of having 1 more unit ÷
Additional receipt if demand for at least one
more unit materialises

then it pays to have 1 more unit.

(b) *Where the stockout penalty is highly significant.* Where we are essentially concerned as to whether or not the demand will be for *exactly* 1 more unit we can use the test:

If P(Exactly 1 more unit) >

Additional cost of having 1 more unit ÷ Stockout penalty

then it pays to have 1 more unit.

> NOTE: (i) We now only need a simple list of the appropriate probabilities relating to each possible ROL—the optimum ROL being identified by inspection.
>
> (ii) The optimum ROL is 1 more than the last ROL to pass the test.
>
> (iii) The "additional cost of having 1 more unit" is the cost price in the case of perishable units, the loss in value in the case of deteriorating units, and merely the unit stockholding cost in the case of non-perishable or non-deteriorating units.

13. Low-price unit situations. So far we have only considered situations where there were a few highly priced units and a step-by-step technique was feasible. The generalised incremental technique developed in the previous paragraph, however, now enables us to handle the more complex but realistic stock control context where there are a great many low-price units. For example, assume during the lead time the demand for a small product forms a normal distribution with a mean of 500 units and a standard deviation (σ) of 100 units (*see* Fig. 27(*a*)). Each unit is nonperishable but costs 4p to store over the lead time period. How can we find the optimum ROLs in the two different stock-control contexts?

First let us assume the unit sells for 20p profit. From **12(a)** we know that providing the probability of selling at least 1 more exceeds (Additional cost of having 1 more unit ÷ Additional receipt if demand for 1 more unit materialises), it pays to stock 1 more unit. Substituting our current values, this probability is $\frac{4}{20} = 0.2$. Now the probability of the demand exceeding any specified figure is given by the normal curve area to the right of that figure. And normal curve tables tell us that the probability is 0·2 when the value is 0.84σ above the mean—and in this instance this means $500 + 0.84 \times 100 = 584$. So the optimum ROL is 585 units (*see* Fig. 27(*b*)).

Next we will take the situation where the cost of a stockout is relatively very high. Let us assume our unit, though small, is crucial to production and a stockout would cost £100. From 12(*b*) we know that providing the probability of the demand for exactly 1 more unit exceeds (Additional cost of having unit ÷

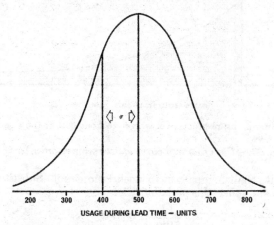

(*a*) Usage during lead time.

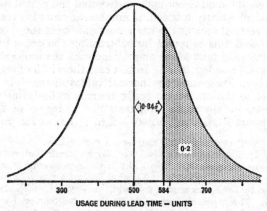

(*b*) Determining re-order level where profit potential is the dominant consideration.

FIG. 27.—*Use of normal curve to determine re-order levels.*

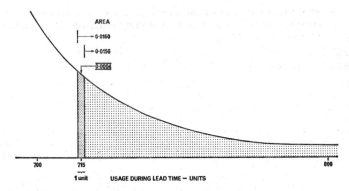

(c) Determining re-order level where stockout cost is the dominant consideration.

FIG. 27.—*Use of normal curve to determine re-order levels.*

stockout penalty), it pays us to stock 1 more unit. Substituting our current values this probability is:

$$\frac{4p}{£100} = 0.0004$$

Now where demand is normally distributed the probability of a demand of exactly a specified number of units is given by the tiny vertical area of the bar 1 unit wide over the specified number—and this is found by subtracting the areas of the two overlapping tails where one tail includes the unit and the other doesn't (*see* Fig. 27(c)). In this case the width of a 1 unit bar is $\frac{1}{100}\sigma$. Inspecting the normal tables again, this time in respect to the differences between areas at 0.01σ intervals we find we obtain values of 0.0004 in the region of 2.15σ. Our optimum ROL, then, is $500 + 2.15 \times 100 = 715$ units.

NOTE: At first glance this may seem rather low. After all, if paying 4p a unit can save £100 stocking a mere 215 above average seems unnecessarily risky. But if we increase our stock by, say, 50 units, *i.e.* to 2.65σ, the probability of a stockout is only reduced by the extra area of this addition—which tables show is 0.0118. The stockout expectation, then, is reduced by only $0.0018 \times £100 = £1.18$ while the extra stockholding cost is increased by $50 \times 4p = £2$.

The point is, of course, that the probability of a stockout is continually receding along this section of the curve though the unit stockholding cost remains the same. Consequently the certain cost of being sure is increasingly greater than the expected cost of being sorry.

PROGRESS TEST 17

1. A trader buys a product for 20p and sells it for 23p. He knows his lead time is constant and that it costs him £5 every time he re-orders the product regardless of his order quantity. He considers that his stockholding cost is simply a 20% p.a. interest charge on the cost value of units held. Past records reveal the annual demand for the product is 16,000 units and that during the lead time the demand is normally distributed with an average of 320 units and a standard deviation of 50 units.

(a) What is the EOQ?

(b) If the retailer wishes to reduce his risk of a stockout to a $2\frac{1}{2}\%$ probability per order:

    (i) Compute the re-order level

    (ii) State how long on average it will be between stockouts

(c) If the retailer is only concerned about having a stockout to the extent of his loss of profits on unmet demand, what will be his appropriate re-order level?

CHAPTER XVIII

NETWORK ANALYSIS

Network analysis is basically a production planning and control technique. In the completion of any major project a number of activities all have to be separately completed. If each activity has to be completed in turn before the next activity can start then the overall completion time is obviously the sum of the times of the component activities. This, however, is a rare condition—far more often a number of activities can be carried on simultaneously (in network terminology "in parallel"). To take a trivial example, a car can be served with petrol at the same time as the windscreen is being cleaned. The complete service time, therefore, is less than the time of the two activities added together—indeed, it is only the time of the longest activity.

In these sorts of situations a *diagrammatic network* can be drawn to show the inter-relationship of the activities involved, and an analysis made to reveal important facts about the project. Although, as we have said, network analysis is basically a production planning and control technique, the economic implications of a more rapid project completion make the economic analysis of networks a worthwhile subject of study. In this chapter, then, we first look at network analysis without monetary figures and then turn to analysing networks in economic terms.

PRINCIPLES OF NETWORK CONSTRUCTION

Let us imagine it is very important that on receipt of a crucial document we must write and post at the earliest possible moment a letter with an enclosed photocopy of the document. We decide to construct a network for this very simple project.

1. Activities. The first thing we must do to construct our network is to list the *activities* and the time each will take. In this illustration the activity schedule may be as follows:

Activity	Time (Minutes)
Dictate letter	5
Type letter	8
Photostat document	10
Type envelope	2
Stamp envelope	1
Insert letter and enclosure in envelope	1
Take to post box	6

Clearly these activities need not follow one after the other—
the envelope can be typed and stamped while the letter is being
dictated and typed and while, at the same time, the document
is being photostatted.

2. Events. Although some activities can be carried out in
parallel, other activities must await the completion of earlier
activities before they can be started—the typing of the letter,
for example, cannot take place before it has been dictated. In
other words, before the activity starts certain *events* have to
have occurred (*e.g.* "dictation complete").

3. Diagrammatic representation of activities and events. In
a diagrammatic representation of such a situation *activities* are
shown as lines (usually with an arrow-head at the end of the
activity) and *events* are shown as circles. Activities that depend
on an event occurring before they can commence are shown as
lines starting from such an event and running to some future
event (circle) that marks the completion of the activity. Thus
before the activity-line "type letter" can be drawn the event-
circle "letter dictated" must have been drawn—and at the end
of the activity-line the event-circle "letter typed" can be shown
(*see* Fig. 28).

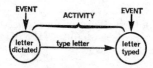

FIG. 28.—*Events and activities.*

The important thing to note here is that activities *take time*,
but events simply mark moments when something has been
done and consequently are timeless.

4. Activity order. In this sort of diagrammatic representation it is, of course, vital to appreciate just what events must have occurred before a given activity can be started—we clearly cannot post our letter until it has been typed. Determining such relationships between activities and events is, in practice, the difficult part of network construction (though in examination questions it is usually given). In our illustration, however, it is simple—the letter must, naturally, be dictated before it can be typed, but meanwhile both the envelope preparation and the photostatting can be carried out. All these activities, however, must be complete before we can insert the letter and photostat into the envelope, and this latter activity must have been completed before we can take it to the post.

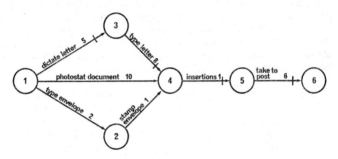

Event schedule: 1. Document received. 2. Envelope typed. 3. Letter dictated. 4. Letter typed, envelope stamped and photostat taken. 5. Letter and photostat inserted in envelope. 6. Letter posted.

Fig. 29.—*Letter posting network. The figures alongside the activity-lines relate to the activity time.*

5. Constructing the network. If we construct the network for our letter-posting project we obtain the diagram shown in Fig. 29. Note that in this network:

(*a*) Time is deemed to run from left to right (it is, therefore, important that one's arrows do not run backwards).

(*b*) The length of the activity-line does *not* relate in any way to the activity time (in other words a network is simply a logic diagram).

(c) Activity times are shown alongside the activity-lines and events are numbered, the event number being shown in the circle.

(d) Where more than one arrow enters a circle the event depicted represents the completion of all activities leading to that circle. Thus event-4 is "letter typed, envelope stamped, and photostat taken."

Note also that conventionally a network must start with a single event and end with a single event.

6. Dummy activities. Sometimes when we have two chains of parallel activities it happens that although the first chain can proceed totally independent of the second chain, there is some activity in the second chain that depends upon some event in the first chain. For example, if in our letter-posting illustration we only had *one* typewriter (but two typists) we obviously couldn't proceed to type the letter until the envelope had been typed—although typing and stamping the envelope could proceed without any reference to dictating and typing the letter. In such a situation we draw a *dummy activity*. Such an activity is shown as a dotted line linking the completion of the crucial activity in the independent chain with the appropriate event circle in the dependent chain (*see* Fig. 30(a). Note the re-structuring of the network so as to avoid activity lines crossing and keep the diagram as clear as possible). As can be seen from Fig. 30(a), event-3 cannot occur until event-2 has occurred—*i.e.* the typing of the letter cannot be started until the typing of the envelope has been completed.

There is a second, relatively minor, context in which a dummy activity is used and this is where two activities have the same start and end events—such as serving a car by supplying petrol and cleaning the windscreen. Rather than draw two curved lines we create an additional event and link this with the final end event by a dummy (*see* Fig. 30(b)).

Note two points about dummies:

(a) The activity time is always zero.

(b) A dummy activity is just as likely to lie on the critical path (see below) as any other activity-line.

7. Coding activities. To avoid ambiguity as to which activity is being referred to in a network reference, all activities are

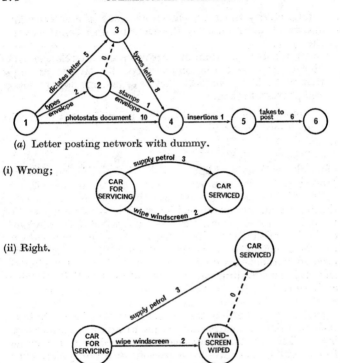

(a) Letter posting network with dummy.

(i) Wrong;

(ii) Right.

(b) Use of dummy to avoid two activities having same start and end events.

FIG. 30.—*Dummies.*

coded in terms of the number of their start event and the number of their end event. For example, "dictate letter" is coded as "1, 3."

CRITICAL PATH METHOD

Having constructed the network the next step is to analyse it. Our first form of analysis will relate to finding the critical path. This is often called critical path method—sometimes abbreviated to CPM.

8. The critical path. If we study our letter project network (Fig. 29) we quickly observe that since the "type and stamp envelope" activity chain and the photostatting activity can both be completed while the letter is being dictated and typed, the completion time of the whole project hinges critically on the time of these two latter activities. Activities which go to determine the completion time of a project are said to lie on the critical path, and the critical path in this case is the chain of activities running between events, 1, 3, 4, 5 and 6. The *critical path*, then can be defined as the longest time chain of activities through the network. Conventionally we mark activities lying along the critical path with a stroke across the activity-line (*see* Fig. 29).

9. Sub-critical paths and float times. All activity chains that do *not* lie on the critical path are called *sub-critical paths*. Clearly, it is not critical to the project completion time if such activities take a little longer than planned. In our letter illustration, for example, it would not affect the project completion time if it took 5 minutes to type the envelope or even 10 minutes if need be.

Although sub-critical activities can safely be allowed to take longer than planned it is naturally important the extra time is not so much that the total chain time exceeds the time along the parallel critical path. It is necessary, therefore, to know the spare time along a sub-critical path. The spare time is called the *float* time, and in our illustration we have the following float times:

$$\text{Path 1, 2, 4} \quad 13 - 3 = 10 \text{ minutes}$$
$$\text{,, } 1, 4 \quad 13 - 10 = 3 \text{ minutes}$$

MORE COMPLEX NETWORKS

So far we have confined ourselves to rather elementary network analysis. In practice networks are usually more complex and problems arise in connection with numbering the events of the network and identifying the critical path. The question of activity time probabilities also tends to be raised. In this section we see how each of these matters can be handled, the points made being illustrated by reference to the network in Fig. 31.

10. Numbering events. Logically when numbering events we should ensure that the start event number of any activity in the network is always lower than the end event number. In our earlier simple network this was done by careful inspection, but in a more complex one, the following numbering procedure may well prove useful:

(*a*) Locate all events which do *not* have an activity leading to them.

(*b*) Give such events the next available numbers (such events can be numbered in any order).

(*c*) Delete all activities that *leave* the numbered events.

(*d*) Repeat steps (*a*) to (*c*) until all events are numbered.

The use of the procedure is illustrated in Fig. 31(*b*).

11. Identifying the critical path. In a simple network the critical path can also be identified by careful inspection, but again this is rarely possible in a more complex network. In such a case the following procedure based on making a forward and a backward pass should be adopted (*see* Fig. 31(*c*)):

(*a*) *Forward pass.* Starting at event-1 move forward through the network and write *above* each event the *earliest time* after the start of the project the event can occur. This is essentially a logical operation. It must be appreciated that such an "earliest" date depends on the *longest* path through the network to that event. For example, in our illustration

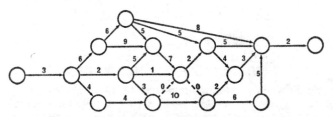

(*a*) Illustrative network (time in days).

FIG. 31.—*More complex network.*

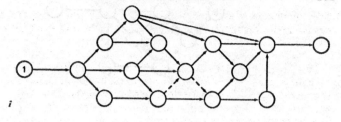

i

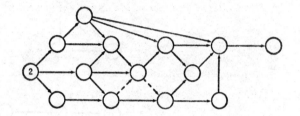

ii

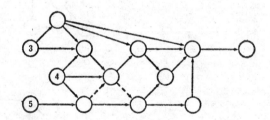

iii

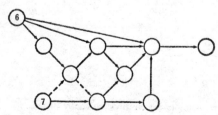

iv

FIG. 31.—*More complex network.*

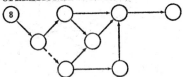

v

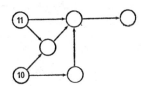

vi

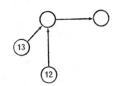

vii

viii

ix

(b) (*i–ix*) Numbering the network.

FIG. 31.—*More complex network.*

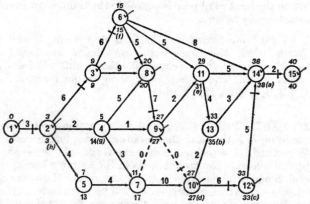

(a) 40—2; (b) 38—3; (c) 38—5; (d) Earliest of 35—2, 33—6; (e) Earliest of 35—4, 38—5; (f) Earliest of 38—8, 31—5, 20—5; (g) Earliest of 17—3, 27—1, 20—5; (h) Earliest of 13—4, 14—2, 9—6.

(c) Identifying the critical path.

FIG. 31.—*More complex network.*

event-7 occurs at the end of chains 1, 2, 4, 7 and 1, 2, 5, 7. These chains can be completed in $3 + 2 + 3 = 8$ days and $3 + 4 + 4 = 11$ days respectively. Since event-7 cannot be said to have occurred until *both* chains are complete the earliest date of that event is 11 days.

When the forward pass is complete the time above the final event will be the *overall project completion time.*

(b) *Backward pass.* Starting at the last event move *backwards* through the network and write *below* the event the latest date the event can occur and *still enable the project to be completed on time.* This involves a little more thought than the forward pass but is still just a logical operation. For example, since it takes 2 days to complete activity 14, 15 then in order to meet the 40 day deadline for event 15, event-14 must occur by day 38 at the latest. Similarly event-11 cannot occur later than day 31 since otherwise there will not be time to complete the chain 11, 13, 14 ($4 + 3 = 7$ days) and meet the 38 day deadline for event-14.

When the backward pass is complete the time below event-1 must naturally be zero.

(c) *Path identification.* The final step is simple—all the events where the times above and below are equal are ticked, and *the activities connecting these events* will form the critical path. The critical path, then, in our illustration is 1, 2, 3, 6, 8, 9, 10, 12, 14, 15.

12. PERT. PERT (Programme Evaluation and Review Technique) is little more than another name for the critical-path method. The technique does, however, add the sophistication of allowing for probabilities in the activity times. The actual times of a repeated activity are rarely the same and neither is it likely their distribution will be symmetrical. If one were, for example, to draw the frequency distribution of the time it took to drive to work it would almost certainly be found that although individual times would *exceed* the average time by, say, 20% or 30% on a number of occasions, time *savings* of this order would be rare. The actual distribution would, in fact, tend to follow what is called a *beta* distribution and the mean and variance of such a distribution can be approximately found from a subjective estimate of the most optimistic, likeliest, and most pessimistic activity times in the following way:

$$\text{Mean time} = \frac{\text{optimistic} + 4 \times \text{likeliest} + \text{pessimistic}}{6}$$

$$\text{Variance} = \left(\frac{\text{pessimistic} - \text{optimistic}}{6}\right)^2$$

By adding the mean times and variances for each activity along the critical path the mean project completion time and the standard deviation of that time can be found.

EXAMPLE: If the estimated times (mins) of the activities in the letter project (*see* Fig. 29) are as given in columns B, C and D below, then columns E and F show the mean activity times and variances:

A ACTIVITY	B MOST OPTIMISTIC TIME	C LIKELIEST TIME	D MOST PESSIMISTIC TIME	E MEAN	F VARIANCE
1,3	3½	5	9½	$\frac{3½ + 4 \times 5 + 9½}{6}$ $= 5.50$	$\left(\frac{9½ - 3½}{6}\right)^2$ $= 1.00$
3,4	5	8	17	$\frac{5 + 4 \times 8 + 17}{6}$ $= 9.00$	$\left(\frac{17 - 5}{6}\right)^2$ $= 4.00$
4,5	0.8	1	1.4	$\frac{0.8 + 4 \times 1 + 1.4}{6}$ $= 1.03$	$\left(\frac{1.4 - 0.8}{6}\right)^2$ $= 0.01$
5,6	3	6	15	$\frac{3 + 4 \times 6 + 15}{6}$ $= 7.00$	$\left(\frac{15 - 3}{6}\right)^2$ $= 4.00$
		20		22.53	9.01

We can, therefore, conclude that the average project completion time will be approximately $22\frac{1}{2}$ minutes with a standard deviation of $\sqrt{9 \cdot 01} \simeq 3$ minutes. If the *final* distribution is normal, then, there will be a 95% probability of the project being completed in a period of $22\frac{1}{2} \pm 2 \times 3$, *i.e.* in between $16\frac{1}{2}$ and $28\frac{1}{2}$ minutes.

PERT/COST

There are very few activity times that cannot in practice be reduced—at a cost. In this section we look at the economics of such reductions.

13. Advantages of reducing the project completion time. Reducing the project completion time can be advantageous for a number of reasons and the following are probably among those met most frequently:

(*a*) Earlier completion may result in possible contract bonuses.

(b) The existing estimated project completion date is beyond the contract date and will result in lateness penalties.

(c) Facilities can be released more quickly for transfer to further profitable work.

(d) Idle time of facilities in sub-critical paths can be reduced.

(e) Company reputation is enhanced and its competitive position improved.

14. Minimum activity times. Although virtually all activity times can be continually reduced by accepting a progressively higher cost, there comes a point when technical factors impose a final limit. The time taken for concrete to harden, for example, cannot be reduced below a set limit no matter how much one is prepared to pay. Similarly, the sheer physical limit to the number of people who can work on a small unit imposes a minimum time limit on such activities. All activities, then, have a minimum activity time which in practice cannot be reduced.

15. Illustrative network. In Fig. 32(a) we show the network we will use to illustrate PERT/COST principles. As can be seen virtually all activity times have three figures alongside them: an ordinary figure indicating the normal activity time; a figure in brackets indicating the minimum activity time; and a monetary figure indicating the cost required to reduce the activity by 1 day (in practice, of course, the reduction cost per unit of time increases progressively, but for simplicity we will take a constant cost here). As can be seen, the initial critical path is 1, 2, 3, 5, 6 and the normal completion time is $3 + 5 + 6 + 5 = 19$ days. Management in this illustration assess the value of time saved on completion at £60 per day.

16. Critical path activities only to be reduced. It is obvious that only activities that lie along the critical path should be considered for reduction. For example, there is no point at the moment in reducing activity 2, 4 since no time saved here can affect the completion date.

17. Basic rule for activity reduction. The basic rule for activity reduction can be stated as follows:

(a) Locate the activity lying along the critical path that has the lowest reduction cost.

(b) Compare the cost of reduction with the value of saved completion time, and if there is a net saving reduce the activity time.

(c) The activity time of the activity should be progressively reduced until either:

(i) the cost of further reductions exceeds the savings; or
(ii) the minimum time is reached; or
(iii) a previous sub-critical parallel path becomes critical as a result of the activity reductions.

Applying this rule to our illustration we see the activity lying along the critical path with the lowest reduction cost is 1, 2 (£10). It must, therefore, be reduced. Since (c)(i) is not applicable in this illustration and there are no parallel paths to this activity, reductions are made until the minimum time is reached, i.e. by 2 days down to a minimum of 1 day.

We now go back to (a) and locate the next lowest critical activity cost—which is obviously 3, 5. This appears to have a potential reduction of 3 days but inspection of the network shows that after a 2-day reduction activity chain 2, 3, 5 is 9 days long—i.e. no longer than the parallel activity 2, 5. This latter (previously sub-critical) path, then, has been thrown critical by the 2-day reduction, and we must, therefore, stop the reduction under part (c)(iii) of our rule. The network remaining after this reduction is shown in Fig. 32(b).

18. Amended rule for parallel critical paths. When two parallel paths are both critical it is obviously pointless to reduce the activity times in one unless the same reduction is made in the activity times of the other, for if this is not done the project completion time remains unaltered. But this means, of course, we must incur the combined costs of *both* sets of reductions, and this leads to an extension of our basic rule which runs:

Where there are two or more parallel critical paths:

(a) Find the lowest combined cost of simultaneously reducing all the parallel critical paths by 1 unit of time; and

(b) Use this cost for this part of the network when applying the basic rule given in **17**(a).

Reverting to Fig. 32(b) of our illustrative network we find the lowest combined cost of reducing the 2, 3, 5 and 2, 5 paths is £30 + £20 (since it is cheaper to reduce 3, 5 than 2, 3) = £50.

Using this cost in our basic rule leads us to next identify activity 5, 6 for reduction, since this has a cost of only £40. This we can reduce by 2 days before we reach the minim activity time of 3 days.

There are now no other reducible activities on the critical path other than the parallel activities, and so we now compare

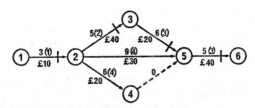

(a) Initial network. Times in days. Completion time—19 days. Value per day saved—£60.

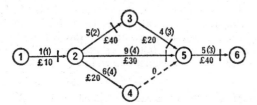

(b) Network after second reduction.

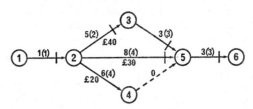

(c) Final network. Minimum cost of reduction = £40 + £30 per day which exceeds £60 value per day saved.

Reduction	Activity	Cost per day (£)	Days saved	Total cost (£)
1st	1, 2	10	2	20
2nd	3, 5	20	2	40
3rd	5, 6	40	2	80
4th	$\begin{pmatrix} 3, 5 \\ 2, 5 \end{pmatrix}$	50	1	50
(Next	$\begin{pmatrix} 2, 3 \\ 2, 5 \end{pmatrix}$	70	Not profitable)	
			7	£190

	£
Saving: 7 days @ £60 per day	420
Costs: As above	190
Net saving	£230

(d) Cost and saving summary.

Fig. 32.—*PERT/COST*.

the £50 combined cost with the £60 value of time saved. Since the comparison is favourable we reduce 3, 5 and 2, 5 simultaneously—only, however, by 1 day, for this is all that 3, 5 can be reduced before it is down to its minimum.

With 3, 5 out of the analysis we now find the combined cost of reducing 2, 3 simultaneously with 2, 5—and discover it amounts to £70 (*see* Fig. 32(c)). As this is above the £60 value per day saved it is uneconomic to make the reductions and so the analysis comes to an end.

19. The final network. As we have just seen, PERT/COST involves repeatedly applying the basic rule (plus the amendment) until the cost of further reductions exceeds the value of the time saved. At this point we have our final network.

The final network of our illustration is given in Fig. 32(c) and a cost-saving summary of the exercise is given in Fig. 32(d). As can be seen, the PERT/COST analysis results in a net saving of £230.

20. Expanding sub-critical activities. It should be appreciated that once the final network has been decided upon it may pay us to *expand the sub-critical activities*. For example, as we see from Fig. 32(c) activity 2, 4 is sub-critical and has a float time of 2 days. This means that it may be possible to allocate less efficient labour or machinery to this activity, and it is also possible that such less efficient resources, while taking a little longer, may well cost a little less. So further cost savings may be made by expanding the activity.

ADVANTAGES OF NETWORK ANALYSIS

The advantages of network analysis can be summarised as follows:

(*a*) It provides a visual and, therefore, more easily grasped record of the logical progression of activities involved in a project.

(*b*) It enables a realistic completion time to be estimated.

(*c*) It identifies the critical path and those activities having completion times that are critical in achieving the planned project completion time. This in turn indicates the priorities of our controls since one day longer on the most trivial activity will delay the whole project by one day if it lies on the critical path.

(*d*) It identifies sub-critical activities which can be allowed to expand and indicates, by means of float times, the degree of such expansion that can be tolerated.

(*e*) It schedules the earliest and latest possible dates of all events in the network.

(*f*) It enables, by means of PERT/COST, the optimum economic scheduling of activities to be achieved.

Perhaps, however, the greatest advantage of network analysis is that the initial construction of the network forces management to think logically and carefully about all aspects of the project *before* actually starting to do anything and incurring commitments.

PROGRESS TEST 18

1. The Mammoth Tent Coy. Ltd. produce on customer's order a "Unique" tent, to which the following production data relates:

Activity	Normal Time (Hrs.)	Minimum Time (Hrs.)	Cost per Hr. Reduction £
Cut from canvas roll: valise, RH, Special, Centre and LH sections	2	1	1
Valise: Sew-in rings	2	1	2
Complete valise	1	1	—
RH section: Sew flaps	2	1	1
Make door	3	2	3
Special section: Treat and then measure	5	5	—
Sew flaps	3	1	2
Centre section: Sew flaps	2	1	3
Using measurement relating to special section cut into top and bottom halves	1	1	—
Top half: sew on lugs	3	1	4
Bottom half: sew on lugs	3	1	4
LH section: Sew flaps	2	1	2
Make door	3	1	3
Sew together top half of centre section, RH section and Special section to make main tent	6	4	2
Sew together bottom half of centre section and LH section to make side tent	4	1	1
Sew together main and side tents to make complete tent	4	2	3
Pack complete tent in valise	1	1	—

(*a*) Prepare a network for this task and identify the critical path.

(*b*) On the basis of every hour saved being worth £6, find the optimum network.

CHAPTER XIX

LINEAR PROGRAMMING

"Linear programming" is a term that covers a whole range
of mathematical techniques that aim to optimise performance
in terms of *combinations* of resources. We have already seen
how to optimise selling prices, stock levels and replacement
periods, but have never considered how to optimise a product
mix, or allocate a variety of tasks among resources, or even
allocate the right resource to the right task. This is the function of linear programming.

Unfortunately linear programming is mathematically very
complex. To avoid such complexity in the actual solving of
problems, mathematicians have reduced their techniques down
to a series of simple if somewhat lengthy procedures. Examiners, therefore, have tended to ask their questions more in
terms of procedures than anything else. We have, then, concentrated in this chapter on these procedures and excluded the
mathematical reasoning. In other words we will discuss the
"how" and not the "why"—students desiring the latter are
referred to any of the standard literature on this subject.

TERMINOLOGY

First, we will look at a few of the terms used in linear programming.

1. Why "linear programming"? In operational research
terminology "programming" means using an optimising technique, and, of course, "linear" means a situation in which the
variables give straight-line curves on graphs—which in this
context usually means that if one doubles the quantity one
doubles the variable cost. "Linear programming," therefore,
is any optimising technique in which the variables are all
linear. Note that in real life costs are not necessarily linear and
so linear programming cannot be used in such situations.

2. Tableaux and transforms. Many linear programming techniques employ a matrix layout, and the routine involves changing the figures within the matrix. Such matrix layouts are called *tableaux*, and changing the figures to produce a new tableau is called a *tableau transform*, or alternatively, an *iteration*.

3. Constraints. In this world there are always factors which set limits on what we can do, *e.g.* production is limited by machine capacity or floor space or cash. Operational research workers refer to such factors as *constraints*. Accounting students will appreciate that "key factors" and "constraints" are the same thing.

GRAPHICAL LINEAR PROGRAMMING

We will start by looking at the simplest linear programming technique—graphical linear programming.

4. Context of use. Graphical linear programming is used where:

   (a) There are two products *only* involved; and
   (b) There are two or more constraints operating so that it is not immediately apparent what product mix will maximise the profit (or minimise the cost).

5. Illustrative figures. To illustrate the graphical technique we will study the following situation:

A factory manufactures Xs and Ys. Production times and profits are as follows:

	X	Y	Capacity
Dept. A	8 hrs.	10 hrs.	11,000 hrs.
Dept. B	4 ,,	10 ,,	9000 ,,
Dept. C	12 ,,	6 ,,	12,000 ,,
Profit	£4	£8	

What production plan maximises profit?

NOTE: (a) The constraints in this illustration are the departmental capacities. (b) The operational researcher's word "profit" is synonymous with the accountant's word "contribution."

6. Constructing the graph. As the name indicates, the graphical linear programming technique is based on a graphical construction that results from adopting the following procedure (*see* Fig. 33):

(*a*) Allocate each product to each of the axes—each axis extending far enough to include the maximum number of units of product that could be manufactured if the least onerous constraint alone operated (*e.g.* 2250 Xs could be made if the capacity in department B alone constrained production, while 2000 Ys could be made if the capacity in department C was the sole constraint).

(*b*) Take the first constraint (*e.g.* Department A) and:

(*i*) Calculate the maximum number of units of the first product that could be possibly manufactured if that constraint alone operated (*e.g.* $\frac{11,000}{8} = 1375$ Xs could be made). Plot this number on the product axis.

(*ii*) Repeat (*i*) for the second product (*e.g.* $\frac{11,000}{10} = 1100$ Ys).

(*iii*) Join the two plotted points with a straight line.

NOTE: If any point is taken on this line it will be found that the product mix given by that point will exactly absorb the capacity of the department (*e.g.* taking point X = 1000, Y = 300 it can be seen that the time required is $1000 \times 8 + 300 \times 10 = 11,000$ hours = capacity of department A). The line, therefore, marks the maximum production possible in the department in respect of every possible mix we may care to consider.

(*c*) Repeat (*b*) for every constraint in the problem.

NOTE: If a constraint only operates on one product the line we draw will run at right-angles to our product axis. Thus, if we had a department D with 6000 hours' capacity through which only Ys passed, each Y requiring 6 hours' work, we would have a horizontal line on our graph passing through the 1000 Y point on our Y axis.

7. Area of feasible solution. Since each line on our graph forms a production "barrier" in respect of each constraint, then the only overall practical product mix is one that falls within *all* the barriers. This area is termed the *area of feasible solution* (*see* Fig. 33). Note, incidentally, that since we can never produce a negative number of units, the axes themselves form barriers. Mathematicians refer to these barriers as the *non-negativity constraints*.

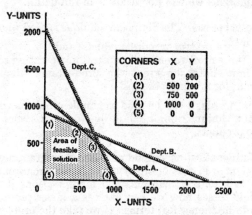

FIG. 33.—*Graphical linear programming.*

8. Finding the optimum mix. It is a mathematical fact that the optimum mix will always be found at one of the corners of the area of feasible solution. Although there is a method of identifying the appropriate corner (which involves constructing the line of equi-profit) the quickest way is probably to test each corner. From the graph in Fig. 33, then, we find the "corner mixes" give us the following contributions:

Corner	X	Y	Profit
1	0	900	$0 + 900 \times 8 = £7200$
2	500	700	$500 \times 4 + 700 \times 8 = £7600$
3	750	500	$750 \times 4 + 500 \times 8 = £7000$
4	1000	0	$1000 \times 4 + 0 = £4000$
5	0	0	$0 + 0 = £0$

Our optimum mix, therefore, is 500 X and 700 Y giving a profit of £7600.

SIMPLEX TECHNIQUE

The next linear programming technique—the Simplex technique—is probably the most complex of the four we shall be examining. However, since the transforms are rarely asked for in examinations we will not study it in full detail.

9. Context of use. The Simplex technique is used where:

(a) There are two or more products; and

(b) There are two or more constraints operating so that it is not immediately apparent what product mix will maximise the profit (or minimise the cost).

In other words, it can be used to handle problems which the graphical technique cannot handle due to the existence of more than two products.

10. Mathematical expression of a linear programming problem. Although in this brief survey of linear programming we will not look at any mathematical manipulations it may be worthwhile to see how we can express a linear programming problem in mathematical terms. If we take the problem given in **5** and let x = number of Xs and y = number of Ys then clearly:

$$8x + 10y \leqslant 11,000$$
$$4x + 10y \leqslant 9000$$
$$12x + 6y \leqslant 12,000$$

Also introducing the non-negativity constraints we can add:

$$x \geqslant 0 \text{ and } y \geqslant 0.$$

Finally we can say that:

$$4x + 8y = \text{PROFIT}$$

This last expression is known as the "objective function" and our aim in the problem given in **5** is to "maximise the objective function."

This set of algebraic expressions details the problem in mathematical terms.

11. Slack variables. One of the difficulties of solving linear programming problems arises because inequalities are mathematically not easy to handle in such a context. This problem can be overcome by pretending *all the unused* units of constraint are in fact used to make a fantasy product, one unit of which requires just one unit of constraint and is, of course, worth zero profit. Such a fantasy product is called a *slack variable*, and in the Simplex technique it is necessary to have a slack variable for each constraint. If we let S = units of slack variable produced then in our illustrative problem we will produce S_A, S_B and S_C units of each slack variable respectively (this means, for example, we can now write $8x + 10y + S_A = 11,000$, and so change the inequality to an equality).

12. The initial tableau. The initial Simplex tableau is set up as follows (*see* Fig. 34(*a*) where 5 constraints are assumed to exist):

(*a*) (*i*) The first three columns are headed PRODUCT, PROFIT and QUANTITY.

    (*ii*) The next group of columns are headed with the names of the real products.

    (*iii*) The final group of columns are headed with the names of the slack variables—one for each constraint.

(*b*) (*i*) In the PRODUCT column are listed *all the slack variables*.

    (*ii*) The PROFIT column shows the profit on the products listed—in this case zero for every product.

    (*iii*) The QUANTITY column shows the units of each constraint available against its associated slack variable.

    (*iv*) Each "real product" column shows the units of constraint required for that product—again against the associated slack variable.

    (*v*) Each "slack variable" column has a "1" where it intersects with the same "slack variable" row—and zero in all other places.

(*c*) The tableau is completed by adding two lines at the bottom—a PROFIT line showing the profit on each of the products that head the columns and a zero in the QUANTITY column, and a Z line which in the initial tableau is identical with the PROFIT line.

13. The final tableau. After a number of relatively complex transforms a final tableau emerges which can be identified by the absence of any values greater than zero in the Z line. This tableau is interpreted as follows (*see* Fig. 34(*b*)):

(a) FIRST TABLEAU

			Products			Slack variables				
Product	*Profit*	*Quantity*	*X*	*Y*	*Z*	S_1	S_2	S_3	S_4	S_5
S_1	0	Capacities	Units of			1	0	0	0	0
S_2	0	of	constraint			0	1	0	0	0
S_3	0	the	per unit			0	0	1	0	0
S_4	0	different	of			0	0	0	1	0
S_5	0	constraints	product			0	0	0	0	1
Profit		0	Profit per unit			0	0	0	0	0
Z		0	of product			0	0	0	0	0

(*a*) First tableau.

(b) FINAL TABLEAU

Product	*Profit*	*Quantity*	*X*	*Y*	*Z*	S_1	S_2	S_3	S_4	S_5
Products to be made	Profit per unit on products to be made	Quantities to be made								
Profit			As per profit row in 1st tableau							
Z										
		Total profit that will be earned	amount by which unit profit must rise to justify inclusion			shadow prices				

(*b*) Final tableau.

FIG. 34.—*Simplex technique.*

(*a*) The PRODUCT and QUANTITY columns list the quantities of each product that must be produced to give the optimum mix. The presence of a slack variable in the PRODUCT column indicates the associated constraint is not fully utilised—the spare units of constraint being shown in the QUANTITY column.

(*b*) The Z row shows (negative signs to be ignored):

(*i*) In the QUANTITY column—the total profit earned by the optimum mix.

(*ii*) In the "real product" columns—the amount by which the product profit must rise for it to be included in the optimum mix (if this is zero the product will be found to be already in the mix).

(*iii*) In the "slack variable" columns—the shadow prices (*see* next paragraph).

14. Shadow prices. Wherever a constraint limits profitable production it is worthwhile buying extra units—at an economical price, of course. The maximum amount one should pay in such circumstances is called the shadow price, and if extra constraint units can be bought below the shadow price, then it pays to buy them (though a further analysis will be needed to ascertain *how many* such units should be bought).

As we saw in (*b*)(*iii*) above, constraint shadow prices can be read from the tableau. Where they happen to be zero it will be noticed that the optimum mix does not, in fact, use all the available constraint units and further such units are, therefore, worthless.

TRANSPORTATION TECHNIQUE

The next linear programming technique we study is called the *transportation technique*, and this we will look at in detail. The necessary routines are shown in Fig. 35 and the technique demonstrated in Fig. 36.

15. Context of use. The transportation technique is normally used where there are a number of sources of supply and a number of destinations for the supplies, and it is desired to minimise the total cost of supplying the destinations.

16. Summary of procedure. The whole procedure is detailed in Fig. 35—Fig. 35(*a*) showing the summary flow chart. As can be seen, after setting up the initial tableau, tableau transforms need to be made until no transport costs (*i.e.* the ones in **23**, below) are less than what will be called the "ringed shadow costs"—at which point the tableau then in being gives the final solution.

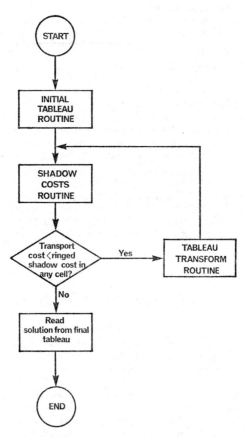

(a) Summary flow chart.

Note: When a subsequent sub-routine states "select next cell," select next cell to the right unless the end of the row has been reached in which case select first cell in next row. If the instruction is given at the end of the bottom row, select top left-hand cell. (The row and column "TOTAL" cells are not classified as "cells" for this technique.)

FIG. 35.—*Transportation technique.*

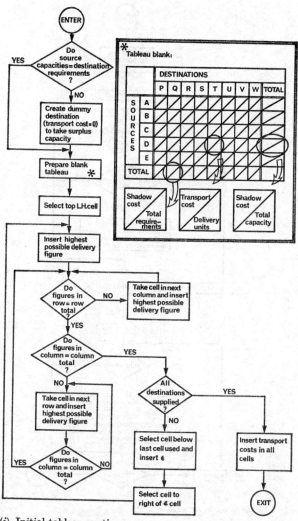

(b) (i) Initial tableau routine.

FIG. 35.—*Transportation technique.*

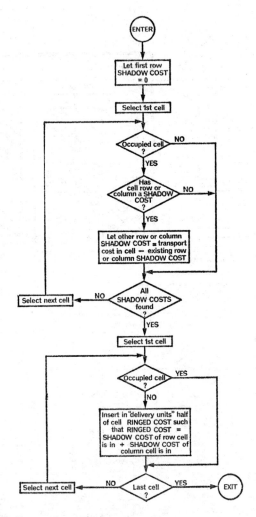

(b) (ii) Shadow costs routine.

FIG. 35.—*Transportation technique.*

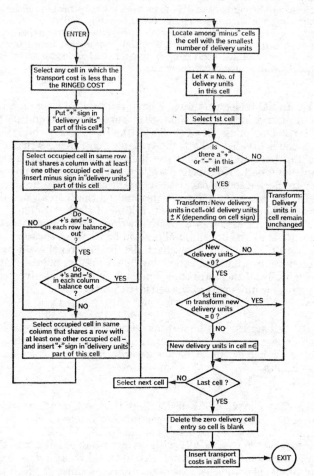

* This cell now has "occupied" status.

(*iii*) Tableau transform routine.

  (*b*) Routines.

FIG. 35.—*Transportation technique.*

NOTE: Although the flow charts may look long and involved, on working through them the principles rapidly become clear so that no great feats of memory are ultimately called for. Charts are used rather than statements of principle because experience has shown this unambiguous, if initially somewhat long-winded, approach enables students to master the procedures in the quickest and most digestible form.

17. Initial tableau routine. The initial tableau is again built up in matrix form—this time with sources as rows and destinations as columns (*see* Fig. 35(*b*)(*i*)). In this case, however, each cell is divided in half, the transport cost being written in the top left-hand half and the delivery units in the bottom right-hand half. Note before setting up the tableau it is necessary to check if source capacities equal destination requirements and if not to create a dummy destination that can absorb the unrequired capacity surplus (*i.e.* a kind of slack variable).

The first allocation of deliveries is done either by an intelligent guess at the optimum allocation or by what is called the *north-west rule*. The flow chart details the north-west rule procedure and its application is shown in Fig. 36(*a*). Note, incidentally, if there are to be no delivery units in a given cell the delivery units part of the cell is left blank.

18. Cell status. An important feature of the transportation technique is the status of a cell. A cell can be *occupied*, when it will carry delivery units, or *unoccupied* when the delivery units part is blank.

19. The ε symbol. In order that this technique functions correctly it is necessary that the number of occupied cells = number of rows + number of columns − 1. Usually this condition is met automatically without any trouble, but where the figures are such that it is *not* met (referred to as a *degenerate* situation) then an otherwise unoccupied cell must be given the status of an occupied cell. This is done by writing an "ε" in the delivery unit's part of the cell. Writing such an ε in no way alters the fact that the cell has zero delivery units—it merely *changes the cell status*. In other words a cell with an ε in it is an occupied cell having zero delivery units.

20. Shadow costs routine. Once the initial tableau has been set up we move to the shadow costs routine shown in Fig. 35(b) (ii) and illustrated in Fig. 36(b). When this routine has been completed we inspect the tableau to see if in any cell the transport cost is less than the ringed shadow cost. If there is such a cell we enter the tableau transform routine—otherwise the tableau is the final tableau.

21. Tableau transform routine. The tableau transform routine is shown in Fig. 35(b)(iii) and illustrated in Fig. 36(c). At the end of the routine we return to the shadow costs routine.

22. Final solution. The tableau transform routine and the shadow costs routine alternate until the transport cost in all cells is equal to, or greater than, the ringed shadow cost (see Fig. 36(e)) when the tableau then existing is the final tableau. The solution to the initial problem can then be read from this tableau (see Fig. 36(f)).

23. Transportation technique illustration.

We will illustrate the transportation technique by means of the following figures:

Sources: A – Capacity 200 units
B – Capacity 600 units
C – Capacity 300 units

Destinations: Y – Requirements 300 units
Z – Requirements 400 units

Costs per unit (pence):

		TO	
		Y	Z
FROM	A	7	9
	B	8	6
	C	4	7

This problem is so simple it can be solved by commonsense, for since the route YC is as low as 4p a unit it will obviously be best to supply all Y's requirements from C. Similarly, it will pay to supply all of Z's requirements from B leaving the 200 units capacity remaining unused along with all A's 200 units. We will, however, demonstrate in Fig. 36 that the procedure given in Fig. 35 leads automatically to this solution.

	Y	Z	*	TOTAL
A	7.*i* / 200.*ii*	9	0	200
B	8 / 100	6 / 400	0 / 100	600
C	4	7	0 / 300	300
TOTAL	300	400	400	1100

(*i*) This and other transport costs come direct from the cost matrix given in the problem (0 cost for *, of course since the units are not, in fact, dispatched).

(*ii*) The routine arbitrarily allocates all A's 200 units to Y leaving Y's remaining 100 units to be supplied by B. The procedure operates similarly in the other cells.

(*a*) Initial tableau routine. Since the capacities of the sources exceed the requirements of the destinations, a dummy destination, represented as * is created having a "requirement" equal to the excess capacity.

	Y	Z	*	SHADOW COST / TOTAL
A	7 / 200	9 / (5) *vii*	0 / (-1) *viii*	0 *i* / 200
B	8 / 100	6 / 400	0 / 100	1 *iii* / 600
C	4 / (8) *ix*	7 / (6) *x*	0 / 300	1 *vi* / 300
SHADOW COST / TOTAL	7 *ii* / 300	5 *iv* / 400	-1 *v* / 400	

(*i*) Given as 0 to begin with. (*ii*) 7−0; (*iii*) 8−7; (*iv*) 6−1; (*v*) 0−1; (*vi*) 0−(−1); (*vii*) 0 + 5; (*viii*) 0 + (−1); (*ix*) 1 + 7; (*x*) 1 + 5. Note that the end of routine the summary shows we must ask "Transport cost < ringed cost in any cell?" Since the answer is "Yes" (see CY) then a transform must be made.

(*b*) 1st shadow cost routine

	Y	Z	*
A	200	(5)	(-1)
B	−*iv* / 100	400	+*iii* / 100
C	+*i* / (8)	(6)	−*ii* / 300

(*i*) +*s* and −*s*. Following the routine given it can be seen +*s* and −*s* will be written in the order given, from i to iv.

	Y	Z	*
A	200		
B		400	200
C	100		200

(*ii*) Transform. Here k = 100 (the BY cell). Note that BY becomes a blank.

(*c*) 1st transform.

	Y	Z	✳	
A	7 / 200	9 / ⑨	0† / ③+	0 / 200
B	8 / ④	6 / 400	0 / 200	-3 / 600
C	4 +/ 100	7 / ⑥	0 -/ 200	-3 / 300
	7 / 300	9 / 400	3 / 400	

† Since transport cost is < ringed shadow cost, a further transform is necessary. For this second transform k = 200.

(d) The 2nd shadow costs and +s and −s.

	Y	Z	✳	
A	7 / ④	9 / ⑥	0 / 200	0 / 200
B	8 / ④	6 / 400	0 / 200	0 / 600
C	4 / 300	7 / ⑥	0 / ε†	0 / 300
	4 / 300	6 / 400	0 / 400	

‡ We write here ε as AY was our first zero (before it became a blank at the end of the routine).

Since no transport cost < ringed cost this is the final transform and the necessary deliveries read directly from it.

(e) The 2nd transform and 3rd shadow costs.

	TO Y	TO Z	UNUSED CAPACITY	TOTAL
FROM A			200	200
FROM B		400	200	600
FROM C	300		§	300
TOTAL	300	400	400	1100

§ The ε = 0, of course.

(f) Final solutions.

Fig. 36.—*Transport technique: illustrations.*

ASSIGNMENT TECHNIQUE

The final linear programming technique we examine is the *assignment technique*. This technique is detailed in Fig. 37 and illustrated in Fig. 38.

24. Context of use. The assignment technique is used when we wish to *pair off* factors—*e.g.* taxis and customers, employees and positions—to find the optimum pairing.

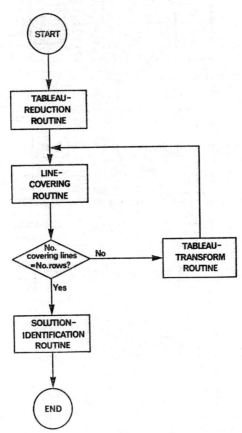

(a) Summary flow chart. In these routines the term "line" is used. A "line" is a row or column. If an instruction says "select 1st line" then the first row should be selected, and at the instruction "select next line" the next row is selected—until all the rows have been selected after which the first column should be selected. The test "last line?" requires all rows and columns to have been selected before an answer in the affirmative can be given.

FIG. 37.—*Assignment technique.*

25. Summary of procedure. In Fig. 37(a) is given the summary flow chart of the procedures. Again the initial tableau is set up in a matrix form so that each cell records the value associated with the pairing of the row factor and the column factor (*see* Fig. 38(b)). The tableau is then "reduced" in accordance with the procedure given in the flow chart in Fig. 37(b)(i) (*see also* Fig. 38(b)). After this the "line-covering" routine is applied (Figs. 37(b)(ii) and 38(c)) and at the end the number of covering lines are counted. If this is equal to the number of rows in the matrix then it remains only to apply the "solution-identification" routine—otherwise it is necessary to move to the "tableau-transform" routine after which it is necessary to return to the "line-covering" routine (*see* Figs. 37(b)(iii) and 38(d) and (e)).

The "solution-identification" routine is a simple routine (Figs. 37(b)(iv) and 38(f)) although it can lead to going "round and round" the matrix a number of times before coming to an end. This is not important in itself, but such repetition must

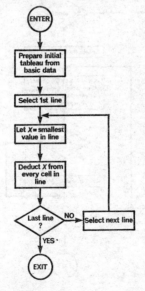

(b) (i) Tableau-reduction routine.

FIG. 37.—*Assignment technique.*

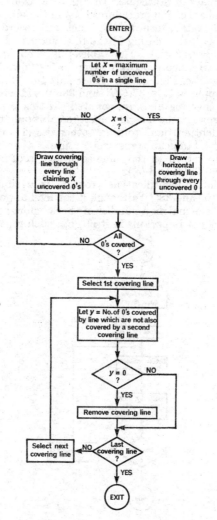

(b) (ii) Line-covering routine.

FIG. 37.—*Assignment technique.*

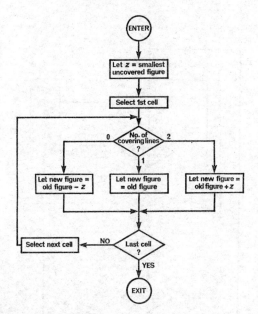

(b) (iii) Tableau-transform routine.

FIG. 37.—*Assignment technique.*

not lead the student to think he is in an endless loop. One is only in an endless loop if, after going *completely* through the matrix once, *nothing* has altered. Where an endless loop does, in fact, arise it simply means there are two optimum solutions, and by arbitrarily crossing out one of the remaining zeros and continuing the routine the loop can be broken and one of these solutions identified.

26. Assignment technique is a minimising technique. The student should be warned the assignment technique is a minimising technique—it gives a solution that minimises the values involved. This is all very well as long as we wish to have a minimum value solution (such as the distance problem in our illustration) but it does mean we have to modify the original data if we want a maximum value solution. For example, if we wished to assign people to jobs on a basis of test marks, using

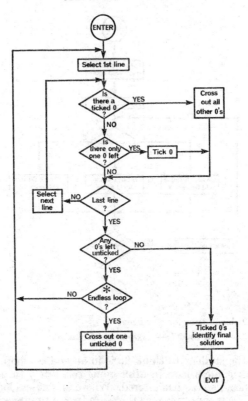

(b) (iv) Solution-identification routine.

*If an endless loop is entered this means there are two optimum solutions. Crossing out one unticked 0 enables one of these solutions to be identified.

(b) Routines.

FIG. 37.—*Assignment technique.*

the marks as they stood it would result in assigning the jobs to the people with the lowest marks.

Fortunately, this problem is easily overcome by *subtracting all the original figures from a constant at least as large as the largest figure* (*e.g.* maximum possible test marks) and building up the initial tableau from these results. In the case of jobs and tests, then, the technique will result in assigning people to jobs

	W	X	Y	Z
A	7	7	5	4
B	6	3	7	5
C	5	3	4	4
D	6	3	7	5

(*a*) Illustrative problem. The manager of a taxi company suddenly receives calls from customers A, B, C, D. He has four roving taxis at points *W*, *X*, *Y* and *Z*. The distance between points and customers is given in the table above. Which taxi should he allocate to which customer? (Only an academic problem really. The manager who solved it using linear programming would very likely find all his customers had walked to their destinations long before his taxis were instructed.)

Initial tableau.

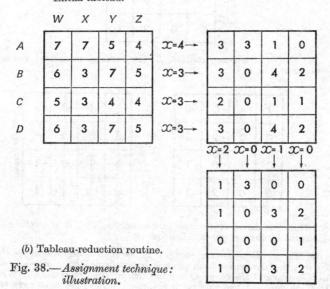

(*b*) Tableau-reduction routine.

Fig. 38.—*Assignment technique: illustration.*

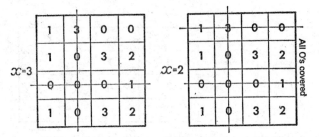

In the right-hand table (i) no covering lines to be removed. (ii) Number of covering lines $\neq$ number of rows.

(c) The 1st line-covering routine.

1	4	0	0
0	0	2	1
0	1	0	1
0	0	2	1

(d) Tableau-transform routine. Z (the smallest uncovered number from above) $= 1$.

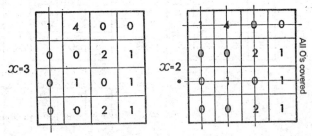

* This line inserted to show an erroneous line is automatically discarded by the next part of the routine.

(e) The 2nd line-covering routine. In the right-hand table above the 0's in the 3rd row are both covered by two covering lines, so $y = 0$ in this case and the covering line in this row must be removed. With this line removed, the number of covering lines = number of rows (4).

1	4	☒	0 ✓
0	0	2	1
☒	1	0 ✓	1
0	0	2	1

1	4	☒	0 ✓
0 ✓	☒	2	1
☒	1	0 ✓	1
☒	0 ✓	2	1

	W	X	Y	Z
A				✓
B	✓			
C			✓	
D		✓		

(*i*) Routine up to the point of endless loop. The letters (*a*) to (*d*) indicate the order in which √s and ×s were made.

(*ii*) 0 in bottom-left corner (*e*) arbitrarily selected for deletion.

(*iii*) The solution: W to B, X to D, Y to C and Z to A.

(*f*) Solution-identification routine.

FIG. 38.—*Assignment technique: illustration.*

on the basis of minimising the lost test marks—*i.e.* maximising the actual test marks.

PROGRESS TEST 19

1. Control Units Ltd. make two types of control units—Light and Heavy (L and H). The Light units require 5 relays but the Heavy require 12. Unfortunately during the coming month only 12,000 relays will be obtainable. Moreover unit bases are also in short supply—there being only 1200 Light bases and 700 Heavy available. Capacity in the Assembly shop is limited as well; being, in fact, equal to 1600 Light assemblies or 1400 Heavy or, of course, an equivalent mix of the two.

Under company policy a minimum of 800 units of all kinds must be manufactured and the contribution from a Heavy must be twice that from a Light.

    (*a*) Show the above information in linear programming mathematical terms.

    (*b*) Using the graphical technique:

        (*i*) show the area of feasible solution; and
        (*ii*) find the optimum mix for the month.

    (*c*) Ignoring the company policy relating to the 800 minimum units, set up the initial Simplex tableau.

2. Interpret the following Simplex tableau:

PRODUCT	PROFIT	QUANTITY	A	B	C	S_1	S_2	S_3	S_4
S_3	0	5000							
A	2	8000							
C	10	400							
S_1	0	2000							
PROFIT (£)		0	2	3	10	0	0	0	0
Z		−20,000	0	−1½	0	0	−¾	0	−2

3. Multishop Ltd. is a trading group with a number of shops and depots. Two of their shops, Y and Z, have notified head office that they require 300 and 200 units respectively of a certain product for the next trading period. These shops can be supplied by any of three depots A, B and C which hold 100, 200 and 250 of these units respectively. The cost of supplying Y from the three depots is 4p, 7p and 2p per unit respectively, while the cost of similarly supplying Z is 6p, 4p and 4p.

How should the required deliveries of units be made? (To parallel suggested answer select BZ at start of first tableau transform).

4. Genoff Ltd. have appointed five new clerks A, B, C, D and E to fill the positions of cashier, invoice clerk, payroll clerk, cost clerk and general ledger clerk. In order to find the optimum assignment of people to posts all the clerks were given a test that covered the five areas of work involved. Each section of the test was marked out of 10 and the scores were as follows:

	Cashier	Invoicing	Payroll	Costing	General Ledger
A	3	3	1	3	5
B	5	8	9	4	4
C	1	9	10	2	7
D	5	5	9	6	7
E	5	5	4	5	6

What is the optimum assignment of people to posts?

CHAPTER XX

GAMES THEORY

In all our analytical studies so far we've assumed the data on which our decisions will be based is independent of those decisions—so that, for example, if we know a process costs £10 per hour to run, the process will not "deliberately" raise its cost to £12 if we decide to run it.

This convenient arrangement unfortunately does not necessarily hold in a competitive situation. We cannot, for example, base a pricing decision on our competitor's selling price, for the decision we make may very well result in our competitor changing his selling price. Where this sort of situation exists, that is where we must make decisions which will influence the decisions of others who are competing with us (and such competitors include anybody whose loss is our gain such as suppliers and labour force as well as other traders), we can say we are in a *games* situation.

Obviously games situations in which the very facts on which our decision depends will change with our decision are much more complex than situations where such basic facts remain unaffected by our decisions. Their full analysis, therefore, is beyond us at the moment. Nevertheless there are a few logical rules and general concepts that can give us improved insight into games situations in practice and this chapter briefly looks at these.

INTRODUCTION

First we must look at a few of the ideas that underlie games theory.

1. "He knows we know he knows we know he knows." The fundamental feature of games theory is the fact that each "player" has the ability to a greater or lesser extent of being able to *reproduce the reasoning of the other*. For example, assume that we, skilled in chess, are playing an equally skilled player. He moves his queen into a position where it can obviously be taken. However, we hesitate to take it since we know he knows it can be taken. So is it a trap? This is most unlikely, since, unless he has grossly underestimated our ability, he knows very well that we know he knows—or in other words, we know he knows we know he knows. And doubtless he knows we know he knows we know he knows. So what do we do?

2. A simple game. Imagine you are to share the cake shown in Fig. 39(*a*) with a "competitor." You've agreed the share-out shall be made by one of you cutting the cake into two sections and the other selecting one of the sections. Now it so happens that you like all parts of the cake equally, but he detests the part that's shaded. You agree to negotiate who shall do the cutting—a failure to agree at this point being resolved by the toss of a coin. What proportion of the cake can you guarantee to obtain for yourself?

To analyse this game logically consider how each of you would cut the cake. These cuts are illustrated in Fig. 39(*b*) and as can be seen, if he cuts it he'll arrange things so you'll select the section containing the shaded part by ensuring it involves just over half the whole cake, while if you cut it you'll arrange things so that to maximise the edible part of the cake for him he'll need to select the section containing just over $\frac{1}{3}$ of the cake. If you always tossed for cutting, then, he'd average:

$$\frac{(\text{just under } \frac{1}{2}) + (\text{just over } \frac{1}{3})}{2} = \frac{5}{12} \text{ of the cake.}$$

You could, then, at the beginning offer him just over $\frac{5}{12}$ of the cake, his section to contain no shaded part, and if he were an intelligent person he would accept your offer. You could, therefore, be sure of obtaining just under $\frac{7}{12}$ of the cake.

| | (*i*) He cuts. | (*ii*) You cut. |

(*a*) The cake to be shared.   (*b*) Strategical cuts.

Fig. 39.—*Game with a cake.*

Logical thinking of this sort underpins all games theory analyses.

3. Games theory terminology. Before we can develop discussion of this logical analysis we must define a few games theory terms.

(*a*) *Two-person game.* A competitive situation in which only two "players" (individuals, teams, or companies) are involved (as in the previous paragraph).

(*b*) *Zero-sum game.* A game in which the winner's winnings always equal the loser's losses. Note that the game in the previous paragraph was *not* a zero-sum game since your "winning" the shaded part of the cake would be no loss to your competitor as he has no wish to win that section.

(*c*) *Strategy.* This is *any* plan that a player has the option of adopting.

(*d*) *Pay-off.* The gain (or loss) to a player that follows from playing a given strategy (and will, of course, depend upon the strategies selected by his opponents).

(*e*) *Pay-off table.* A table showing for a given player all the pay-offs that can arise in a game. Such a table, then, must show the pay-off for every possible combination of playable strategies. In a two-person, zero-sum game constructing the pay-off table simply involves preparing a matrix with player A's strategies shown, by convention, in rows and player B's strategies in columns—each cell containing A's pay-off from the intersecting strategies. There is, of course, no need to prepare a second pay-off table for B since B's pay-offs are, in a zero-sum game, naturally identical to A's except that the sign is reversed.

(*f*) *Value of the game.* The value of a game is the average pay-off that would result if the game were played over and over again.

In the previous paragraph we were clearly looking at a two-person, non-zero-sum game where the methods of cutting the cake represented the strategies of the players and the value of the game was $\frac{7}{12}$ for you and $\frac{5}{12}$ for your opponent.

4. Practical limitation of games theory. In the main games theory has only been developed in terms of two-person, zero-sum games. However most competitive business situations involve more than two companies and, moreover, are virtually never zero-sum (a contract for which two companies are competing may be worth £50,000 to one and £70,000 to the other). Games theory, then, has limited direct practical application, but as we said earlier, the logic and concepts in the theory have definite value in analysing even the most complex of commercial game situations.

PURE STRATEGY GAMES

The simplest kind of game analysis relates to pure strategy games, and we start by looking at these sorts of games.

5. A typical pure strategy game. Imagine I've lost a bet with a friend and now owe him a free foreign holiday. I've agreed he shall select the *type* of holiday—seaside, mountains or city—by writing his choice on a piece of paper. I, meanwhile, will select the *country*—Spain, Italy or Portugal—by writing my choice on a piece of paper. We then swap papers and so find out where my friend is going. Clearly he will want the dearest holiday he can squeeze out of me and I will want him to have the cheapest possible. Before making our selection we both study the following holiday costs:

Spain:	sea £95	Italy:	sea £75	Portugal:	sea £85
	mountains £35		mountains £55		mountains £80
	city £100		city £60		city £40

What selection should each of us make?

6. The pay-off table. Constructing the pay-off table here is very simple—the pay-off to him is always the value of the holiday he wins and so we just reproduce the holiday cost data in the form of a games pay-off table (*see* Fig. 40(*a*)).

7. Maximin. To start our analysis let us first study the pay-off table from the point of view of my friend. Clearly a Spanish city holiday is the ideal for him, but if he writes down "city" he could end up with a £40 Portuguese holiday. It makes sense for him, then, to note the *minimum* he would get from each of his strategies (*see* MINIMUM column Fig. 40(*b*)). Now if he identifies the maximum of these minima (£75 in this case) and selects the associated strategy ("sea"), he guarantees himself a holiday of at least this value. And we refer to the *maximum of the minima* as the *maximin*. We have, then, a maximin of £75.

8. Minimax. Now let's look at the table from my point of view. The Spanish mountains at £35 is what I want, but selecting Spain could cost me £100 if he selects "city." So it makes sense for me to note the *maximum* each of my strategies could cost me (*see* MAXIMUM row Fig. 40(*b*)) and select the strategy with the *minimum* of these. This means I'd select "Italy," and the value of this *minimum of the maxima* is known as the *minimax*. In this case the minimax is £75.

He selects:	I select: SPAIN	ITALY	PORTUGAL
SEA	95	75	85
MOUNTAINS	35	55	80
CITY	100	60	40

(*a*) Holiday pay-off table.

He selects:	I select: SPAIN	ITALY	PORTUGAL	MINIMUM
SEA	95	75	85	75 ⟵MAXIMIN
MOUNTAINS	35	55	80	35
CITY	100	60	40	40
MAXIMUM	100	75	85	

MINIMAX

(*b*) Game analysis. Since the maximin and minimax are the same amount (75) then the game has a saddlepoint (SEA/ITALY) and is, therefore, a pure strategy game. The two strategies are: He selects SEA, I select ITALY.

FIG. 40.—*Pure strategy game.*

9. Saddlepoint. Having identified the maximin and the minimax the next step in our analysis is to compare them. *If they are the same* then we say the game has a *saddlepoint*, the saddlepoint being identified as the point where the maximin and minimax strategies intersect.

Since the maximin and the minimax in our illustration *are* the same we have a saddlepoint—and this saddlepoint is at the place where the two respective strategies intersect, namely "sea" and "Italy."

10. Pure strategy game. A *pure strategy game* is one in which it always pays the players to keep to the same strategy. If a game has a saddlepoint then it will be a pure strategy game—the appropriate strategies of each player being indicated by the saddlepoint.

Our game, then, is a pure strategy game. The validity of this conclusion can easily be seen by envisaging what would happen if one of us deviated from the correct pure strategy. If, for example, he stuck to playing his correct strategy "sea," I could only lose by selecting anything else but "Italy." Similarly, if I kept to "Italy" he could only lose by not selecting "sea." Only a foolish gambler would, therefore, deviate from his correct strategy on the rather remote chance that his opponent was an equally foolish gambler. But games theory is essentially for intelligent businessmen rather than foolish gamblers.

It should be noted as a matter of interest that if a game has a saddlepoint there is, in fact, no need for intelligent players to play it at all since the saddlepoint will indicate the only feasible strategy for either player. In this case there is no need for any writing on papers—inevitably my friend will be spending his holiday by the sea in Italy.

11. Value of the game. The value of a pure strategy game is given by the saddlepoint. In this case, then, it is £75 (which is obviously correct since every time the game is "played" my friend will win—and I'll pay for—a £75 holiday).

MIXED STRATEGY GAMES

There are frequently occasions when a pure strategy game is not called for and when players must mix their strategies. We must now consider these kinds of games.

12. Initial analysis of a game. First it must be made clear that *all* game analyses must start by finding the maximin and minimax and checking to see if there is a saddlepoint. If there is, the analysis is complete. Only if there is no saddlepoint does the analysis extend to a mixed strategy analysis.

13. Mixed strategy games. If a game has no saddlepoint then players must mix their strategies and play a *mixed strategy game*. Look, for example, at the following game:

B secretly writes £3 or £4 on a piece of paper and A guesses the amount. If he guesses correctly he is paid the amount written; if he guesses wrongly he is paid nothing.

In this situation B may reason that by writing £3 he will stand to lose less than by writing £4. However, if A correctly reproduces B's reasoning he will know just what B will write—and he'll guess, and win, £3. Conversely if A decides to go for the "big" win of £4 and B realises this then he'll write £3 and A will lose. And even if neither out-thinks the other but one adopts a pure strategy, it will not take the other long to observe this and select his own strategy accordingly. So it is imperative for both players to mix their strategies.

14. Analysis of a mixed strategy game. Analysis of all games starts by checking to see if there is a saddlepoint. In this case we find we have a maximin of 0 and a minimax of 3 (*see* Fig. 41). There is, then, no saddlepoint so we move to the next stage of the analysis which involves finding the proportion of time a player should use a given strategy. To ascertain this in the case where each player has only two strategies we write against each strategy *the difference between the two pay-offs relating to the* ALTERNATIVE *strategy*. For example, looking at A's "guess £3" strategy we see the pay-offs of the alternative, "guess £4," strategy are 0 and 4—and since the difference between these is 4 we write "4" opposite the £3 strategy of A. We can, then, list the appropriate differences as follows:

Strategy considered	Differences between pay-offs of alternative strategies
A's "guess £3"	0 and 4 = 4
A's "guess £4"	3 and 0 = 3
B's "write £3"	0 and 4 = 4
B's "write £4"	3 and 0 = 3

We can, then, complete our analysis as in Fig. 41 which tells us that A should guess £3 four times out of seven and £4 three times, while B should write £3 and £4 four and three times out of seven respectively.

	B writes: £3 £4		MINIMUM	A's MIX
A guesses: £3	3	0	0	4
£4	0	4	0	3
MAXIMUM	3	4		
B's MIX	4	3		7

FIG. 41.—*Mixed strategy game. Maximin = 0. Minimax = 3. Maximin does not equal minimax so there is no saddlepoint. Final analysis shows both A and B must select £3 and £4 in the ratio of 4 : 3.*

15. Selecting a strategy for a specific game. Knowing our strategy proportions is all very well, but how does one know just which strategy to play in a specific game? Using a formula or rule of thumb can, of course, be very dangerous since if our opponent can deduce our method we will be no better off than if we had used a pure strategy. The escape from this quandary is to use random numbers to select our strategy. Thus A, faced with guessing £3 or £4 in the ratio of 4:3 could designate digits 1, 2, 3 and 4 as representing "guess £3" and digits 5, 6 and 7 as representing "guess £4" (and disregard digits 8, 9 and 0). Looking up a digit in a random number table would, then, indicate which strategy he should play.

Note that using this method:

(*a*) It is impossible for his opponent to deduce his, A's, strategy.

(*b*) Over a large number of games A will guess £3 and £4 in the required ratio of 4:3.

16. Value of a mixed strategy game. To find the value of a mixed strategy game the following procedures should be adopted:

(*a*) Select arbitrarily a particular strategy of a particular player (*e.g.* B's strategy "write £4").

(*b*) Find the average pay-off that will result if the second player plays his correct mixed strategies continuously against the selected strategy of the first player. This average pay-off will be the value of the game; *e.g.* if A guessed £3 and

£4 in the ratio of 4:3 while B always wrote £4, the average pay-off would be:

$$\frac{£0 \times 4 + £4 \times 3}{7} = \frac{£12}{7}$$

NOTE: This procedure is a purely *mathematical* one for finding the value of the game—it in no way implies the game would actually be played that way (for obvious reasons). Note, too, the value can also be found by probability theory since the expectation of A winning if both players play their correct optimum strategy is:

A guesses £3 AND B writes £3 to gain £3 win $= \dfrac{4}{7} \times \dfrac{4}{7} \times 3 = \dfrac{48}{49}$

A guesses £4 AND B writes £4 to gain £4 win $= \dfrac{3}{7} \times \dfrac{3}{7} \times 4 = \dfrac{36}{49}$

TOTAL $= \dfrac{12}{7}$

17. Significance of the value of the game. The value of a mixed strategy game gives the average pay-off that would follow if each player played his optimum strategy. We can see from the value, then, who would win in the long run and his average winnings per game. In the above game, for example, A would win $\dfrac{£12}{7}$ per game. If the game is to be a "fair" game, therefore, A must pay B $\dfrac{£12}{7}$ for the right to play a game.

The value of a game, however, not only indicates the fair playing price but also gives the *optimum* pay-off, for provided one of the players keeps to his computed mixed strategies it is inevitable that he will ensure winnings or limit his losses to the game value. Conversely, if his opponent keeps to his computed mixed strategy, a player who deviates from his own correct strategy will be unable to improve on his winnings (employing the probability calculation approach demonstrated in the previous paragraph you can show that as long as one player keeps to the correct strategy no changing of the mix by the other player will alter the expectation).

18. Dominance. In games theory, dominance arises whenever one of a player's strategies is better in every respect than another of his strategies—which means the latter strategy should *never* be played and therefore can be deleted from the analysis. An example of dominance arises in Fig. 40, for there it can be seen that my friend should never select "mountains," for whatever country I select he would always be better off if he'd selected "sea." Thus the "sea" strategy dominates the "mountains" strategy which consequently can be deleted.

If at first glance a game appears too complex for analysis, a careful study of the pay-off table will often reveal a dominated strategy which can be deleted so making the game simpler to handle.

PROGRESS TEST 20

1. Charles and I both belong to the Upper and Lower Clubs. He goes to one club or the other every Friday night. I can either stay at home or visit one of the clubs—and in the latter event I decide which club to visit simply on the basis of where I think Charles will be, because if I can catch him I can always talk the poor devil into buying drinks, which cost him £4 at the Upper Club but only £1 at the Lower Club. I understand Charles selects his club for the night solely with the object of avoiding me, and, what's more, the crafty Scrooge has been taking a course in Games Theory to improve his rate of success. I'm wondering now how often I ought to visit the Upper Club and, what's more, since the subscription is twenty guineas a year, whether it wouldn't pay me to give up my membership.

CHAPTER XXI

EXPONENTIAL SMOOTHING

Exponential smoothing is a statistical averaging technique (and strictly speaking should appear in a statistics book rather than an operational research book—but the tendency of examiners to include exponential smoothing questions in operational research papers warrants its brief mention here). It is, in fact, no more than a special kind of moving average.

1. Defect of a normal moving average.

A normal moving average is computed by adding the actual figures in a time series and then dividing by the number of periods (*see Statistics,* 2nd edition, Chapter VI in this HANDBOOK series). It is at once obvious that the earliest figure involved in computing such an average carries just as much weight as the latest. This is an unfortunate feature of the average, since the later figures will tend to reflect the more up-to-date average of the series and it would be better if they could be given more weight than the earlier figures in the calculation.

2. Exponential weighting.

One way of achieving this desirable end would be to simply allocate straightforward progressively increasing weights to the figures in the series—for example, if we wanted a 5-period moving average we could allocate weights of 1, 2, 3, 4 and 5 to the five consecutive figures involved in the computation. Note, incidentally, the last step would require us to divide the weighted total by the sum of the weights (*see Statistics* again)—in this case by $1 + 2 + 3 + 4 + 5 = 15$.

Exponential weighting is, however, a neater and easier method of achieving such a progressive form of weighting. In this technique all one does each period is to suitably weight and then add together the current figure and the *previous period's moving average*. This computation gives the new period's moving average.

3. The smoothing constant. The key figure in this simply-applied technique is called the *smoothing constant* (symbolised as α). The selection of a value for this constant gives the selector a measure of control over the degree of smoothing induced in the series. The value must, however, always lie between 0 and 1. The effect of different values is discussed below after the operation of the technique has been demonstrated.

4. Exponentially smoothing a series. A series is exponentially smoothed by applying the following formula:

New moving average = [Current actual figure in series $\times$ α] + [Previous average $\times$ $(1 - \alpha)$]

EXAMPLE: Exponentially smooth the series shown in column 2 of Fig. 42(a) (using a smoothing constant α of 0·2).

Since the period 1 actual is 500, the period "average" is obviously 500 too. Period 2, then, will be $(700 \times 0\cdot2) + 500 \times (1 - 0\cdot2) = 540$. The moving averages for the subsequent periods are similarly calculated and shown in the end column of Fig. 42(a).

5. Selecting the smoothing constant value. The selection of the value of α depends on how much weight it is desired to give later periods relative to earlier periods. As a quick calculation will show giving α a value of 0 means the moving average will always be the first figure in the series (since all the later figures will be multiplied by 0 before being incorporated in the average), while a value of 1 means the average will always be the last figure (since all previous "averages" will be multiplied by 0). This means that the higher α is, the greater the weightings of the later figures. The effect of using, for example, a smoothing constant of 0·8 in the series shown in Fig. 42(a) is demonstrated in Fig. 42(b).

Although a high smoothing constant keeps the average more closely aligned to the actual figures it suffers the disadvantage that it does little to smooth the series and is unduly influenced by random variations. Consequently in practice α is generally chosen so that it lies between 0·1 and 0·3.

Period	Actual figure	Exponentially smoothed moving average (To nearest whole number)	
1	500	Actual Figure	= 500
2	700	[700 × 0·2] + [500 × (1 − 0·2)]	= 540
3	600	[600 × 0·2] + [540 × (1 − 0·2)]	= 552
4	550	[550 × 0·2] + [552 × (1 − 0·2)]	= 552
5	900	[900 × 0·2] + [552 × (1 − 0·2)]	= 622
6	1300	[1300 × 0·2] + [622 × (1 − 0·2)]	= 758

(a) Smoothing a given series with a smoothing constant of 0·2.

Period	Average	
1	Actual figure	= 500
2	[700 × 0·8] + [500 × (1 − 0·8)]	= 660
3	[600 × 0·8] + [660 × (1 − 0·8)]	= 612
4	[550 × 0·8] + [612 × (1 − 0·8)]	= 562
5	[900 × 0·8] + [562 × (1 − 0·8)]	= 832
6	[1300 × 0·8] + [832 × (1 − 0·8)]	= 1206

(b) Smoothing previous series using 0·8 smoothing constant.

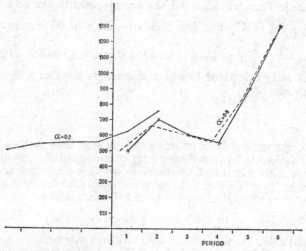

(c) Graph of actual values in the series and the two exponentially-weighted moving averages.

FIG. 42.—*Exponential smoothing.*

6. Sum of the weights in exponential smoothing. Some statistically-minded students may be a little worried that the procedure for computing an exponentially-weighted average omits a division by the sum of the weights. However, the formula for the exponentially weighted average is such that the sum of the weights is 1—as the reader who tackled question 4 in Progress Test 4 will appreciate. Since dividing by 1 does not alter the figure on which the division is carried out the step is "omitted" in the smoothing procedure.

7. Plotting an exponentially smoothed average. Students of statistics are always told they must be very careful where they plot a moving average. In the case of an ordinary moving average this has to be at the mid-point of the period covered by the average. Where, however, can one plot an exponentially smoothed moving average?

The answer to this question is that the average must be plotted with a $\dfrac{1 - \alpha}{\alpha}$ period *lag* (*i.e.* prior to the current period). Thus, when α is 0·2, the average must be plotted with a $\dfrac{1 - 0·2}{0·2} = 4$ period lag. Similarly, an α of 0·8 requires a $\dfrac{1 - 0·8}{0·8} = \dfrac{1}{4}$ period lag. Fig. 42(*c*) shows the plotting of our previously calculated two sets of averages together with the original series.

8. Forecasting from an exponentially smoothed average. If it is desired to forecast figures from an exponentially smoothed average then it is first necessary to determine a period trend value. Once this is done by whatever technique the forecaster may elect to use, the forecast is made by first extrapolating the last average up to the current period (*i.e.* adding "$\dfrac{1 - \alpha}{\alpha} \times$ trend value" to the last average) and then extrapolating on to the required future period (*i.e.* adding a further trend value $\times$ number of periods that the required period lies ahead).

PROGRESS TEST 21

1. Exponentially smooth (to two decimal places) the following series of period figures using a 0·25 smoothing constant: 8, 12, 15, 14, 17, 20, 25, 23, 28, 30, 33.

On the basis of a 2·5 period trend estimate, forecast values for the next two periods.

APPENDIXES

APPENDIX 1

EXPONENTIAL VALUES

x	e^x	e^{-x}
0·02	1·0202	0·9802
0·04	1·0408	0·9608
0·06	1·0618	0·9418
0·08	1·0833	0·9231
0·10	1·1052	0·9048
0·11	1·1163	0·8958
0·12	1·1275	0·8869
0·13	1·1388	0·8781
0·14	1·1503	0·8694
0·15	1·1618	0·8607
0·16	1·1735	0·8521
0·17	1·1853	0·8437
0·18	1·1972	0·8353
0·19	1·2092	0·8270
0·20	1·2214	0·8187
0·21	1·2337	0·8106
0·22	1·2461	0·8025
0·23	1·2586	0·7945
0·24	1·2712	0·7866
0·25	1·2840	0·7788
0·26	1·2969	0·7711
0·27	1·3100	0·7634
0·28	1·3231	0·7558
0·29	1·3364	0·7483

x	e^x	e^{-x}
0·30	1·3499	0·7408
0·31	1·3634	0·7335
0·32	1·3771	0·7261
0·33	1·3910	0·7189
0·34	1·4050	0·7118
0·35	1·4191	0·7047
0·36	1·4333	0·6977
0·37	1·4477	0·6907
0·38	1·4623	0·6839
0·39	1·4770	0·6771
0·40	1·4918	0·6703
0·41	1·5068	0·6636
0·42	1·5220	0·6570
0·43	1·5373	0·6505
0·44	1·5527	0·6440
0·45	1·5683	0·6376
0·46	1·5841	0·6313
0·47	1·6000	0·6250
0·48	1·6161	0·6188
0·49	1·6323	0·6126
0·50	1·6487	0·6065
0·60	1·8221	0·5488
0·70	2·0138	0·4966
0·80	2·2255	0·4493
0·90	2·4596	0·4066

x	e^x	e^{-x}
1·0	2·7183	0·3679
1·1	3·0042	0·3329
1·2	3·3201	0·3012
1·3	3·6693	0·2725
1·4	4·0552	0·2466
1·5	4·4817	0·2231
1·6	4·9530	0·2019
1·7	5·4739	0·1827
1·8	6·0497	0·1653
1·9	6·6859	0·1496
2·0	7·3891	0·1353
2·1	8·1662	0·1225
2·2	9·0250	0·1108
2·3	9·9742	0·1003
2·4	11·023	0·0907
2·5	12·182	0·0821
2·6	13·464	0·0743
2·7	14·880	0·0672
2·8	16·445	0·0608
2·9	18·174	0·0550
3·0	20·085	0·0498
3·1	22·198	0·0450
3·2	24·532	0·0408
3·3	27·113	0·0369
3·4	29·964	0·0334

x	e^x	e^{-x}
3·5	33·115	0·0302
3·6	36·598	0·0273
3·7	40·447	0·0247
3·8	44·701	0·0224
3·9	49·402	0·0202
4·0	54·598	0·0183
4·1	60·340	0·0166
4·2	66·686	0·0150
4·3	73·700	0·0136
4·4	81·451	0·0123
4·5	90·017	0·0111
4·6	99·484	0·0100
4·7	109·95	0·00910
4·8	121·51	0·00823
4·9	134·29	0·00745
5·0	148·41	0·00674
5·1	164·02	0·00610
5·2	181·27	0·00552
5·3	200·34	0·00499
5·4	221·41	0·00452
5·5	244·69	0·00409
5·6	270·43	0·00370
5·7	298·87	0·00335
5·8	330·30	0·00303
5·9	365·04	0·00274
6·0	403·43	0·00248

RANDOM NUMBERS

05858	78210	09287	00009	61147	20482	71797	27159	98336	31938
69771	09735	00656	66214	07977	90029	80831	51618	43888	27336
47831	16079	92331	36444	80659	59991	67358	45638	89427	86607
26338	56443	84299	39328	23229	17073	64889	91229	52082	93342
50975	00398	91290	38684	62113	81710	36105	97136	96896	69298
91865	63682	15919	30415	19312	92798	91594	41117	51038	10012
47232	31544	65278	21163	52880	76850	96354	88210	73185	65912
80614	01402	77979	68944	49254	10563	25234	50041	89506	48441
58279	28347	91842	01549	83729	24749	19012	05056	57865	23525
01274	84685	29684	85021	24511	21108	79646	21015	12544	03452
80239	50800	80285	77560	38258	47492	54533	65726	10806	86451
82606	04734	89479	73340	48828	07527	63980	62640	07544	79488
23987	39758	10429	72572	95846	12260	37124	77395	58374	52611
42053	81580	74717	92003	50640	33821	78506	23315	40243	29904
67565	53427	70514	51303	33566	62521	62237	98610	21451	92641
25916	52499	82893	53860	97540	60487	35197	24491	30004	97277
83265	57092	15374	97997	50951	69691	47331	58129	00093	02857
32302	20854	36943	62515	51985	21436	34791	06716	46371	11335
54315	67390	90354	30571	32065	54442	60270	16054	01527	11474
62629	33592	19845	15715	10325	98776	73118	37987	63807	90224
00158	62981	15279	99025	45789	94853	58727	67769	55471	85688
55185	51872	56397	16441	91586	25696	57841	16028	37720	78916
99854	67007	73619	72347	30789	41691	47109	90774	53268	29392
11512	54189	81503	30503	17028	27596	26623	32674	93479	48217
16758	25618	71319	63673	88337	04053	66070	99310	33215	35275
91766	23325	38907	07476	42553	06899	70293	02352	35230	61402
86963	92962	93562	83355	03063	48759	40768	91387	02926	67706
99508	12314	42080	16966	65292	94222	14905	07045	75733	72137
45038	69548	05961	22126	44082	02233	45140	75578	95540	97012
73273	24201	11029	19814	74990	10343	75464	58187	76364	59449
65153	23717	45349	22218	20860	40387	50430	38611	52512	65142
58791	80665	65948	55645	80190	20034	05251	83245	79194	46852
54075	06040	07083	16012	29042	26103	03489	54566	67181	83641
43742	40869	36107	80737	49387	38073	07584	68739	42435	68805
77319	39531	12505	89042	18142	47322	32160	07432	47276	20228
48719	38945	92765	31827	81260	55396	81441	60743	10816	14958
76564	04577	89917	24760	62441	96534	41500	90128	13142	06463
12128	25590	75917	81812	03265	00029	21362	80119	85620	87281
33334	19816	89493	39607	35203	37985	38430	45498	93798	50284
81117	11995	04007	32506	63084	78787	58363	99221	14220	07647

EXAMINATION TECHNIQUE

To pass any examination you must:

1. Have the knowledge.
2. Convince the examiner you have the knowledge.
3. Convince him within the time allowed.

In the book so far we have considered the first of these only. Success in the other two respects will be much more assured if you apply the examination hints given below.

1. Answer the question. Apart from ignorance, *failure to answer the question is undoubtedly the greatest bar to success.* No matter how often students are told, they always seem to be guilty of this fault. If you are asked to use difference equations then *don't* use a step-by-step technique; if asked when you would run a simulation *don't* describe how you would run one. You can write a hundred pages of brilliant exposition, but if it's not in answer to the set question you will be given no more marks than if it had been a paragraph of utter drivel. To ensure you answer the question:

(a) *Read the question carefully.*
(b) *Decide what the examiner wants.*
(c) *Do just what the examiner asks.*
(d) *Keep returning to the question as you work on the answer.*

2. Put your ideas in logical order. It is quicker, more accurate and gives a greater impression of competence if you follow a pre-determined logical path instead of jumping about from place to place as ideas come to you.

3. Maximise the points you make. Examiners are more impressed by a solid mass of points than an unending development of one solitary idea—no matter how sophisticated and exhaustive. Do not allow yourself to become bogged down with your favourite hobby-horse.

4. Allocate your time. Question marks often bear a close relationship to the time needed for an appropriate answer. Consequently the time spent on a question should be in proportion to the marks. Divide the total exam marks into the total exam time (less planning time) to obtain a "minutes per mark" figure, and allow that many minutes per mark of each individual question.

5. Attempt all questions asked for. Always remember that the first 50% of the marks for any question is the easier to earn. Unless you are working in complete ignorance, you will always earn more marks per minute while answering a new question than while continuing to answer one that is more than half done. So you can earn many more marks by half-completing two answers than by completing either one individually.

6. Don't show your ignorance. Concentrate on displaying your knowledge—not your ignorance. There is almost always one question you need to attempt and are not happy about. In answer to such a question put down all you *do* know—and then devote the unused time to improving some other answer. Certainly you will not get full marks by doing this, but nor will you if you fill your page with nonsense. By spending the saved time on another answer you will at least be gaining the odd mark or so.

7. If time runs out. What should you do if you find time is running out? The following are the recommended tactics:

(*a*) If it is a mathematical answer, do not bother to work out the figures. Show the examiner by means of your layout that you know what steps need to be taken and which pieces of data are applicable. He is very much more concerned with this than with your ability to calculate.

(*b*) If it is an essay answer, put down your answer in the form of notes. It is surprising what a large percentage of the question marks can be obtained by a dozen terse, relevant notes.

(*c*) Make sure that every question and question part has some answer—no matter how short—that summarises the key elements.

(*d*) Don't worry. Shortage of time is more often a sign of knowing too much than too little.

8. Avoid panic, but welcome "nerves." "Nerves" are a great aid in examinations. Being nervous enables one to work at a much more concentrated pitch for a longer time without fatigue. Panic, on the other hand, destroys one's judgment. To avoid panic:

(*a*) Know your subject (this is your best "panic-killer").

(*b*) Give yourself a generous time allowance to read the paper. Quick starters are usually poor performers.

(*c*) Take two or three deep breaths.

(*d*) Concentrate simply on maximising your marks. Leave considerations of passing or failing until afterwards.

(*e*) Answer the easiest questions first—it helps to build confidence.

(*f*) Do not let first impressions of the paper upset you. Given a few minutes, it is amazing what one's subconscious will throw up. Moreover it is often only the unfamiliar presentation of data that makes a question look difficult: once you have looked carefully at it, it often shows itself to be quite simple.

PROGRESS TESTS—SUGGESTED SOLUTIONS

Progress Test 2

1. $y = 64 \times 8^{-\frac{5}{3}} + (64 \times 8)^{-\frac{5}{3}} + 3^{0 \cdot 5 \times 8} = 64 \times \dfrac{1}{\sqrt[3]{8^5}}$

$$+ \dfrac{1}{\sqrt[3]{(64 \times 8)^5}} + 3^4$$

$$= \dfrac{64}{32} + \dfrac{1}{32768} + 81 = 83\dfrac{1}{32768}$$

2. $h = (1 \times 7) + (2 \times 3) + (3 \times 5) + (4 \times 2) + (5 \times 1)$
$$= \underline{\underline{41}}$$

3.

When $r = 1$ then $a_r = 6 - 1 = 5$ and
$r^{r-3} = 1^{1-3} = 1^{-2} = 1$ ∴ $a_r r^{r-3} = 5 \times 1 = \underline{5}$

When $r = 2$ then $a_r = 6 - 2 = 4$ and
$r^{r-3} = 2^{2-3} = 2^{-1} = \frac{1}{2}$ ∴ $a_r r^{r-3} = 4 \times \frac{1}{2} = \underline{2}$

When $r = 3$ then $a_r = 6 - 3 = 3$ and
$r^{r-3} = 3^{3-3} = 3^0 = 1$ ∴ $a_r r^{r-3} = 3 \times 1 = \underline{3}$

When $r = 4$ then $a_r = 6 - 4 = 2$ and
$r^{r-3} = 4^{4-3} = 4^1 = 4$ ∴ $a_r r^{r-3} = 2 \times 4 = \underline{8}$

When $r = 5$ then $a_r = 6 - 5 = 1$ and
$r^{r-3} = 5^{5-3} = 5^2 = 25$ ∴ $a_r r^{r-3} = 1 \times 25 = \underline{25}$

$$\therefore L = \sum_{r=1}^{5} a_r r^{r-3} = \underline{\underline{43}}$$

4. When $i = 1$, $\displaystyle\sum_{j=2}^{4} ij = (1 \times 2) + (1 \times 3) + (1 \times 4) = 9$

When $i = 2$, $\displaystyle\sum_{j=2}^{4} ij = (2 \times 2) + (2 \times 3) + (2 \times 4) = 18$

When $i = 3$, $\displaystyle\sum_{j=2}^{4} ij = (3 \times 2) + (3 \times 3) + (3 \times 4) = 27$

$$\therefore \sum_{i=1}^{3} \sum_{j=2}^{4} ij = \underline{\underline{54}}$$

5. First $e^{-1\cdot2} = 0\cdot3012$ (from Table Appendix I)

(i) So when $x = 0$, $P(x) = e^{-1\cdot2}\dfrac{1\cdot2^0}{0!} = 0\cdot3012 \times 1$
$$= \underline{\underline{0\cdot3012}}$$

(ii) So when $x = 1$, $P(x) = e^{-1\cdot2}\dfrac{1\cdot2^1}{1!} = 0\cdot3012 \times \dfrac{1\cdot2}{1}$
$$= \underline{\underline{0\cdot3614}}$$

(iii) When $x = 2$, $P(x) = e^{-1\cdot2}\dfrac{1\cdot2^2}{2!} = 0\cdot3012 \times \dfrac{1\cdot44}{2 \times 1}$
$$= \underline{\underline{0\cdot2169}}$$

(iv) When $x = 3$, $P(x) = e^{-1\cdot2}\dfrac{1\cdot2^3}{3!} = 0\cdot3012 \times \dfrac{1\cdot728}{3 \times 2 \times 1}$
$$= \underline{\underline{0\cdot0867}}$$

(v) When $x = 4$, $P(x) = e^{-1\cdot2}\dfrac{1\cdot2^4}{4!} = 0\cdot3012$
$$\times \dfrac{2\cdot0736}{4 \times 3 \times 2 \times 1}$$
$$= \underline{\underline{0\cdot0260}}$$

6. If $n = 5$ and $p = \frac{1}{2}$, then $P(x \leqslant 2)$
$$= \sum_{x=0}^{2} \binom{5}{x} (\tfrac{1}{2})^x (1 - \tfrac{1}{2})^{n-x}$$
$$= \sum_{x=0}^{2} \binom{5}{x} (\tfrac{1}{2})^x (\tfrac{1}{2})^{n-x}$$

When $x = 0$, $\binom{5}{x}(\tfrac{1}{2})^x(\tfrac{1}{2})^{n-x} = \dfrac{5!}{(5-0)!0!} \times (\tfrac{1}{2})^0 \times (\tfrac{1}{2})^{5-0}$
$$= \dfrac{1}{32}$$

When $x = 1$, $\binom{5}{x}(\tfrac{1}{2})^x(\tfrac{1}{2})^{n-x} = \dfrac{5!}{(5-1)!1!} \times (\tfrac{1}{2})^1 \times (\tfrac{1}{2})^{5-1}$
$$= \dfrac{5}{32}$$

When $x = 2$, $\binom{5}{x}(\tfrac{1}{2})^x(\tfrac{1}{2})^{n-x} = \dfrac{5!}{(5-2)!2!} \times (\tfrac{1}{2})^2 \times (\tfrac{1}{2})^{5-2}$
$$= \dfrac{10}{32}$$

$$\therefore \sum_{x=0}^{2} \binom{5}{x}(\tfrac{1}{2})^x(\tfrac{1}{2})^{n-x} = P(x \leqslant 2) = \dfrac{16}{32} = \underline{\underline{\tfrac{1}{2}}}$$

Progress Test 3

1. (a) *See* Fig. 43(a). As these curves are straight lines they are referred to as *linear curves*.

(b) *See* Fig. 43(b).

(c) *See* Fig. 43(c). This is called an exponential curve and is very much used in problems of growth.

(d) *See* Fig. 43(d). This is called a negative exponential curve and is used in problems relating to decay.

(e) *See* Fig. 43(e). This is a binomial distribution. Since, as we will see later, x can only take discrete values (whole numbers) rectangles are plotted rather than a line curve.

(f) *See* Fig. 43(b). This is a Poisson distribution. Again, x can only take discrete values.

(g) *See* Fig. 43(g). This is called a Gompertz curve. It can sometimes be used to depict the growth of a new product or project where in the long-term growth is limited to a definite ceiling.

(h) *See* Fig. 43(h). This is, of course, a normal curve. The various values of y can be calculated as follows:

Since $\sigma = 1$ and $\bar{x} = 0$,

$$\text{then } y = \frac{1}{\sigma\sqrt{2\pi}}\, e^{-\frac{1}{2}\left(\frac{x-\bar{x}}{\sigma}\right)^2} = \frac{1}{1 \times \sqrt{2\pi}}\, e^{-\frac{1}{2}\left(\frac{x-0}{1}\right)^2}$$

$$= \frac{1}{2\cdot5}\, e^{-\frac{x^2}{2}}$$

Value of x	x^2	$\dfrac{x^2}{2}$	$e^{-\frac{x^2}{2}}$ (from Appendix I)	$\frac{1}{2\cdot5}e^{-\frac{x^2}{2}}$ ($= y$)
-3	9·00	4·500	0·0111	0·0044
$-2\frac{1}{2}$	6·25	3·125	0·0440*	0·0176
-2	4·00	2·000	0·1353	0·0541
$-1\frac{1}{2}$	2·25	1·125	0·3247*	0·1299
-1	1·00	0·500	0·6065	0·2426
$-\frac{1}{2}$	0·25	0·125	0·8825*	0·3530
0	0	0	1·0000	0·4000
$+\frac{1}{2}$	0·25			0·3530
$+1$	1·00			0·2426
$+1\frac{1}{2}$	2·25	CURVE		0·1299
$+2$	4·00	SYMMETRICAL		0·0541
$+2\frac{1}{2}$	6·25			0·0176
$+3$	9·00			0·0044

* By interpolation.

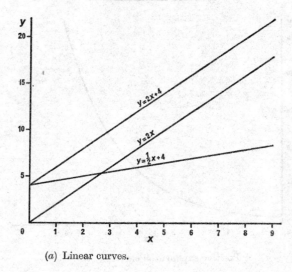

(a) Linear curves.

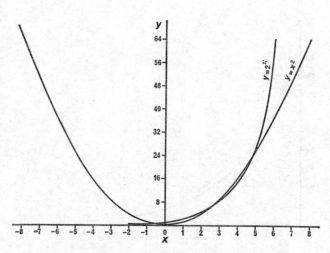

(b) x^2 and 2^x curves.

FIG. 43.—*Mathematical curves.*

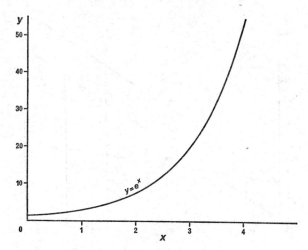

(c) Positive exponential curve.

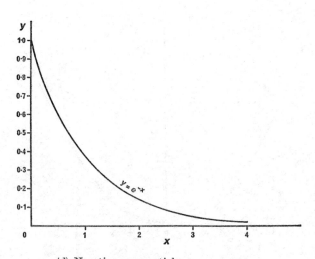

(d) Negative exponential curve.

FIG. 43.—*Mathematical curves.*

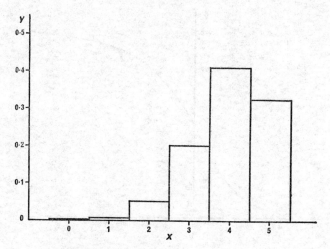

(e) Binomial distribution — n = 5, p = 0·8.

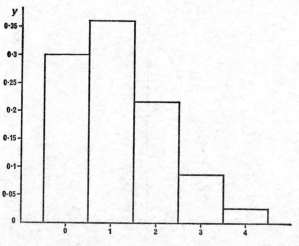

(f) Poisson distribution — a = 1·2.

Fig. 43.—*Mathematical curves.*

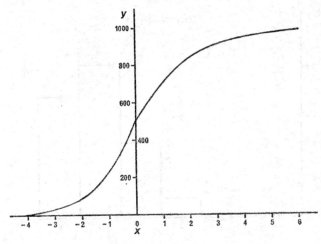

(g) Gompertz curve.

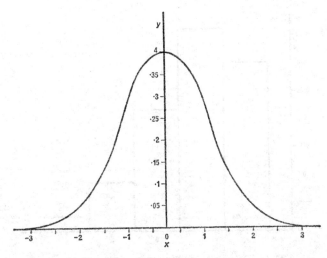

(h) Normal curve.

FIG. 43.—*Mathematical curves.*

Progress Test 4

1. (a) Sum of series $= \dfrac{20 + 100}{2} \times 21 = \underline{\underline{1260}}$

(b) This is a combination of two series 5, 10, 15, . . . 45 and 7, 12, 17, . . . 47. The sum, then,

$$= \frac{5 + 45}{2} \times 9 + \frac{7 + 47}{2} \times 9 = \underline{\underline{468}}$$

2. (a) The hash total is the sum of the three separate arithmetic progressions formed by the serial numbers of the used requisitions.

Hash total, then $= \left(\dfrac{132 + 145}{2} \times 14 \right) +$

$$\left(\frac{288 + 296}{2} \times 9 \right) + \left(\frac{344 + 377}{2} \times 34 \right)$$

$$= 1939 + 2628 + 12{,}257$$
$$= \underline{\underline{16{,}824}}$$

(b)

    (i) $16{,}824 - 16{,}461 = 363$
                 ∴ Requisition 363 missing.
    (ii) $17{,}121 - 16{,}824 = 297$
                 ∴ Requisition 297 included by mistake.
    (iii) $16{,}824 - 14{,}196 = 2628$
                 ∴ 200 series missing.

3. This is a geometric progression with a constant term of 1·4 (*i.e.* costs each year are 1·4 times those of previous year).
∴ 16th year (*i.e.* 17th term) $= 2000 \times 1{\cdot}4^{17-1} \simeq \underline{\underline{\pounds 440{,}000}}$

4. Let $b = (1 - a)$ So $A_t = ax_t + bA_{t-1}$
Expanding the formula we obtain:
$A_t = ax_t + b(ax_{t-1} + b[ax_{t-2} + b\{ax_{t-3} + b(\ldots$
Removing brackets:
$A_t = ax_t + abx_{t-1} + ab^2x_{t-2} + ab^3x_{t-3} \ldots$
Considering the weights only, then, we have the series: a, ab, ab^2, ab^3 . . . which is a geometric progression with constant b. Now where the constant is less than 1 the sum of a geometric progression to infinity is $\dfrac{\text{1st term}}{1 - \text{constant}}$ (*see* **5**)

∴ Sum of weights $= \dfrac{a}{1 - b}$

But $b = 1 - a$.

$\therefore$ Sum of weights $= \dfrac{a}{1 - (1 - a)} = \dfrac{a}{a} = \underline{\underline{1}}$

Progress Test 5

1. (a) $\displaystyle\sum_{i=0}^{4} \binom{4}{i} = 1 + 4 + 6 + 4 + 1 = 16$

   (b) $\displaystyle\sum_{i=0}^{6} \binom{6}{i} = 1 + 6 + 15 + 20 + 15 + 6 + 1 = 64$

2. (a) Permutation of 7 items taking 7 at a time $= {}^7P_7 = 7!$
   $$= 5040$$

   (b) This involves finding the number of combinations of four out of seven projects that can be linked with the permutation formed by the remaining three projects. No. of combinations
   $$= \binom{7}{4} = \frac{7!}{4!3!} = 35$$
   No. of permutations $= 3! = 6$
   Since each combination can be linked with each permutation total number of programmes $= 35 \times 6 = 210$

3. No. of different teams $= \binom{19}{4} = \dfrac{19!}{15!4!}$
   $$= \frac{19 \times 18 \times 17 \times 16 \times 15!}{15! \times 4 \times 3 \times 2 \times 1}$$
   $$= \underline{\underline{3876}}$$

If 1 individual must be in the team then this leaves 3 men to be selected from the remaining 18. 3 men can be selected from 18 in

$$\binom{18}{3} \text{ ways} = \frac{18!}{15!3!} =$$

$$\frac{18 \times 17 \times 16 \times 15!}{15! \times 3 \times 2 \times 1} = \underline{\underline{816}}$$

Progress Test 6

1. (a) (i) $dy/dx = 20x^3 + 30x + 12$

   (ii) $dy/dx = 270x^8 - 12x^2 + 9x^{-\frac{1}{2}} - 16x^{-3} + 30x^{-4}$

   (b) (i) $\int y \, . \, dx = x^5 + 5x^3 + 6x^2 + 8x + c$

   (ii) $\int y \, . \, dx = 3x^{10} - x^4 + 12x^{1\frac{1}{2}} + x - 8x^{-1} + 5x^{-2}$
   $$+ c$$

2. $dy/dx = 12 - 6x$

   (a) Slope at $x = 0$ is 12

   (b) y at maximum when $12 - 6x = 0$, *i.e.* when $x = 2$.

      $\therefore$ Since $y = 12x - 3x^2$,

      maximum value of $y = 12 \times 2 - 3 \times 2^2 = 12$

3. (a) $dy/dx = 120 - 8x$

     $\therefore$ When $120 - 8x = 0$, $x = 15$; when y is at a maximum.

   (b) $dy/dx = 4x^3 - 32$

     $\therefore$ When $4x^3 - 32 = 0$, $x = 2$; when y is at a minimum.

4. $\int (12x - 3x^2) \, . \, dx = 6x^2 - x^3 + c$

   (a) $\left[6x^2 - x^3 + c \right]_0^1 = 5$

   (b) $\left[6x^2 - x^3 + c \right]_1^2 = 11$

   (c) $\left[6x^2 - x^3 + c \right]_2^3 = 11$

   (d) $\left[6x^2 - x^3 + c \right]_3^4 = 5$

Progress Test 7

1. (a)

Tool Capacity	Mfg Cost	Tool Depreciation ($£120 \div$ capacity)	Total Cost of Part
	p	p	p
1000	10	12	22
2000	$10\frac{1}{2}$	6	16·5
3000	11	4	15
4000	$11\frac{1}{2}$	3	14·5
5000	12	2·4	MIN → 14·4
6000	$12\frac{1}{2}$	2	14·5
7000	13	1·7	14·7
8000	$13\frac{1}{2}$	1·5	15
9000	14	1·3	15·3
10000	$14\frac{1}{2}$	1·2	15·7

The optimum tool capacity, therefore, is 5000 units.

(b) First we must generalise the total unit cost, letting n = tool capacity.

The tool depreciation is straightforward being simply $\dfrac{120 \times 100}{n}$ pence per unit. As regards the manufacturing cost, since this is 10p at 1000 units capacity and increases by $\frac{1}{2}$p per 1000 units, there is a theoretical cost of $9\frac{1}{2}$p per unit at 0 capacity. At n capacity, then, this cost is $9\frac{1}{2} + \frac{1}{2} \times \dfrac{n}{1000}$ pence.

The total cost, therefore, is $\dfrac{12,000}{n} + 9\frac{1}{2} + \dfrac{n}{2000}$.

Next, at the optimum capacity two consecutive capacity costs will be about equal—*i.e.* if n is near the optimum the cost per unit at $n \simeq$ cost per unit at $n + 1000$.

$\therefore$ Cost at n − cost at $(n + 1000) = 0$

$$\therefore \frac{12,000}{n} + 9\frac{1}{2} + \frac{n}{2000} - \left(\frac{12,000}{n + 1000} + 9\frac{1}{2} + \frac{n + 1000}{2000} \right) = 0$$

$$\therefore \frac{12,000}{n} + 9\frac{1}{2} + \frac{n}{2000} - \frac{12,000}{n + 1000} - 9\frac{1}{2} - \frac{n}{2000} - \frac{1}{2} = 0$$

$$\therefore \frac{12,000}{n} - \frac{12,000}{n + 1000} - \frac{1}{2} = 0$$

Multiply both sides by $2n(n + 1000)$.

$$\therefore 2 \times 12,000(n + 1000) - 2 \times 12,000n - \frac{2(n^2 + 1000n)}{2} = 0$$

$$\therefore 24,000n + 24,000,000 - 24,000n - n^2 - 1000n = 0$$

$$\therefore n^2 + 1000n - 24,000,000 = 0$$

We can avoid solving this rather awkward quadratic by using the fact that we know n must be a round 1000. A few tests quickly show the optimum lies between 4000 and 5000 and further testing of these two possibilities shows 5000 is the optimum.

The most convenient method in this case is obviously the step-by-step. However, if the tool could be designed to produce any number of units the difference equation method would be the more convenient, even though it would involve solving an awkward quadratic very similar to that obtained above.

Progress Test 8

1. (a) $\begin{pmatrix} 6 & 8 \\ 1 & 4 \end{pmatrix} + \begin{pmatrix} 3 & 5 \\ 4 & 0 \end{pmatrix} = \begin{pmatrix} 9 & 13 \\ 5 & 4 \end{pmatrix}$

(b) $\begin{pmatrix} 6 & 8 \\ 1 & 4 \end{pmatrix} - \begin{pmatrix} 3 & 5 \\ 4 & 0 \end{pmatrix} = \begin{pmatrix} 3 & 3 \\ -3 & 4 \end{pmatrix}$

(c) $\begin{pmatrix} 6 & 8 \\ 1 & 4 \end{pmatrix} \times \begin{pmatrix} 3 & 5 \\ 4 & 0 \end{pmatrix} = \begin{pmatrix} 6 \times 3 + 8 \times 4 & 6 \times 5 + 8 \times 0 \\ 1 \times 3 + 4 \times 4 & 1 \times 5 + 4 \times 0 \end{pmatrix}$

$= \begin{pmatrix} 50 & 30 \\ 19 & 5 \end{pmatrix}$

2. (a)

$$\begin{array}{c} \textit{Pay rates} \\ \textit{Low} \quad \textit{Medium} \quad \textit{High} \\ (0\cdot50 \quad 0\cdot75 \quad 1) \end{array} \times \begin{array}{c} \textit{Store Staffing:} \\ \begin{array}{ccc} & & \textit{Sub-} \\ & \textit{City} & \textit{Town} & \textit{urban} \end{array} \\ \begin{array}{c} \textit{Low} \\ \textit{Labour} \; \textit{Medium} \\ \textit{Grade:} \quad \textit{High} \end{array} \begin{pmatrix} 6 & 10 & 8 \\ 16 & 12 & 4 \\ 6 & 3 & 1 \end{pmatrix} \end{array}$$

$$\times \quad \begin{array}{c} \textit{Stores} \\ \begin{array}{c} \textit{City} \\ \textit{Store:} \quad \textit{Town} \\ \textit{Suburban} \end{array} \begin{pmatrix} 3 \\ 11 \\ 30 \end{pmatrix} \end{array}$$

(b) $(0\cdot50 \quad 0\cdot75 \quad 1) \times \begin{pmatrix} 6 & 10 & 8 \\ 16 & 12 & 4 \\ 6 & 3 & 1 \end{pmatrix} \times \begin{pmatrix} 3 \\ 11 \\ 30 \end{pmatrix}$

$= (21 \quad 17 \quad 8) \times \begin{pmatrix} 3 \\ 11 \\ 30 \end{pmatrix} = 490$

∴ Total wage bill $= \underline{\underline{£490}}$

NOTE: Though matrix algebra is not really suitable for a calculation as simple as this, where the number of different categories is very much more then by writing the data initially in matrix form the calculations can be handled by a computer programmed to perform matrix algebra. The time-saving then can be considerable (particularly where the figures are liable to frequent change).

Progress Test 9

1. (a) (i) $\frac{1}{2} \times \frac{1}{2} = \underline{\underline{\frac{1}{4}}}$

   (ii) $\frac{1}{6} \times \frac{1}{6} = \underline{\underline{\frac{1}{36}}}$

   (b) $\frac{1}{6} + \frac{1}{6} = \underline{\underline{\frac{1}{3}}}$

   (c) $\frac{1}{52} + \frac{1}{52} + \frac{1}{52} + \frac{1}{52} = \underline{\underline{\frac{1}{13}}}$

   (d) String-events are H AND T, T AND H.
   ∴ Probability $= (\frac{1}{2} \times \frac{1}{2}) + (\frac{1}{2} \times \frac{1}{2}) = \underline{\underline{\frac{1}{2}}}$

   (e) String-events giving a total of 11: 5 AND 6, 6 AND 5
   $= (\frac{1}{6} \times \frac{1}{6}) + (\frac{1}{6} \times \frac{1}{6}) = \underline{\underline{\frac{1}{18}}}(a)$

   (f) String-events giving a total of 7: 1 AND 6, 2 AND 5, 3 AND 4, 4 AND 3, 5 AND 2, 6 AND 1.
   ∴ Probability $= (\frac{1}{6} \times \frac{1}{6}) + (\frac{1}{6} \times \frac{1}{6}) + (\frac{1}{6} \times \frac{1}{6}) + (\frac{1}{6} \times \frac{1}{6}) + (\frac{1}{6} \times \frac{1}{6}) + (\frac{1}{6} \times \frac{1}{6}) = \underline{\underline{\frac{1}{6}}}$

   (g) This is the AT LEAST situation, so probability of backing at least one winner is 1 minus probability of backing none. We need, then, 1 minus probability of all four horses losing $= 1 - (\frac{2}{3} \times \frac{3}{5} \times \frac{27}{40} \times \frac{5}{9}) = \underline{\underline{0 \cdot 85}}$

   NOTE: (a) It should be appreciated that the probability of throwing a 5 and a 6 is *not* the same as throwing two 6s. The reason is that there are two different combinations of 5 and 6 but only one of double 6.

2. *See* Fig. 44. It should be appreciated any die score over 2 terminates the branch (since the score from three dice cannot be 4 or less if one of them is over 2), while even a score of over 1 terminates the branch if there is already a 2 along it.

3. If we let Y = "Yes" and N = "No" to the question "does the retailer allow himself to be interviewed?", then all the possible string-events are listed in the left-hand column below. Note that once the survey worker has achieved his quota he stops visiting retailers and the probability of subsequent potential interviewees accepting or refusing does not arise.

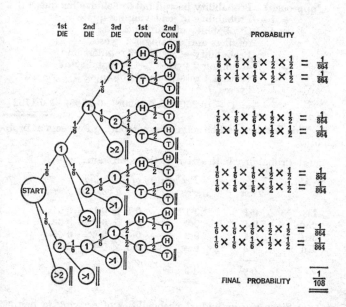

FIG. 44.—*Probability-tree.*

Quota	Question	Visits				Probability	
		1	2	3	4		
F	(a)(i)	Y	Y	—	—	0·6 × 0·6	= 0·3600
I	(a)(ii)	N	Y	Y	—	0·4 × 0·6 × 0·6 = 0·1440	} = 0·2880
L		Y	N	Y	—	0·6 × 0·4 × 0·6 = 0·1440	
L	(a)(iii)	N	N	Y	Y	0·4 × 0·4 × 0·6 × 0·6 = 0·0576	
E		N	Y	N	Y	0·4 × 0·6 × 0·4 × 0·6 = 0·0576	} = 0·1728
D		Y	N	N	Y	0·6 × 0·4 × 0·4 × 0·6 = 0·0576	
	(b)	N	N	N	N	0·4 × 0·4 × 0·4 = 0·0640	
NOT		N	N	Y	N	0·4 × 0·4 × 0·6 × 0·4 = 0·0384	} = 0·1792
FILLED		N	Y	N	N	0·4 × 0·6 × 0·4 × 0·4 = 0·0384	
		Y	N	N	N	0·6 × 0·4 × 0·4 × 0·4 = 0·0384	

CROSS-CHECK: Probability quota filled OR not filled   1·0000

Alternative
approach: Probability he will fail to achieve his quota
= 1 — Probability of achieving his quota
= 1 — (Probability of visiting 2
retailers and obtaining 2 "yeses" +
Probability of visiting 3 retailers and
obtaining 2 "yeses" + Probability of
visiting 4 retailers and obtaining 2
"yeses")
= 1 — (0·3600 + 0·2880 + 0·1728) = 0·1792

4. This problem can be solved by computing four sets of prob-abilities.

(a) Probability both arrive by the same train:

| Train | *Probability of Arriving* | | |
	Tom	Jerry	Tom and Jerry
1st	0·1	0·1	0·1 × 0·1 = 0·01
2nd	0·1	0·2	0·1 × 0·2 = 0·02
3rd	0·4	0·2	0·4 × 0·2 = 0·08
4th	0·3	0·4	0·3 × 0·4 = 0·12
	0·9	0·9	0·23

(b) Since the individual probabilities of arriving in neither case adds to 1, there is no certainty either of them will arrive.
Now probability Tom does not arrive   = 1 − 0·9 = 0·1
And probability Jerry does not arrive   = 1 − 0·9 = 0·1
∴ Probability neither arrives is 0·1 × 0·1 = 0·01

(c) Tom will arrive before Jerry if he catches an earlier train. So probability Tom arrives first can be calculated as follows:

Train	Tom on Train	*Jerry comes Later (or not at all)*		Tom arrives First
1st	0·1	1 − 0·1	= 0·9	0·1 × 0·9 = 0·09
2nd	0·1	1 − (0·1 + 0·2)	= 0·7	0·1 × 0·7 = 0·07
3rd	0·4	1 − (0·1 + 0·2 + 0·2)	= 0·5	0·4 × 0·5 = 0·20
4th	0·3	1 − (0·1 + 0·2 + 0·2 + 0·4)	= 0·1	0·3 × 0·1 = 0·03
				0·39

(d) Now it is certain that either Tom and Jerry will arrive together, OR neither will arrive, OR Tom will arrive first, OR Jerry will arrive first. Therefore probability Jerry will arrive first is 1 minus sum of the other probabilities—*i.e.*

$$1 - (0.23 + 0.01 + 0.39) = \underline{0.37}$$

THEREFORE: Probability that Angela will:

(i) Go dancing = 0.39
(ii) Go to the cinema = 0.37
(iii) Go for a drink = 0.23
(iv) Wash her hair = 0.01

Progress Test 10

1. The marble chosen from A must be either black or white. We have, then, two string-events—one starting with a white marble and one with a black marble. The analysis, therefore, runs as follows:

Marble from A	Probability	Marbles now in B	Probability of White Marble	String-Event Event	Probability
White	$\frac{1}{3}$	1B, 3W	$\frac{3}{4}$	W — W	$\frac{1}{3} \times \frac{3}{4} = \frac{1}{4}$
Black	$\frac{2}{3}$	2B, 2W	$\frac{1}{2}$	B — W	$\frac{2}{3} \times \frac{1}{2} = \frac{1}{3}$

Probability Final Marble is White $\frac{7}{12}$

2. First note that since the three machines collectively can produce 600 units per hour, of which 300 are from A, 200 from B and 100 from C, the probabilities of a unit being allocated to these machines is $\frac{300}{600} = \frac{1}{2}$, $\frac{200}{600} = \frac{1}{3}$ and $\frac{100}{600} = \frac{1}{6}$ respectively.

(a) Probability a unit produced on A AND emerges substandard = P(unit allocated to A) $\times$ P(unit emerges substandard|unit allocated to A)

$$= \frac{1}{2} \times \frac{1}{10} = \underline{0.05}$$

(b) Probability a unit emerges substandard = Probability made on A AND is substandard, OR made on B AND is substandard OR made on C AND is substandard = [P(allocated to A) $\times$ P(substandard|A)] + [P(allocated to B) $\times$ P(substandard|B)] + [P(allocated to C) $\times$ P(substandard|C)]

$$= [\tfrac{1}{2} \times \tfrac{1}{10}] + [\tfrac{1}{3} \times \tfrac{15}{100}] + [\tfrac{1}{6} \times \tfrac{24}{100}]$$
$$= 0.05 + 0.05 + 0.04 = \underline{0.14}$$

(c) This is a straight application of Bayes' Theorem. Since the probability of a given unit being allocated to A and proving substandard is 0·05 (see (a)) and the probability that a unit will in any event be substandard is 0·14 (see (b)) the probability a substandard unit was in fact produced on A—i.e. P(unit allocated to A|unit substandard)—is:

$$\frac{0·05}{0·14} = \underline{\underline{0·357}}$$

NOTE: In other words the probability is greater than $\frac{1}{3}$ despite the fact that A has the lowest rate of substandard units. The reason the probability is so high is, of course, because A produces by far the most units and although its substandard *rate* is low, its proportion of substandard units actually produced is relatively high.

Progress Test 11

1. (a) Here $np = 12 \times 0·25 = 3$. Since this is less than 5, therefore, the Normal Curve cannot be used and it is, then, a BINOMIAL situation.

(b) Here $np = 12 \times 0·5 = 6$ and so this is a NORMAL situation.

(c) Here $np = 12 \times 0·05 = 0·6$. Since this is less than 1 it can be considered a POISSON situation.

(d) Here the population is very small and therefore we have a HYPOGEOMETRIC situation.

2. This is a BINOMIAL situation. The required probabilities can therefore be found from the formula:

$$P(x) = \binom{8}{x} \left(\frac{1}{2}\right)^x \left(\frac{1}{2}\right)^{8-x} = \binom{8}{x} \left(\frac{1}{2}\right)^8 = \binom{8}{x} \times \frac{1}{256},$$

i.e.

No. Males in Sample	Probability
0	$\binom{8}{0} \times \frac{1}{256} = \frac{1}{256}$
1	$\binom{8}{1} \times \frac{1}{256} = \frac{8}{256}$
2	$\binom{8}{2} \times \frac{1}{256} = \frac{28}{256}$
3	$\binom{8}{3} \times \frac{1}{256} = \frac{56}{256}$

$$4 \qquad \binom{8}{4} \times \frac{1}{256} = \frac{70}{256}$$

$$5 \qquad \binom{8}{5} \times \frac{1}{256} = \frac{56}{256}$$

$$6 \qquad \binom{8}{6} \times \frac{1}{256} = \frac{28}{256}$$

$$7 \qquad \binom{8}{7} \times \frac{1}{256} = \frac{8}{256}$$

$$8 \qquad \binom{8}{8} \times \frac{1}{256} = \frac{1}{256}$$

$$\overline{1}$$

3. This is also a BINOMIAL situation in which our formula becomes:

$$P(x) = \binom{4}{x} \times 0 \cdot 3^x \times 0 \cdot 7^{4-x},$$

i.e.

No. of Failures in Year	Probability

$$0 \qquad \binom{4}{0} \times 0 \cdot 3^0 \times 0 \cdot 7^4 = 1 \times 1 \quad \times 0 \cdot 7^4 = 0 \cdot 2401$$

$$1 \qquad \binom{4}{1} \times 0 \cdot 3^1 \times 0 \cdot 7^3 = 4 \times 0 \cdot 3 \quad \times 0 \cdot 7^3 = 0 \cdot 4116$$

$$2 \qquad \binom{4}{2} \times 0 \cdot 3^2 \times 0 \cdot 7^2 = 6 \times 0 \cdot 3^2 \times 0 \cdot 7^2 = 0 \cdot 2646$$

$$3 \qquad \binom{4}{3} \times 0 \cdot 3^3 \times 0 \cdot 7^1 = 4 \times 0 \cdot 3^3 \times 0 \cdot 7^1 = 0 \cdot 0756$$

$$4 \qquad \binom{4}{4} \times 0 \cdot 3^4 \times 0 \cdot 7^0 = 1 \times 0 \cdot 3^4 \times 1 \quad = 0 \cdot 0081$$

$$\overline{1 \cdot 0000}$$

4. This is a POISSON situation where the formula is

$$P(x) = e^{-3}\frac{3^x}{x!}.$$

Using the incremental technique discussed on pages 57–8 we can say

$$P(x) = P(x-1) \times \frac{3}{x}$$

and $P(0)$ is, of course, $e^{-3} = 0 \cdot 0498$

The probabilities, then, are:

No. of Blemishes	Probability
0	$0 \cdot 0498$
1	$0 \cdot 0498 \times \frac{3}{1} = 0 \cdot 1494$
2	$0 \cdot 1494 \times \frac{3}{2} = 0 \cdot 2240$*
3	$0 \cdot 2240 \times \frac{3}{3} = 0 \cdot 2240$
4	$0 \cdot 2240 \times \frac{3}{4} = 0 \cdot 1680$
5	$0 \cdot 1680 \times \frac{3}{5} = 0 \cdot 1008$
	$\underline{0 \cdot 9160}$
6 and over	$1 - 0 \cdot 9160 = \underline{0 \cdot 0840}$
	$\underline{\underline{1 \cdot 0000}}$

*This is the correct probability, the $0 \cdot 2241$ one obtains from the calculation containing a small rounding error that arises as a result of taking e^{-3} to only four decimal places.

5. This is a NORMAL situation in which the mean number of failures is $np = 2100 \times 0 \cdot 3 = 630$, and the standard deviation is $\sqrt{2100 \times 0 \cdot 3 \times 0 \cdot 7} = 21$. The value of 650 is, then, virtually 1 standard deviation above the mean and so the probability of more than this number of components failing is to all intents and purposes $\frac{1}{6}$.

Progress Test 12

1. Let x = selling price

Demand (units) $= 20,000 - 1000x$

New contribution per unit $= x - 11$

∴ New total contribution $= (20,000 - 1000x)(x - 11)$

$$= 20,000x - 220,000 - 1000x^2 + 11,000x$$

$$= 31,000x - 1000x^2 - 220,000.$$

∴ $\dfrac{d(\text{total contribution})}{dx} = 31,000 - 2000x.$

∴ Total contribution is at a maximum when $31{,}000 - 2000x = 0$
i.e. when x (selling price) $= £15\frac{1}{2}$.

2.　　(*a*) Let x = selling price.
Then sales in £'s $= 10{,}000/x$
∴ sales in units $= (10{,}000/x) \div x = 10{,}000/x^2$

$$\therefore \text{PROFIT} = \frac{10{,}000}{x} - \left(1000 + 2 \times \frac{10{,}000}{x^2} \right)$$

$$= \frac{10{,}000}{x} - 1000 - \frac{20{,}000}{x^2}$$

(*b*) To maximise profit:
$$\text{PROFIT} = 10{,}000x^{-1} - 1000 - 20{,}000x^{-2}$$

$$\therefore \frac{d(\text{PROFIT})}{dx} = -10{,}000x^{-2} + 40{,}000x^{-3}$$

Set equal to 0:
$-10{,}000x^{-2} + 40{,}000x^{-3} = 0$
∴ $x = 4$
∴ Selling price must be £4.

3. Let TA = Time allowed; TT = Time taken; R = Rate of pay per hour.
　　(*a*) Wages model:
$$\text{Wages earned} = (TT \times R) + \left(TT \times R \times \frac{TA - TT}{TA} \right)$$

$$= TT \times R\left(1 + \frac{TA - TT}{TA} \right)$$

(*b*) Let x = Time to be booked to "10 hour" job.
Then $8 - x$ = Time to be booked to "8 hour" job.

Wages earned on "10 hour" job =

$$x \times R\left(1 + \frac{10 - x}{10} \right) = Rx\left(2 - \frac{x}{10} \right)$$

Wages earned on "8 hour" job =

$$(8 - x) \times R\left(1 + \frac{8 - (8 - x)}{8} \right) = (8R - Rx)\left(1 + \frac{x}{8} \right)$$

$\therefore$ Total wages earned $=$

$$Rx\left(2 - \frac{x}{10}\right) + (8R - Rx)\left(1 + \frac{x}{8}\right)$$

$$= 2Rx - \frac{Rx^2}{10} + 8R + \frac{8Rx}{8} - Rx - \frac{Rx^2}{8}$$

$$= 2Rx - \frac{Rx^2}{10} + 8R + Rx - Rx - \frac{Rx^2}{8}$$

$$= 2Rx + 8R - \frac{Rx^2}{10} - \frac{Rx^2}{8}$$

$$= 2Rx + 8R - Rx^2\left(\frac{1}{10} + \frac{1}{8}\right)$$

$\therefore$ To maximise wages earned, differentiate above expression, set equal to zero, and solve for x, i.e.

$$\frac{d(\text{Total wage earned})}{dx} = 2R - 2Rx\left(\frac{1}{10} + \frac{1}{8}\right) = 0$$

Divide both sides by $2R$ $\therefore$ $1 - x \times \frac{18}{80} = 0$

$$\therefore x = \frac{80}{18} = 4\frac{4}{9}$$

$\therefore$ Worker should book $4\frac{4}{9}$ hours to the "10 hour" job and $8 - 4\frac{4}{9} = 3\frac{5}{9}$ hours to the "8 hour" job.

4. Note first that no matter what the production volume is, £5000 will always be spent on direct labour.
Now let $x =$ Tons of metal poured in week.
Then actual costs for week:

Metal	£6x
Direct labour	5000
Variable overhead	x
Fixed costs	8000
	$13{,}000 + 7x$

And sales for the week as per the price fixing formula will be:

Metal	£$6x$
Direct labour	5000
Overheads (200% D.L.)	10000
	$15,000 + 6x$
Profit (10% on cost)	$1500 + 0\cdot6x$
Sales	$16,500 + 6\cdot6x$

$\therefore$ Profit for week = Sales — Costs
$$= (16,500 + 6\cdot6x) - (13,000 + 7x)$$
$$= 16,500 + 6\cdot6x - 13,000 - 7x$$
$$= 3500 - 0\cdot4x$$

The anomaly here is that since the x expression is negative it means the larger x, *i.e.* the more work done, the *less* the profit.

5. Let n = number of units to be produced per tool.
Since the cost of finishing increases by £$0\cdot01$ for each unit produced, then cost of jth unit = £$0\cdot01j$.

$$\therefore \text{Total finishing cost} = £ \sum_{j=1}^{n} (0\cdot01j)$$

$$= 0\cdot01 \frac{1 + n}{2} \times n \text{(since this is an arithmetic progression)}$$

$$= 0\cdot005(n + n^2)$$
$$\therefore \text{Total cost} = 50 + 0\cdot005(n + n^2)$$
$$= 50 + 0\cdot005n + 0\cdot005n^2$$
$$\therefore \text{TOTAL COST PER UNIT} = \frac{50 + 0\cdot005n + 0\cdot005n^2}{n}$$
$$= 50n^{-1} + 0\cdot005 + 0\cdot005n^1$$

Differentiating, etc.:

$$-50n^{-2} + 0\cdot005 = 0$$

$$\therefore n = \sqrt{\frac{50}{0\cdot005}} = \sqrt{10,000} = 100$$

The tool should, therefore, be scrapped after 100 units.

Progress Test 13

1. (a)

Event	Value (Hire Income)	Probability	Expectation (£)
0 lorries	£0	0·1	0
1 lorry	£20	0·2	4
2 lorries	£40	0·3	12
3 lorries	£60	0·2	12
4 lorries	£80	0·2	16
		1·0	44

Less cost of keeping 4 lorries @ £9 each   36

Profit expectation per day   £8

(b)

Event			Expectation No. of Lorries Company Buys :		
Lorries Demanded	Value (Hire)	Probab.	1	2	3
0	£0	0·1	0	0	0
1	£20	0·2	20 × 0·2 ⎫	20 × 0·2 4	20 × 0·2 4
2	£40	0·3	20 × 0·3 ⎪ 18	40 × 0·3 ⎫	40 × 0·3 12
3	£60	0·2	20 × 0·2 ⎬	40 0·2 ⎬ 28	60 × 0·2 ⎫
4	£80	0·2	20 × 0·2 ⎭	40 0·2 ⎭	60 × 0·2 ⎭ 24
Total expected hire value			18	32	40
Less fixed lorry cost @ £9 each			9	18	27
Profit expectation per day			£9	£14	£13

Profit expectation from 4 lorries (see (a)): £8

Therefore 2 lorries should be bought since this maximises the daily expectation.

2. (a) First note that if there is a certain demand for at least 1 machine per period and a 0·4 probability of demand for 2 machines there must be 1 − 0·4 = 0·6 probability the demand will be for exactly one machine.

As can be seen in the opposite table, the optimum number of machines is 3.

(b) If the company had perfect information it would know exactly how many machines would be demanded and would pur-

EVENT				NO. MACHINES COMPANY ORDERS					
				2		3		4	
SALES PERIOD 1	SALES PERIOD 2	TOTAL SALES	PROBABILITY	REVENUE	EXPECTATION	REVENUE	EXPECTATION	REVENUE	EXPECTATION
				£	£	£	£	£	£
1 mach.	1 mach.	2	0.6 × 0.6 = 0.36	2000	720	2000	720	2000	720
1 mach.	2 mach.	3	0.6 × 0.4 = 0.24	2000	480	3000	720	3000	720
2 mach.	1 mach.	3	0.4 × 0.6 = 0.24	2000	480	3000	720	3000	720
2 mach.	2 mach.	4	0.4 × 0.4 = 0.16	2000	320	3000	480	4000	640
			1.00		2000		2640		2800
LESS PURCHASE COST OF MACHINES					1200		1700		1900
NET EXPECTATION					£ 800		£ 940		£ 900

chase just this number. In these circumstances its expectation would be as follows:

Total Demand	Probability of Demand	Profit (£)	Expectation (£)
2 mach.	0·36	2000 − 1200 = 800	800 × 0·36 = 288
3 mach.	0·48	3000 − 1700 = 1300	1300 × 0·48 = 624
4 mach.	0·16	4000 − 1900 = 2100	2100 × 0·16 = 336
	1·00		£1248

Since knowing the actual demand in advance would enable the company to earn on average £1248 profit, while without this information it will only make £940 on average, the value of "perfect information" will be 1248 − 940 = £308.

3. *See* Fig. 45. As the decision-tree in this Fig. shows, you should adopt plan B and if it is successful advertise it lightly.

It should, perhaps, be observed that the difference between the two plans is a mere £20,000 expectation, and the decision, therefore, could be taken on other grounds than this marginal economic differential. Moreover, even plan B is forecast to return an expectation of only £220,000 which in practice may hardly justify the time and effort required to run it. On the other hand, only £0·5m

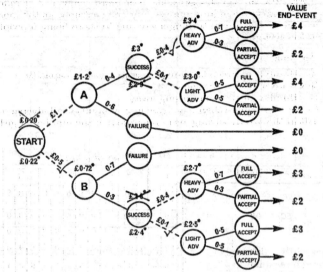

FIG. 45.—*New product decision-tree: all amounts in £M. Ticks and
's indicate backward pass entries.*

will be at risk initially, and if the research proves successful, a
mere additional £100,000 advertising will guarantee at least a £2m
return.

Progress Test 15

1. The Poisson distribution developed in the answer to question
4, Progress Test 11 is shown below together with the logical allocation of random number digits:

No. of Arrivals During any Minute	Probability (to 3 decimal places)	Cumulative Probability	Random Number Allocation	
0	0·050	0·050	000–	049
1	0·149	0·199	050–	198
2	0·224	0·423	199–	422
3	0·224	0·647	423–	646
4	0·168	0·815	647–	814
5	0·101	0·916	815–	915
6 or more	0·084	1·000	916–	999
	1·000			

NOTE: We can end the series at "6 or more" since if 6 or more customers arrive in any minute only one customer at the most will wait—the others turning away due to there being 6 people in the system.

Columns:

A—Number of arrivals joining system (system capacity = 6, therefore A ≤ 6 − previous C)

B—Number of arrivals turning away

(NOTE: Since more than 6 arrivals in any minute will always result in the excess turning away regardless of the number of girls

minute	RANDOM number	NO OF arrivals	NO. OF GIRLS														
			1.			2			3			4			5		
			A	B	C	A	B	C	A	B	C	A	B	C	A	B	C
1	319	2	2	0	1	2	0	0	2	0	0	2	0	0	2	0	0
2	273	2	2	0	2	2	0	0	2	0	0	2	0	0	2	0	0
3	866	5	4	1	5	5	0	3	5	0	2	5	0	1	5	0	0
4	933	6	1	5	5	3	3	4	4	2	3	5	1	2	6	0	1
5	692	4	1	3	5	2	2	4	3	1	3	4	0	2	4	0	0
6	100	1	1	0	5	1	0	3	1	0	1	1	0	0	1	0	0
7	659	4	1	3	5	3	1	4	4	0	2	4	0	0	4	0	0
8	484	3	1	2	5	2	1	4	3	0	2	3	0	0	3	0	0
9	235	2	1	1	5	2	0	4	2	0	1	2	0	0	2	0	0
10	034	0	0	0	4	0	0	2	0	0	0	0	0	0	0	0	0
11	864	5	2	3	5	4	1	4	5	0	2	5	0	1	5	0	0
12	794	4	1	3	5	2	2	4	4	0	3	4	0	1	4	0	0
13	526	3	1	2	5	2	1	4	3	0	3	3	0	0	3	0	0
14	299	2	1	1	5	2	0	4	2	0	2	2	0	0	2	0	0
15	926	6	1	5	5	2	4	4	4	2	3	6	0	2	6	0	1

	1	2	3	4	5
Total turning away	29	15	5	1	0
Value lost sales @ 20p each	£5.80	£3	£1	£0.20	0
Girls' wages at £1 each	£1	£2	£3	£4	£5
Total cost	£6.80	£5	£4	£4.20	£5

and opening state of the system, the retailer will inevitably lose such customers. They can, therefore, be ignored in this study which is aimed at identifying the *relatively* most profitable policy regarding the employment of girls.)

C—Number left in the system at the end of the minute—*i.e.* opening number + arrivals joining system − (1 × number of girls).

CONCLUSION: The optimum number of girls to employ indicated by this simulation is 3 — although further runs need to be made before a firm conclusion can be reached.

2. *See* Fig. 46.

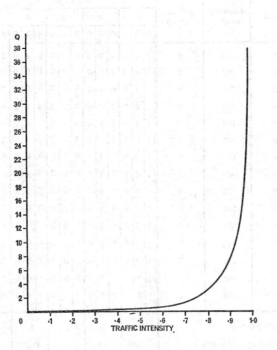

FIG. 46.—*Queue length and traffic intensity in a steady state simple queue.* $Q = \dfrac{i^2}{1-i}$; (**10**(*b*)(*ii*))

Progress Test 16

REPLACEMENT PERIOD	TOTAL DEPRECIATION	ANNUAL COSTS				TOTAL COST	AVERAGE ANNUAL COST
		MAINTEN-ANCE		BREAKDOWN EXPECTATION			
	£	YR.	£	YR.	£*	£	£
1 year	1250	1	100	1	100	1450	1450
2 years	1750	1	200	1	100		
		2	100	2	500		
			300		600	2650	1325
3 years	2000	1	200	1	100		
		2	300	2	500		
		3	100	3	1300		
			600		1900	4500	1500

*Probability of breakdown during year × £2000.

1. As can be seen above, the average annual cost is minimised by replacing the equipment at the end of the second year.

2. This clearly is a POISSON situation, components failing in a given period following a Poisson distribution. Our first task, therefore, is to use the Poisson formula to give us the probability of a breakdown occurring during each of the possible inspection periods. Since the probability of more than one component failing —i.e. $P(> 1)$ — is given by $1 - [P(0) + P(1)]$ we can find this by means of the following layout:

INSPECTION PERIOD (WEEKS)	AV. NO. OF COMPONENTS FAILING DURING PERIOD (i.e. a)	$P(0)^*$ i.e. e^{-a}	$P(1)$ i.e. $e^{-a} \times a$	$P(0) + P(1)$	$P(>1)$ i.e. $1 - [P(0) + P(1)]$
1	½	0.6065	0.3032	0.9097	0.0903
2	1	0.3679	0.3679	0.7358	0.2642
3	1½	0.2231	0.3346	0.5577	0.4423
4	2	0.1353	0.2706	0.4059	0.5941
5	2½	0.0821	0.2052	0.2873	0.7127
etc					

*From Appendix I.

Knowing these breakdown probabilities we can find the breakdown cost expectation by multiplying them by the appropriate service charge. Adding next the £120 weekend inspection and maintenance charge gives the total cost over the inspection period

—and this total divided by the number of weeks in the period gives the average weekly cost, so:

INSPECTION PERIOD (WEEKS)	BREAKDOWN			W/E CHARGE	TOTAL CHARGE	AVERAGE WEEKLY COST*
	CHARGE	PROBA- BILITY	EXPEC- TATIONS*			
1	£100	0.0903	£ 9	£120	£129	£129
2	£200	0.2642	£ 53	£120	£173	£ 86
3	£300	0.4423	£133	£120	£253	£ 84
4	£400	0.5941	£238	£120	£358	£ 89
5	£500	0.7127	£356	£120	£476	£ 95

*To nearest £.

From these figures an inspection period of 3 weeks will give us a minimum average weekly cost of £84.

Considering the alternative maintenance scheme, since 1 component fails on average every 2 weeks, 2 components will fail on average every 4 weeks. There will, then, be a breakdown on average every four weeks which will cost £350. This gives an average weekly cost of $350 \div 4 = £87\frac{1}{2}$ which is more than the 3 week inspection period scheme and therefore should not be adopted.

Progress Test 17

1. Note first the annual stockholding cost per unit per annum will be 20% of 20p = 4p.

    (a) $\text{EOQ} = \sqrt{\dfrac{2PN}{S}}$

             $= \sqrt{\dfrac{2 \times 5 \times 16{,}000}{0\cdot04}}$

             $= \underline{\underline{2000 \text{ units.}}}$

    (b) (i) Since only $2\frac{1}{2}$% of the area under the normal curve lies beyond the average plus two standard deviations, then there is only a $2\frac{1}{2}$% probability the demand during the lead time will exceed $320 + 2 \times 50 = 420$ units. The re-order level, then, should be set at $\underline{\underline{420 \text{ units.}}}$

(b) (ii) Since the annual demand is 16,000 units and the re-order quantity is to be 2000 units, then the product will be re-ordered $16{,}000 \div 2000 = 8$ times a year. If there is a $2\frac{1}{2}\%$ probability of suffering a stockout, then such a stockout will occur only once in 40 times—*i.e.* once every 40 orders. At the rate of 8 orders a year this means there will be an average of $\frac{40}{8} = 5$ years between stockouts.

(c) If a unit is unsold at the end of the lead time, then clearly the average stock held until the product is again re-ordered is raised by one unit. Since the product is re-ordered 8 times a year this means an unsold unit incurs a stockholding cost of $\frac{1}{8} \times 4\text{p} = \frac{1}{2}\text{p}$. The trader, then, must balance the certain cost of holding a unit of $\frac{1}{2}\text{p}$ against the expectation of there being a demand for that unit. And this expectation is, of course, the 3p per unit profit $\times$ the probability of there being a demand for at least one more unit—*i.e.* expectation $= 3 \times P(\text{Demand} \geqslant x)$, where x is the number of units held at the moment of re-ordering. So we can say, then, optimum re-order point occurs when:
$\frac{1}{2} = 3 \times P(\text{Demand} \geqslant x)$ *i.e.* when $P(\text{Demand} \geqslant x) = \frac{1}{6}$.

Now since $\frac{1}{6}$ of the area under a normal curve lies beyond the average plus one standard deviation, $P(\text{Demand} \geqslant x) = \frac{1}{6}$ will occur when x is $320 + 50 = 370$ units.

The trader should in these circumstances, therefore, set his re-order level at 370 units.

Progress Test 18

1. (a) *See* Fig. 47(a).
   (b) *See* Fig. 47(b).

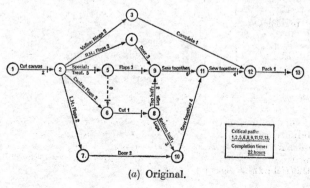

(a) Original.

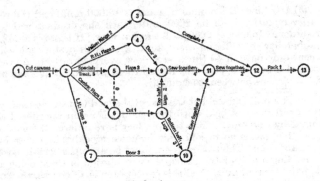

(b) Optimum.

Fig. 47.—*"Unique" tent network.*

The reductions were made as follows:

Activity	Cost per Hr (£)	Reduction (Hrs)	Total Cost (£)
1, 2	1	1	1
9, 11	2	2	4

(Note this now throws path 8, 10, 11 critical)

Activity	Cost per Hr (£)	Reduction (Hrs)	Total Cost (£)
11, 12	3	2	6
$\left\{\begin{matrix} 8, 9 \\ 10, 11 \end{matrix}\right\}$	$\left\{\begin{matrix} 4 \\ 1 \end{matrix}\right\}$	1	5

(Note this now throws path 5, 9 critical.)

$\left\{\begin{matrix} 8, 9 \\ 10, 11 \\ 5, 9 \end{matrix}\right\}$	$\left\{\begin{matrix} 4 \\ 1 \\ 2 \end{matrix}\right\}$	Cost per hour exceeds saving, so reduction not profitable

TOTAL		6	£16

	£
Value of reduction time— 6 hours @ £6	36
Cost of reduction time	16
NET SAVING	£20

Progress Test 19

1. (a)
$$5L + 12H \leqslant 12,000$$
$$L \leqslant 1200$$
$$H \leqslant 700$$
$$\frac{L}{1600} + \frac{H}{1400} \leqslant 1^{(a)}$$
$$L + H \geqslant 800$$
$$L \geqslant 0; H \geqslant 0$$

Objectives function:

Let c = contribution from 1 Light unit

∴ Total contribution = $c(L + 2H)$

(b) (i) See Fig. 48.

(ii) Testing corners of area of feasible solution in Fig. 48.

Corner:
(1) $c(100 + 2 \times 700) = 1500c$
(2) $c(720 + 2 \times 700) = 2120c$
(3) $c(873 + 2 \times 636) = 2145c$
(4) $c(1200 + 2 \times 350) = 1900c$
(5) $c(1200 + 2 \times 0) = 1200c$
(6) $c(800 + 2 \times 0) = 800c$

∴ Optimum mix is at corner 3, *i.e.* 873 Light and 636 Heavy.

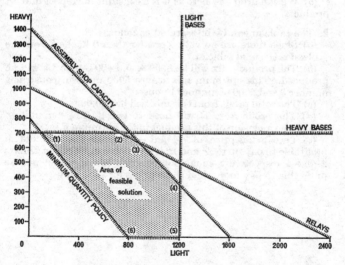

Fig. 48.—*Graphical linear programming: Control Units Ltd.*

(c) Initial Simplex tableau:

PRODUCT	PROFIT	QUANTITY	L	H	S_R	S_{LB}	S_{HB}	S_A
S_R	0	12000	5	12	1	0	0	0
S_{LB}	0	1200	1	0	0	1	0	0
S_{HB}	0	700	0	1	0	0	1	0
S_A	0	1	$\frac{1}{1600}^{(a)}$	$\frac{1}{1400}^{(a)}$	0	0	0	1
PROFIT:		0	$1^{(b)}$	$2^{(b)}$	0	0	0	0
Z.		0	1	2	0	0	0	0

NOTES:

(a) We can regard capacity of the Assembly shop as being "1" month. Since 1600 Light units can be made in 1 month 1 Light unit will require $\frac{1}{1600}$ months, and so L Light units will require $\frac{L}{1600}$ months. Similarly H Heavy units will require $\frac{H}{1400}$ months, and, of course the total production time of all units cannot exceed 1 month.

(b) We can drop "c" here as it is a constant in respect of both products.

2. The tableau can be interpreted as follows:

(a) Since there are no values greater than 0 in the Z row the tableau is the final tableau.

(b) The product mix will be 8000 A and 400 C. No Bs will be produced. This optimum mix leaves 5000 units of constraint number 3 and 2000 of number 1 unused.

(c) The total profit from this mix will be £20,000.

(d) The profit from B will need to rise by £1½ per unit to justify the inclusion of this product in the optimum mix.

(e) The shadow prices of $-\frac{3}{4}$ and -2 indicate that it would be profitable to pay up to £$\frac{3}{4}$ and £2 if additional units of constraints 2 and 4 respectively could be acquired, but it would not be profitable to pay more than these prices for such units.

1st Tableau

	Y	Z	*	TOTAL
A	4 / 100	6 / ⑥	0 / ②	0 / 100
B	7 / − 200	4 / + ⑨	0 / ⑤	3 / 200
C	2 / + ε	4 / − 200	0 / 50	−2 / 250
TOTAL	4 / 300	6 / 200	2 / 50	550

Transport cost in BZ < ring cost

$k = 200$

2nd Tableau

	Y	Z	*	TOTAL
A	4 / − 100	6 / ⑥	0 / + ②	0 / 100
B	7 / ②	4 / 200	0 / ⓪	−2 / 200
C	2 / + 200	4 / ε	0 / − 50	−2 / 250
TOTAL	4 / 300	6 / 200	2 / 50	550

Transport cost in A* < ring cost

$k = 50$

* Dummy destination

3rd Tableau

	Y	Z	*	TOTAL
A	4 50	6 (6)	0 50	0 100
B	7 (2)	4 200	0 (-2)	-2 200
C	2 250	4 e	0 (-2)	-2 250
TOTAL	4 300	6 200	0 50	550

No transport cost < ringed cost,
∴ tableau is final tableau

Solution

		TO Y	TO Z	REMAIN IN STOCK	TOTAL
F	A	50		50	100
R	B		200		200
O					
M	C	250			250
	TOTAL	300	200	50	550

4.

(i) Initial data

(ii) Initial tableau

Deduct marks in (i) from 10 to adjust for technique being a minimisation technique

	Ca	I	P	Co	GL
A	3	3	1	3	5
B	5	8	9	4	4
C	1	9	10	2	7
D	5	5	9	6	7
E	5	5	4	5	6

7	7	9	7	5
5	2	1	6	6
9	1	0	8	3
5	5	1	4	3
5	5	6	5	4

(iii) Tableau reductions

2	2	4	2	0	1	1	4	1	0
4	1	0	5	5	3	0	0	4	5
9	1	0	8	3 →	8	0	0	7	3
4	4	0	3	2	3	3	0	2	2
1	1	2	1	0	0	0	2	0	0

(iv) Line covering

(v) Tableau transform & 2nd line covering

$z = 2$

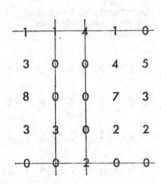

No. of covering lines ≠ No. of rows

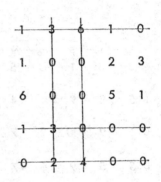

No. of covering lines = No. of rows

(vi) Solution Identification

(vii) Solution

	1	3	6	1	0 ✓
	1	✗ (a)	0 ✓	2	3
	6	0 ✓	✗	5	1
	1	3	✗	0 ✓	✗
	0 ✓	2	4	✗	✗

(a) This zero is deleted to break endless loop

	Ca	I	P	Co	GL
A					✓
B			✓		
C		✓			
D				✓	
E	✓				

Note: In the alternative optimum solution B and C simply interchange jobs

Progress Test 20

		Charles goes to		MIN	MIX
		Upper	Lower		
I go to:	Upper	4	0	0	1
	Lower	0	1	0	4
	MAX	4	1		
	MIX	1	4		5

NOTE: The strategy "stay home" has pay-offs of 0, 0 and so is dominated by both the other two strategies. It is, therefore, eliminated from the pay-off table.

Maximin = 0 ⎱ No saddle-point. Therefore game is a mixed
Minimax = 1 ⎰ strategy game.

Further analysis shows we both go to Upper Club 1 in 5 times.

$$\text{Value of the game} = £\frac{4}{5}$$

Now probability we both go to the Upper Club $= \frac{1}{5} \times \frac{1}{5} = \frac{1}{25}$

i.e. twice a year.

On the face of it paying £21 to win £8 of drinks is uneconomical, but if the subscription is unpaid then Charles will always go to the

Upper Club and I shall win nothing. Since I win £$\frac{4}{5}$ per week, this is

£40 per annum, so the net gain of being an Upper Club member is £40 − 21 = £19.

Progress Test 21

1. 8, × 0·75 + 12 × 0·25 = 9, × 0·75 + 15 × 0·25
= 10·5, × 0·75 + 14 × 0·25
= 11·38, × 0·75 + 17 × 0·25 = 12·78, × 0·75 + 20 × 0·25
= 14·58, × 0·75 + 25 × 0·25 = 17·18, × 0·75 + 23 × 0·25
= 18·64, × 0·75 + 28 × 0·25 = 20·98, × 0·75 + 30 × 0·25
= 23·24, × 0·75 + 33 × 0·25 = 25·68

Average lag $= \dfrac{1 - 0 \cdot 25}{0 \cdot 25} = 3$ periods.

$\therefore$ Average brought up to date $= 25 \cdot 68 + 3 \times 2 \cdot 5 = 33 \cdot 18$
$\therefore$ Forecast for next period $= 33 \cdot 18 + 2 \cdot 5 = \underline{\underline{35 \cdot 68}}$

And forecast for period after $= 35 \cdot 68 + 2 \cdot 5 = \underline{\underline{38 \cdot 18}}$

EXAMINATION QUESTIONS

1. (a) *Draw the graph* of the equations:

$$2x + y = 8$$
$$y = x^2 - 2x + 4$$

for the values of x from and including -2 to $+4$.

(b) From the graph *state the points where the two equations intersect* and prove the accuracy of your graph by solving the simultaneous equations.

(c) *Prove* the minimum value of:

$$y = x^2 - 2x + 4$$

by differentiation. (ICMA *May '72*)

2. Between the sales range of 30 and 80 units the management has determined that the sales income follows the function:

sales income (in £'s) = £20 × (sales units) − £0·15
× (sales units)^2

while the total cost follows the function:

total cost (in £'s) = £450 + £2 × (sales units)

(a) Draw a graph showing the income and cost lines.

(b) By derivation find the output which will give maximum income and calculate the maximum profit.

(c) Calculate the point where the two lines intersect, *i.e.* where neither a profit nor a loss is made. (ICMA *Dec '72*)

3. (a) Derive a formula for the sum of n terms of the arithmetic series:

$$a + (a + d) + (a + 2d) + (a + 3d) \ldots \ldots$$

(b) A firm retains out of profits, £100 in the first month, £120 in the second month and continues to increase the amount retained by £20 each month for 36 months. Use the formula to calculate how much the firm will have accumulated at the end of 36 months. (ICMA *Dec '72*)

4. A company buys for its computer room an air-conditioning plant at a cost of £2500. It is estimated that its value will depreciate during each year by 20% of its value at the beginning of the year. *Find the value of the air-conditioning plant (to the nearest £1) at the end of five years.*

At the beginning of each of the five years the company sets aside a certain fixed sum £x to accumulate at 6% per annum (compound interest) in order to be able to buy, at the end of five years, a new plant costing £3125. If the company trades in the old air-conditioning plant in part exchange for the new at the value calculated above, how much will have to be set aside each year to cover the balance due on the new air-conditioning plant? (ICMA *Dec '71*)

5. (*a*) On 1st January John Smith owes £12,000. To reduce the debt he agrees to pay £1200 at the end of each 6 months together with interest at $2\frac{1}{4}\%$ on the opening balance of each period.

The formula for the sum of an arithmetic progression is:

$$S = \frac{n}{2}\left[2a + (n - 1)d\right]$$

Using this formula find the total interest which he pays.

(*b*) It is estimated that a machine costing £5000 will have a saleable value of £2048 after 4 years. *Derive a suitable formula for the reducing balance method of depreciation and find the depreciation rate per cent* to be applied during the four year life.

(ICMA *May '72*)

6. A company, in which the training period for apprentices is five years, is considering its intake for the coming year. Information concerning apprentices recruited in previous years is given below:

Year of intake				1963	1964	1965	1966
Number of apprentices recruited				700	500	150	250
Number of apprentices leaving in:							
First year	..	..	..	28	18	8	14
Second year	..	..	..	29	18	6	10
Third year	..	..	..	17	8	2	1
Fourth year	..	..	..	13	8	1	2
Fifth year	..	..	..	2	2	1	1

(*a*) *What is the probability that an apprentice will qualify?*

(*b*) *What is the probability that an apprentice will stay for longer than two years?* (ICMA *June '71*)

7. Inspection samples of four items are chosen from large batches containing 10 per cent defectives. In a long run of samples what percentage of all samples would you expect to contain 0, 1, 2, 3, 4 defectives? State briefly how these results can be used in connection with quality control. (ICMA *Specimen question*)

8. A component required in a main assembly is supplied to a company by one of its subsidiaries. Inspection of the component is carried out by the parent company and it is considered by them that the rejection rate is too high; this is thought to be due to poor machining of certain critical dimensions of the component. If a

component has to be scrapped, the cost is £5. Production is in batches of 1000 components.

The parent company proposes to send a trained operator to the subsidiary each time a batch of these components goes into production, to carry out the machining of the critical dimensions. It will cost £150 each time to send one of its operators to the subsidiary, but it is expected that the scrap rate will be held at 2%.

The prior probabilities of the percentage defectives under the present circumstances are given in the following table:

Defective components %	Prior probability
2	0·07
4	0·23
6	0·29
8	0·35
10	0·06

You are required:

(a) To explain the likely derivation of a 'prior' probability distribution in this case.

(b) From the data given, to determine whether or not the proposed action should be taken. (ICMA *May '72*)

9. A company is considering whether to work one of its North Sea natural gas concessions. It has two options, *either* to conduct an initial study which would cost £100,000 *or* not to conduct it. Experience in similar areas has been that initial studies indicated a 5% probability that a workable gas field was likely to exist in the area, and a 95% probability that there would not be one. If the company decides to start drilling, the cost will be £2,000,000. If gas were found, the present worth of the gas obtained would be £20,000,000 but if gas were not found the return would be nil.

The probabilities of finding gas are as follows:

(a) if an initial study is conducted, and the likelihood of the existence of a field is indicated, the probability is 90%;

(b) if an initial study is conducted, and the likelihood of the existence of a field is found to be remote, the probability is 2%;

(c) if no initial study is conducted, the company believes that in its particular area the probability is 6·4%.

What advice, with supporting arguments and figures, would you give the company? (CMI *'68*)

10. You are required using the information given below to:

(a) draw a decision tree diagram to illustrate the relationships between the two sets of outcomes;

(b) calculate the net expected monetary value of undertaking both investments.

The following table gives the probabilities associated with three possible outcomes of two investments. The outcomes relate to a set of mutually exclusive, mutually exhaustive and independent events.

Investment Y Net Outcomes (£)	Investment X Net Outcomes (£)			
	0	2000	4000	
0	0·04	0·12	0·04	0·20
2000	0·12	0·36	0·12	0·60
4000	0·04	0·12	0·04	0·20
	0·20	0·60	0·20	

(ICMA Nov '72)

11. At the market in the morning, before any customers are about, a retailer buys bunches of flowers which cost him £0·10 each to sell at £0·25 each. The retailer buys only in the morning, does not reduce his price and gives any stock not sold by the evening to the local hospital. The various quantities he can buy each morning are 100, 200, 300 or 400 bunches.

He estimates the demand characteristics each day to be:

Bunches				Probability
0	..	..	..	0·05
100	..	..	..	0·20
200	..	..	..	0·40
300	..	..	..	0·25
400	..	..	..	0·10
500 or more	..	..	0·00
				1·00

You are required to calculate:

(a) the expected value for each alternative purchasing policy;

(b) the most probable result of a day's trading if the retailer bought 400 bunches;

(c) the maximum the retailer should agree to pay for advance knowledge of the exact demand for the following day.

(ICMA June '71)

12. A baker makes a special loaf each day which cost 10p each and sells at 15p each. Any loaves not sold at the end of the day must be thrown away. Experience shows that he sells 48, 49, 50, 51 or 52 loaves per day and that the probability of specific sales are 0·1, 0·3, 0·4, 0·1, 0·1.

(a) How many loaves should the baker produce?

(b) Discuss the advantages and limitations of a decision theory approach to this problem.

(CMI '71)

13. (a) *You are required to state the properties relevant to a simple queue.*

(b) Assuming that a simple serving system has been in operation long enough for it to have settled down, some simple results about average characteristics can be derived.
You are required to define traffic intensity and calculate the expected length of time a customer will be in a queue if the service rate is 10 per hour and the traffic intensity is 0·8. (ICMA *May '72*)

14. (a) Explain the characteristics of problems that arise in commerce and industry which would be amenable to solution by use of queueing theory. In what way does simulation help?

(b) A bulk milk collecting depot is equipped with one pump that can empty a tanker in 5 minutes. If the tankers arrive at the depot in a random manner at an average of 10 per hour, calculate:

(i) the average length of the queue of tankers waiting to be emptied, excluding the tanker being handled;

(ii) the average length of time that tankers will have to wait before being emptied;

(iii) the probability that the queue will be longer than three tankers. (CMI *'68*)

15. Show graphically how the average time that one has to wait for a sole telephone operator to answer varies with the number of calls made per hour if the operator can deal with 60 calls per hour. Discuss how the principles behind your graph can be applied to a wide variety of situations. (CMI *'70*)

16. An enquiry desk was set up in the hallway of a company's offices. Callers, all of whom were on the company's business, arrived at the rate of 20 per hour and were dealt with on average at the rate of 30 per hour. If the cost of one clerk to staff the desk for an 8-hour day is 50p per hour and the average cost of the visitor's time is £2 per hour, consider the case for employing a second clerk at the desk at 50p per hour. Discuss the usefulness to a management accountant of the ideas behind your solution.

(CMI *'69* (adapted))

17. A factory manager has to decide which of two shop maintenance engineers, A or B, to employ. Machines break down on average at one per hour. The cost of a machine being idle is estimated at £2 per hour. A asks for £1 per hour while B asks for 75p per hour. It is known that A can repair 2 machines per hour while B can only repair 1½ machines per hour. Advise the manager as to the more economical engineer to employ. Discuss the assumptions that have to be made in using queueing theory to solve this problem. (CMI *'71*)

18. (a) What statistical or operational research techniques can be employed in deciding when capital equipment should be replaced?

(b) A transport company buys road tankers costing £5000 each. From the data given below advise management when a tanker should be replaced:

Year	1	2	3	4	5	6
Operating costs	750	800	850	900	1000	1225
Resale price	4500	4050	3750	3600	3450	3325

(CMI '68)

19. The manager of a fleet of 10 lorries costing £2200 each knows that every lorry will on average require a major overhaul every 2 years. There is, however, a 30% probability that a lorry will have a major breakdown at the end of the first year but not before. The vehicle supplier with whom the manager deals is prepared to replace the whole fleet at a cost of £15,000 at the end of one year's life; £17,500 at the end of two years' life, or £20,000 at the end of three years' life. What is the most economic policy for the fleet manager to follow:

    (a) replace the whole fleet after one year
    (b) replace the whole fleet after two years
    (c) replace the whole fleet after three years
    (d) replace each lorry individually?

You may assume that the cost of a major breakdown and overhaul is the same, i.e. £2200 and that after the first year, surviving lorries are subject to the same annual risks of breakdown.

Explain in detail the reasons for your choice of policy and what assumptions are involved.   (CMI '70)

20. A company is about to install a new manufacturing process. Essential to the success of the process is a control unit for which the probability distribution of failures during the lifetime of the installation is estimated to be:

Number of failures	0	1	2	3	4
Probability	0·30	0·25	0·20	0·15	0·10

Spares of the unit can be purchased only at the time of the initial order when their cost will be £2,000 each. If there is a failure and no spare is available it has been estimated that the loss of production while the control unit is being repaired together with the direct cost of the repair will cost the company £10,000.

You are required to:

    (a) calculate the expected number of failures;
    (b) state the number of spares, if any, the company should purchase at the time of the initial order;
    (c) state how many spares the company would have purchased if the probabilities of failure were not known but that it was considered extremely unlikely there would be more than four failures during the life of the machine.   (ICMA Dec '71)

21. (*a*) Derive the formula for the economic order quantity.

(*b*) A firm is able to obtain quantity discounts on its orders of material as follows:

Price per ton £	Tons
6·0	less than 250
5·9	250 and less than 800
5·8	800 and less than 2000
5·7	2000 and less than 4000
5·6	4000 and over

The annual demand for the material is 4000 tons.
Stock holding costs are 20% of material cost per annum.
The delivery cost per order is £6·00.
You are required to calculate the best quantity to order.

(ICMA *Nov '72*)

22. (*a*) Use the square root formula to determine the economic order quantity and total supply costs of tyres costing £5 each for a transport undertaking that uses 500 tyres per year. The holding cost is 15% of the average stock value and the average cost per order is 60p.

(*b*) Discuss critically the square root formula for stock control purposes. (CMI *'67* (adapted))

23. (*a*) *You are required to state the advantages and disadvantages of the Periodic Review system of inventory control.*

(*b*) Best Value Supermarkets Limited buys an economy size instant coffee to market under its own brand name. The monthly sales in all its stores, assuming 25 days in a month are 50,000 units. The sales occur evenly throughout the month.

The company currently orders in lots of 50,000 at a time at a price of £0·25 per unit with a lead time of 15 days. A base inventory of 20,000 units is kept as a buffer stock.
You are required to calculate the re-order point.

(*c*) The supplier has offered to reduce the price to £0·23 per unit if the order size is increased to 200,000 units for delivery within 30 days. If these terms were accepted the company would still keep a base inventory of 20,000 units but would have to rent additional storage space at a cost of £6000 per annum. Carrying costs to the company, excluding additional storage space, are 20% per annum. Terms of settlement are the same under both current and proposed delivery patterns.
You are required to state, and support with calculations, whether or not the new terms be accepted. The only costs to be considered are those given above. (ICMA *June '71*)

24. You have been instructed to investigate the ordering of raw

materials in your company with a view to making cost savings on the amount of stocks carried at the moment.

The present procedure for controlling stocks and ordering raw materials is a physical inspection of the amount of stock on hand; if stock is thought to be 'low' an amount is ordered to bring it up to a satisfactory level.

After investigation it is found that the annual carrying cost of stock is £0·10 per unit. Production is steady throughout the year, there are no delivery problems with suppliers, so safety stocks need not be held. It is therefore decided to time purchases to be received just as the stocks of raw material reach zero. Each raw material order incurs a procurement cost of £20 which includes invoicing, transportation etc. The annual demand for raw material is 1,000,000 units.

You are required to:

(*a*) *report on the economic order quantity*, for the raw material, at which costs are minimised;

(*b*) *graph this specific solution* to help management understand your recommendation. (ICMA *May '72*)

25. (*a*) How do the following factors affect economic reorder quantities of a stocked item?

(*i*) frequency of ordering;

(*ii*) cost of running out of stock due to fluctuations in demand;

(*iii*) fluctuations in stock usage;

(*iv*) fluctuations in stock prices;

(*v*) storage costs.

(*b*) What other factor(s) enter into the calculation of economic reorder quantities? (J.D.M.A.S.)

26.

Job	1 man	2 men	3 men	4 men	Constraints
		Duration, days			
Smelt	30	18	10	5	after joining
Join	16	10	6	6	after preparation
Cleave	2	2	2	2	after grooving and chasing
Prepare	10	10	10	10	—
Groove	10	10	10	10	after breaking
Break	—	20	16	12	after preparation
Carry	20	10	5	5	after cleaving, grouting and smelting
Chase	12	8	8	8	after breaking
Grout	50	30	30	30	after preparation

The above table sets out a list of activities on a work-site, together with the time for each activity (under alternative manpower assumptions) and the constraints affecting each activity.

17 men are available on the site: each can undertake each activity.

(a) Draw up a network for completion of the work in the shortest possible time, using appropriate conventions.

(b) On your network write in, in brackets beside the duration of each activity, the manpower usage for that activity.

(c) Identify the critical path. Why is it critical?

(J.D.M.A.S.)

27. From the following activities construct a network indicating the critical path and the sub-critical activities. Discuss fully the value of such an analysis, giving examples of its application.

Initial activity Node	Terminal activity Node	Activity time (days)
0	1	2
0	2	4
1	3	3
2	4	5
3	4	12
3	5	11
3	6	10
4	7	14
5	8	4
6	8	6
7	8	7
8	9	3

(CMI '70)

28. A project consists of six activities A to F inclusive, with the following sequential relationships:

A must follow C and E.
B must follow A and F.
D must follow B.
F must follow C.

Activities C and E may take place at the same time; and similarly activities A and F.

The normal duration of each activity is, in weeks:

Activity ..	..	..	A	B	C	D	E	F
Duration ..	..	..	4	5	4	1	2	3

Associated with each activity are the following crash durations and the corresponding extra cost which is linearly related for each activity.

Activity	..	..	..	A	B	C	D	E	F
Crash duration, in weeks				1	3	2	1	2	1
Associated extra cost, in £'s				240	200	120	—	—	80

The customer requires the project to be completed in 13 weeks and there is a penalty of £200 per week for excess time with a bonus of £90 per week for earlier completion.

You are required to:

(a) draw a logical network based on normal durations for the project and show on the network the duration, earliest start time and the latest start time for each activity;

(b) indicate the critical activities and the normal duration of the project;

(c) derive the data which would enable you to plot the cost/time curve for the project;

(d) state with reasons, whether or not the normal duration for the project should be changed.

(ICMA *Dec '71*)

29. You have been provided with the following durations and costs of the activities necessary to complete project K:

Activity	Normal duration, days	Normal cost £	Crash duration, days	Crash cost £
0–1	4	80	4	80
0–2	3	60	3	60
1–3	6	150	5	180
1–4	3	80	2	150
2–4	5	100	4	120
3–5	8	160	8	160
4–5	15	300	10	400
5–6	10	200	8	290

You are required to:

(a) construct the network;

(b) calculate the shortest time within which the project can be completed at normal cost;

(c) calculate the total float for each activity;

(d) calculate the normal cost of completing the project;

(e) calculate the revised cost and duration of the optimal programme if the project will produce profits at the rate of £40 per day saved and there are no physical limits on the resources needed.

(ICMA *June '71*)

30. Four machines I, II, III and IV are used to manufacture four products A, B, C and D from two materials X and Y.

You are given the following information with regard to the four products:

Production rates per hour in units of product	Machine I	Machine II	Machine III	Machine IV
Product				
A	100	35	—	60
B	—	40	100	60
C	—	—	175	90
D	150	60	200	120
Machine hour costs	£	£	£	£
Variable costs: direct labour and variable overhead ..	25	70	50	45
Fixed costs: absorbed on basis of maximum time available ..	150 hours	40 hours	200 hours	60 hours
Maximum machine time available	1728	1824	1824	1632

Raw material costs and selling prices per unit of product are:

	Material X £	Material Y £	Selling price £
Cost per unit	0·20	0·40	
Product	units	units	
A	1·0	2·0	6·0
B	2·5	—	4·5
C	3·0	3·0	5·0
D	—	1·5	4·0

Market research has shown there is a limit in the market of 150,000 units for product A and 120,000 units for product C.

You are required to formulate the equations and the initial Simplex tableau for the above as a profit maximising linear programme.

(ICMA *May '72*)

31. Given the following information about a problem:

Maximise $\qquad 4x_1 + 8x_2 + 10x_3$

Subject to $\qquad x_1 \geqslant 0, \; x_2 \geqslant 0, \; x_3 \geqslant 0$

$$x_1 + x_2 + x_3 \leqslant 1000$$
$$0 \cdot 5x_1 + 0 \cdot 5x_2 + 0 \cdot 5x_3 \leqslant 1500$$
$$0 \cdot 5x_1 + x_2 + x_3 \leqslant 2000$$

You are required to:

(a) Formulate the first feasible solution.

(b) Using the Simplex method, carry out the first iteration to improve the first solution.

(c) Interpret the position of the problem as it stands after the first iteration.   (ICMA *Nov '72*)

32. A steel company is concerned with the problem of distributing imported ore from three ports to four steel mills situated throughout the country.

The supplies of ore arriving at ports are:

Port	Tons per week
a	20,000
b	38,000
c	16,000

Demands at the steel mills are:

Steel mill	Tons per week
A	10,000
B	18,000
C	22,000
D	24,000

Transportation costs are £0·05 per ton mile. The distances between the ports and the steel mills are given below:

	A	B	C	D
a ..	50	60	100	50
b ..	80	40	70	50
c ..	90	70	30	50

You are required to calculate the transportation plan which will minimise ore distribution costs for the steel company. State the cost of this distribution plan.   (ICMA *Dec '71*)

33. A manufacturer wishes to produce 100 tons of a product containing at least 50% of factor A and 30% of factor B. He can use two ingredients, X costing £20 per ton, which will yield 60% of A and 20% of B, and Y costing £40 per ton which will yield 40% of A and 50% of B.

You are required (i) to determine by graphical methods the mix of X and Y to yield the minimum material cost of production, (ii) to discuss the usefulness of graphical as opposed to Simplex methods of solving this type of problem. You may assume that the relationship is linear.   (CMI *'69*)

34. (a) A company manufactures two products x_1 and x_2. The contribution margin per unit of $x_1 = $ £8 and of $x_2 = $ £10.

There are three machine centres through which the products pass. Product x_1 requires one hour's machining time in machine centre 1, and two and one hours respectively in machine centres 2 and 3. The machining time requirements for product x_2 are one, one and two hours respectively in machine centres 1, 2 and 3. The maximum machine time available is 80 hours in machine centre 1, 100 hours in machine centre 2, 120 hours in machine centre 3. The company wishes to maximise the total contribution from these two products.

Construct the initial tableau for a linear programme based on the Simplex approach.

(b) The final iteration to the above problem is given as follows:

	Product x_1	Product x_2	Machine centre 1	Machine centre 2	Machine centre 3	
Machine centre 1	0	0	1	$-\frac{1}{3}$	$+\frac{2}{3}$	6·63
Product x_1	1	0	0	$+\frac{2}{3}$	$-\frac{1}{3}$	26·67
Product x_2	0	1	0	$-\frac{1}{3}$	$+\frac{1}{3}$	46·66
Z	0	0	0	-2	-6	680

Interpret this statement.   (ICMA *Specimen question*)

35. Three operational research teams have a working capacity of 200, 300 and 500 man hours per week respectively. Four minor research problems must be resolved within one week and will require an estimated 300, 150, 400 and 150 man hours. The cost per hour in £'s of each team working on each problem is given below.

Team	Job	A	B	C	D
1		5	5	20	25
2		5	10	15	20
3		8	5	10	5

(a) Using linear programming techniques find the least cost solution of resolving the four research problems in one week.

(b) Discuss the advantages and practical limitations of linear programming techniques for the solution of management problems.   (CMI '71)

36. The owner of a small mini-cab firm controls three small garages in various parts of a town containing respectively 2, 3 and 4 cabs. At one point of time in the evening the owner receives three requests for cabs in various quantities from three parties

going on in the town. He calculates the distances in miles from his garages to the parties as follows:

	Party A needing 1 car	Party B needing 3 cars	Party C needing 5 cars
Garage X—containing 2 cars	6	3	10
Garage Y—containing 3 cars	4	9	5
Garage Z—containing 4 cars	3	6	6

Calculate an optimum solution that minimises the total distances from garages to parties explaining how you are sure that the solution is an optimum.

What other applications of this technique are there? How can any lack of equality between demand and supply be overcome?

(CMI '70)

37. A company manufactures two types of stainless steel dish, type A and type B. The following data refers to the material content, manufacturing process times and variable costs of each type:

	Type A	Type B
Material content (pounds per unit) ..	1	1
Cost per pound	£0·06	£0·10
Manufacturing time (seconds per unit):		
Press shop	20	20
Polishing	20	10
Manufacturing costs (direct labour + variable overhead)		
	£	£
Press shop, per press hour	3·60	3·60
Polishing, per hour:		
machine 1	3·60	—
machine 2	—	5·40

Material supplies each week are limited to 16,000 lbs. for the type A dish and 21,000 lbs. for the type B dish.

There are available each week 200 press hours and 120 hours each for both types of polishing machine.

Overtime working may be used to increase the hours available up to a limit of 10% for each machine group. However, overtime also adds 10% to the manufacturing costs of each machine group.

The type A dish sells for £0·12 each and the type B dish for £0·16 each.

The company wishes to know how many it should produce in order to maximise contribution.

You are required to formulate the initial Simplex tableau for the linear programme which would lead to the optimum production plan.

(ICMA Dec '71)

38. A ladies' fashion shop wishes to purchase the following quantities of summer dresses:

Dress size	I	II	III	IV
Quantity	100	200	450	150

Three manufacturers are willing to supply dresses. The quantities given below are the maximum they are able to supply of any given combination of orders for dresses:

Manufacturer	A	B	C
Total quantity	150	450	250

The shop expects the profit per dress to vary with the manufacturer as given below:

Manufacturer	Sizes			
	I	II	III	IV
	£	£	£	£
A	2·50	4·00	5·00	2·00
B	3·00	3·50	5·50	1·50
C	2·00	4·50	4·50	2·50

You are required to:

(a) use the transportation technique to solve the problem of how the orders should be placed on the manufacturers by the fashion shop in order to maximise profit;

(b) explain how you know that there is no further improvement possible, showing your workings. (ICMA *Nov '72*)

39. A company manufactures two models of power tool; a single speed model and a two speed model.

The manufacturing requirements of the two models and the available manufacturing capacity are:

	Machining hours	Assembly hours	Testing hours	Warehouse space square feet
Model:				
single speed	2·0	1·5	0·5	1·0
two speed	2·5	1·0	1·0	1·0
Capacity available	40,000	24,000	14,000	30,000

You are required to:

(a) *produce a graphic solution to the problem of maximising the contribution*, taking into account the above production requirements and constraints and given that the contribution per unit is £3 and £5 for the single speed and two speed models respectively; the graph should clearly indicate the feasible region for the solution;

(b) *state the number of each model to be produced*, the contribution from this production and which constraints are binding in the solution. (ICMA *June '71*)

40. (a) What do you understand by "game theory"? What relevance has it to decision making in a competitive industry?

(b) Define the following terms as used in game theory:
(a) strategy, (b) pay-off, (c) zero-sum games and (d) saddle-point.

(c) Given the following matrix what is the best strategy for (1) player A and (2) player B, to adopt.

	B	
A	6	2
	−1	−4

(CMI '66)

41. Two companies selling a similar product to the general public are considering their advertising programmes. They have the alternative of advertising either in the press or on television.

The following pay-off matrix shows the gains and losses in £000s of these alternative policies.

Company B

Company A	Do nothing	Advert in Press	Advert on TV
Do nothing	0	−50	−250
Advert in Press	50	0	−50
Advert on TV	300	150	100

On the basis of the above data indicate the policy which each company should follow. Expand upon your answer to indicate generally the application of games theory to economic activity.

(CMI '69)

42. Moving averages and simple exponentially weighted moving averages are statistical smoothing techniques often applied in short-term forecasting.

You are required to:

(a) *State* how the data is weighted in each case. *Describe the effect* of raising the 'α' values in the exponentially weighted moving average systems and state the formula which gives the equivalent moving average period for any chosen 'α' value.

(b) *Calculate* a three-month moving average and an exponentially weighted moving average ('α' (or 'a') = 0·2) from the following data:

Period reference	Actual demand	Old forecast
1	16	16
2	20	
3	15	
4	19	
5	17	
6	21	
7	25	

(c) *Give the principal advantages* of using a simple exponentially weighted moving average over an ordinary moving average in a forecasting system.

(d) *State* the kind of demand conditions in which either technique will operate most successfully to give (reasonably) good forecasts.   (ICMA *May '72*)

43. Write a report to your managing director on:

Either: The applications and principles of queueing theory, explaining the help given by the Monte Carlo method in solving complex queueing situations.

Or: The case for introducing a method of statistical stock control in your company. Outline any such method with which you are familiar and state the assumptions upon which the method is based.   (CMI *'66*)

44. (a) Explain briefly in layman's terms, and in not more than 50 words, the basic concepts of each of the following techniques:

(i) Queueing theory.
(ii) Linear programming.
(iii) Simulation.

(b) Give, in not more than 50 words, an example of the type of problem that can be resolved quantitatively, by each of these techniques, the sort of help it can provide, and the type of complexity with which the technique can cope.   (J.D.M.A.S.)

45. Define and illustrate with a simple numerical example or diagram, where appropriate, any four of the following terms:

> Traffic intensity
> Sequential sampling
> Free float
> Normal distribution
> Slack variables
> Zero sum two person games

(ICMA *Nov '72*)

INDEX

For full details of other Macdonald & Evans
Handbooks send for the FREE M & E
Handbook list, available from: Department E6
Macdonald & Evans Ltd., Estover Road,
Plymouth PL6 7PZ